The
BAC Three-Eleven
THE BRITISH AIRBUS THAT SHOULD HAVE BEEN

The
BAC Three-Eleven
THE BRITISH AIRBUS THAT SHOULD HAVE BEEN

GRAZIANO FRESCHI

TEMPUS

To Bluebird

Sic transit Gloria Mundi
(philosophical aphorism of the ancient Church)

First published 2006

Tempus Publishing Limited
The Mill, Brimscombe Port,
Stroud, Gloucestershire, GL5 2QG
www.tempus-publishing.com

© Graziano Freschi 2006

The right of Graziano Freschi 2006 to be identified as the Author
of this work has been asserted in accordance with the
Copyrights, Designs and Patents Act 1988.

British Library Cataloguing in Publication Data.
A catalogue record for this book is available from the British Library.

ISBN 0 7524 3913 8

Typesetting and origination by Tempus Publishing Limited
Printed in Great Britain

Contents

Acknowledgements

I could not have written this book without the help and assistance of several people. I wish first of all to thank the Rt Hon. Tony Benn, MP, who was Minister of Technology for most of the period covering the BAC Three-Eleven project evaluation by Her Majesty's Government. Mr Benn answered, via private correspondence, several questions I had in respect of the thinking of the British Government of the time in relation to supporting major aerospace projects like the Three-Eleven.

I owe a very substantial debt of gratitude to Frank Armstrong FREng, FRAeS, former chairman of the Royal Aeronautical Society's Historical Group. I entrusted Mr Armstrong with reviewing the full manuscript. In return he gave generously of his time and shared with me his considerable insight into the British aircraft industry of the 1960s and 1970s. Frank Armstrong also provided me with priceless suggestions aimed at improving and refining the finished work.

I also had the good fortune to meet, or correspond with, several former BAC senior personnel who were deeply involved in the Three-Eleven programme. Amongst them special thanks go to former BAC Commercial Aircraft Director of Sales Engineering John Prothero Thomas, whom I met at Brooklands in June of last year. Mr Prothero Thomas enriched my knowledge with his personal recollections of the project and gifted me with a substantial pack of very useful engineering and marketing material on the Three-Eleven. I am also most grateful to Christopher Hamshaw Thomas, former BAC market development manager, who took the trouble to review chapters 3, 4 and 5 of the book and who provided me with many helpful insights and a very useful 'behind the scenes' understanding of the political undertones surrounding the project. In addition, Mr Hamshaw Thomas's files on the Three-Eleven, now stored at Brooklands, were a mine of precious information for me.

Particular thanks are also due to Roger Back, former chief aerodynamicist on the BAC Three-Eleven and later design project manager on the Airbus A320, and Mike Salisbury, former chief aerodynamicist at BAC Commercial Aircraft and later chief engineer (UK) Airbus A320. Both Mr Back and Mr Salisbury kindly undertook to review chapters 3 and 4 of the book and fed back to me pertinent and constructive comments as well as their own personal recollections of the Three-Eleven project and of the civil projects that BAC and then Airbus undertook following the Three-Eleven's demise.

Other ex-BAC people who helped me in understanding the Three-Eleven aircraft programme include Doug Halloway, who worked in the Weybridge design office and was responsible for the Three-Eleven's flight deck, and Steve McDonald, who worked as a junior executive in the personnel department that was tasked with promoting the Three-Eleven's employment opportunities in the Weybridge and Surrey areas. I am grateful to both for taking time to answer my queries.

Neil Gaunt of Central African Airways visited the BAC Three-Eleven cabin mock-up in the late 1960s and provided me with a potential customer's impressions of the aircraft.

I am indebted to Brian Riddle, Royal Aeronautical Society librarian, who indefatigably dug out all the information on the BAC Three-Eleven available in the Society's vast library, and who enthusiastically supported me in my voracious research needs.

I would also like to thank Julian Temple, aviation curator at the Brooklands Museum, and Nik Read, the 'guru' on BAC One-Eleven prototype G-ASYD, also of the Brooklands Museum, for allowing me access to the BAC Three-Eleven photographic archives and technical archives, and for helping me obtain the photographic material on the aircraft that illustrates this book. Fellow author Richard Anthony Payne also kindly made available to me some BAC Three-Eleven photographs from his private collection.

The staff at Tempus Publishing helped make sure that everything ran smoothly once the manuscript and photographs were delivered to them. Amongst the key personnel at Tempus, I wish to thank Amy Rigg for her continuous support in seeing the book to fruition.

Finally I wish to thank my parents Ledo and Joan, and my better half Rebecca for supporting me in this endeavour.

Of course, notwithstanding the enormous and dedicated contribution of the people mentioned above, all errors of fact, repetitions, misunderstandings and opinions expressed in this book are entirely my own.

Graziano Freschi
Twickenham
July 2006

Foreword

My interest in the British commercial aerospace industry goes back a long way – to the summer of 1965, to be precise. It was then that, as a four year old, I boarded a BEA Trident 1C jet airliner for the relatively short flight from Venice to London. The purpose of the trip was to meet my grandparents here in England (my mother is British). That Trident flight was my first ever and, as it happened, it was on a British-built airliner that I undertook that exciting experience.

As I got older, I developed a strong interest in the aircraft industry in general and in the British civil aircraft industry in particular. I therefore grew to admire the proud technical achievements of the UK commercial aircraft industry in the 1950s and early 1960s. One only needs to mention the world's first jet airliner (de Havilland Comet), the world's first turboprop (Vickers Viscount) and the Anglo-French Concorde SST as prime examples of the industry's technical brilliance. Other fine airliners introduced into service in the early 1960s, such as the Vickers VC-10, HS Trident and BAC One-Eleven, confirmed the UK's technical leadership in Europe in commercial airliners.

Unfortunately for Britain, her European leadership was undermined in the late 1960s when two very poor industrial policy decisions by the British Government led first to Britain's withdrawal from the A.300B European Airbus project when the country was co-leader with France (1969), and later to the cancellation of the broadly equivalent, all-British, BAC Three-Eleven wide-body twinjet airliner in 1970. In the wake of those two highly damaging decisions, leadership on large civil aircraft was transferred from Britain to France by default. Britain has never recovered her leading position in Europe, and to this very day France leads large civil aircraft development in Europe via the Airbus joint venture, of which Britain is a relatively junior partner.

There is absolutely no doubt in many people's minds that from a technical viewpoint the UK could have produced a large wide-bodied jet transport like the BAC Three-Eleven on its own. Indeed, at the time, the UK was the only European country capable of launching a Three-Eleven Class aircraft on its own, but unfortunately politics and Treasury-imposed budgetary constraints played a key part in the demise of this very promising aircraft. And so it came to pass that Britain opted out of independent development of large civil transports at the very time when demand for such equipment was about to show exponential growth.

It is my firm belief that Britain's decision not to launch the BAC Three-Eleven into production marked a watershed in the country's position as a major civil aircraft developer and this is the main reason why I decided to write a book on this all-too-often overlooked aircraft project.

Why did the British decision-makers elect to forego an enormous market opportunity in a sector where the country was still leading Europe at the time? As we shall see in this book, the reasons are several, but overriding them all there was a loss of nerve and lack of vision among the country's elite, which reflected above all a deep-seated defeatism and pessimism about Britain's future role in the world. During the lifespan of the people governing the country in the 1960s, Britain had gone from the position of world's greatest industrial and military power to the much more limited role of regional power. As an acute observer has noted, 'managed decline' became the byword among the country's ruling classes.

Today there is only one small consolation for the supporters of the UK's commercial aerospace industry (and small it is indeed, given the country's past achievements in this sector). In addition to producing the Rolls-Royce family of large jet engines, a market in which the British company occupies the No.2 slot in the world, the UK still designs and manufactures all the wings for the Airbus family of large jet transports. BAE SYSTEMS also retains a 20 per cent stake in the Airbus Integrated Company (the remaining 80 per cent being owned by the Franco-German-Spanish giant EADS). Alas, BAE SYSTEMS' recent decision to sell its 20 per cent stake to EADS will mean that the UK will have no equity interest in civil aircraft manufacture. There is no question that this sad state of affairs would not have come to pass had the BAC Three-Eleven been allowed to go ahead, or had the UK played its European Airbus cards better.

In recent years I had the good fortune, in my capacity as Principal Analyst Aerospace & Defence at PricewaterhouseCoopers, to work closely with a large number of senior people in the UK aerospace industry. I therefore met industry leaders across the whole spectrum of the supply chain, from the primes to the smallest of contractors. I know, from the conversations I had with them, that many industry people share my views that Britain could have done more to pro-tect its strong post-war position in aircraft production and that an enormous amount of intellectual property (engineering, technical and commercial know-how) was given away to other European countries for little or no consideration. It is to them, and to all those who care about the British aerospace industry, that I dedicate my book.

Graziano Freschi
Twickenham
England

Introduction

2 December 1970: The then UK Minister for Aviation, Mr Frederick Corfield, announces in the House of Commons that, due to the continuing funding of Rolls-Royce and to the financial demands of the Concorde project, the Government has no spare cash to fund either the BAC Three-Eleven airliner or Hawker Siddeley's re-entry as a full partner in the European Airbus consortium. Rolls-Royce was to collapse and call in the receivers only a few weeks later.

That announcement sounded the death knell for the BAC Three-Eleven wide-bodied airliner project. With the demise of the Three-Eleven in December 1970, Britain effectively opted out of independent development of large civil aircraft. In April 1969, little more than a year before, the British Government had opted out of the European Airbus consortium, leaving Hawker Siddeley to negotiate a private venture contract with its French and German partners.

We believe that few people outside the UK aerospace industry at the time realised the significant impact on the UK's civil aircraft industry of the December 1970 decision not to fund development and production of the BAC Three-Eleven. Fewer still will be aware that the technological, economic and financial fallout of such a decision have negatively affected the scale and the role of Britain's civil aerospace industry to this very day. The negative implications for the industry can be summarised as follows:

Loss of large transport aircraft design & development capability
Leadership on the design, development and manufacture of large civil aircraft in Europe, up to then largely a UK preserve, was transferred to France by default. That country's Government had the foresight to realise that a leading role in commercial aerospace would yield France massive technological, economic, financial and political benefits over many decades. From the early 1960s onwards France's political and industrial elite, with a series of enlightened moves, set about achieving that role by means of international partnerships with Britain, then the only serious competitor to the might of the US commercial aerospace industry. This goal was achieved in two broad steps. Firstly, in 1962, the French Government successfully negotiated that France would have design leadership on

the Concorde supersonic transport (SST) airframe, with 60 per cent of the work going to France's Sud Aviation, and 40 per cent to the British Aircraft Corporation (BAC).[1] Secondly, in 1967, when Britain, France and Germany agreed in principle to launch preliminary development of a European Airbus wide-bodied aircraft, France successfully negotiated for Sud Aviation to have leadership of the airframe design, development and production, in return for conceding exclusivity to Rolls-Royce on the engine and British leadership on engine development. Eventually, due to Rolls-Royce's decision to concentrate on the RB.211 engine for the Lockheed L.1011 TriStar, the British company was dropped in favour of US suppliers.

The final, tragic outcome of this loss of leadership for Britain is that now the UK civil airframe sector and its supplier base depend on programmes led by, and centred in, France, the US, Brazil and Canada. All the major programme strategic decisions are taken in Toulouse, Seattle, Sao José Dos Campos and Montreal. The programme key tasks, such as overall aircraft design, systems integration, final assembly, flight-testing and certification, also take place in those centres.[2] The UK's Bristol, Chester and Belfast design and manufacturing facilities only play a supporting role to these parent centres located abroad. To put it bluntly, they are designers and suppliers of aircraft subsystems and components. The damage extends to the large and profitable civil aircraft after-market (aircraft support, maintenance, repair & overhaul (MRO), financing, etc.). Most high-value-added MRO work on Airbus, Boeing, Embraer or Bombardier aircraft takes place in France, Germany, the US, Brazil and Canada. The highly lucrative aircraft financing and leasing business is mainly in the hands of American, Canadian or French and German banks and institutions.[3]

The foregoing of a tremendous market opportunity

The commercial aerospace market is currently worth in excess of US$60 billion in revenues per annum, and this relates to new build activity alone. The after-market is easily worth another US$40–50 billion per annum. We are therefore talking of a huge market opportunity in a sector which is generally regarded as high-value-added with significant technological spin-offs. The UK's *de facto* decision to opt out of independent development of large civil aircraft *and* its agreeing to French leadership on joint international projects have not *per se* meant that Britain has not retained a reasonable share of the commercial aerospace market. Indeed the UK today has an estimated 10–12 per cent share of this market, mainly through the Airbus joint venture and exports of Rolls-Royce aero-engines. Nevertheless the UK's self-inflicted decision to forego leadership on large airliners has meant that its share is much smaller than it might otherwise have been. It is difficult to quantify the magnitude of this differential, but we would estimate that the current UK share of the commercial aircraft market is something between one third and one half of what it would be, had it opted to either continue independent development of large civil transports or to lead on the Airbus joint venture.[4]

Loss of substantial spin-off benefits

Spin-off benefits can range from those measurable in purely economic terms, such as direct employment and revenue and associated multiplier effects (for example, support services, the attraction of sub-contractors to the geographical area chosen for aircraft final assembly, growth of ad hoc higher education institutions and training colleges, Commercial Off The Shelf ('COTS') technology that can be applied to other industries, etc.) to the more intangible, such as political clout and international prestige. The latter arise from the identification, in the world at large, of the country leading the aircraft project as a beacon of technological prowess and industrial muscle. The direct and indirect economic, financial and employment benefits are usually easy to understand and quantify. More difficult to measure are the intangible benefits accruing to the country producing the aircraft. In this respect a commercial airliner is a highly visible and internationally operated product that is associated in people's minds with high technology. The intangible 'spin-off' benefits for a country producing such equipment are very powerful indeed. It is no wonder then that all the major developed countries have historically striven to nurture or acquire those capabilities, with varying degrees of success, and that any self-respecting newly industrialised nation is eager to step on to the civil airliner design and manufacturing world stage.

The principal aim of this book is to tell the story of the BAC Three-Eleven project, which represented the UK's last attempt at preserving its hard-earned status as Europe's leading producer of large commercial aircraft, and the second largest in the Western world after the USA. Eventually, as we shall see, this noble attempt was defeated not by the lack of engineering, technical or marketing skills in the UK aircraft industry, but by mind-numbing myopia on the part of the UK Government and other senior decision-makers. We must emphasise at this point, however, that the British aerospace industry and its leaders are not entirely free of blame in bearing responsibility for this state of affairs: prior to the Three-Eleven project there had been too many occasions when British companies had launched civil aircraft that were either too late for the market for which they were intended or had the wrong specifications. Although this observation does not apply to the Three-Eleven project or to other successful British airliners that did sell well worldwide, the industry has to share the fault for the Government-backed launch of several aircraft that did not stand a chance in the marketplace: it was up to industry, not the Government, to get these projects right.

In order to set the history of the BAC Three-Eleven airliner project in the correct context, we shall review and analyse the evolution of Britain's civil aerospace industry after the Second World War, with its initial technological breakthroughs, its commercial successes and painful commercial failures. We shall also analyse developments in other European countries, principally France. It was mainly due to French ambitions in the sector and to British political goodwill towards Europe that Anglo-French co-operation on the Concorde SST, and the later success of the Pan-European Airbus, came to fruition.

On a broader canvas, the book is also an attempt to analyse exhaustively the reasons why Britain decided to commit technological and economic suicide by pulling out of independent development of large civil airframes when it had at last devised the right product for the market, and at the very point in time when the air transport industry was on the verge of entering a period of exponential growth.

The reader may wonder why there is a need for a book on a project that did not see the light of day as a full production airliner. Industry insiders and aviation enthusiasts alike are aware that a considerable number of books and articles have been written on the subject of Airbus and of its rise from a Pan-European effort aimed at challenging American supremacy in large civil airliners, to it having overtaken Boeing as world leader in the sector. In addition, many well-researched and insightful books have been written on the historical evolution of Britain's aircraft industry. Analyses of the structure of the industry and of the resulting economic benefits to the country have also been undertaken. However, apart from sporadic, if well-researched, articles in the specialist press, we have not come across a comprehensive history of the BAC Three-Eleven project and of the implications of its demise in 1970 for the UK commercial aerospace sector. This book aims to redress this perceived imbalance, as we firmly believe that the Three-Eleven programme has not yet received the attention it deserves.[5]

The remainder of this book is structured as follows:

Chapter 1

This chapter covers the post-Second World War commercial airliner developments in Europe, from the late 1940s up to 1970, the year when the Airbus versus Three-Eleven go-ahead decision loomed large for the UK Government. The chapter, out of necessity, concentrates on British and, to a lesser degree, French developments, as these two countries at the time accounted for the lion's share of the work in this area. The aim of this chapter is to draw the reader's attention to Britain's almost unassailable technological and market leadership in modern civil turbine-powered airliners vis-à-vis France and other European nations.

Chapter 2

This chapter deals with the events that led to the formation of Airbus and with the factors which were to play a part in the conversion of the UK Government of the day to the doctrine of international cooperation in aerospace in general, and commercial aerospace in particular. In this regard reference is made to the substantial influence that the Plowden Report had on Government thinking. We also provide a brief review of BAC's stillborn alternative to the Airbus A.300, the BAC Two-Eleven.

Chapter 3

This chapter traces the history of the BAC Three-Eleven aircraft project from internal launch to cancellation. This includes the project's genesis, a technical description of the aircraft (including comparisons with the A.300B European Airbus), and the financial arrangements that were being discussed between BAC, the aircraft's manufacturers, and the UK Government for the project. This chapter also includes a summary of an economic study carried out in 1970 aimed at estimating the cost-benefit for the UK economy of investing in the Three-Eleven versus the A.300B Airbus and a comprehensive review of Her Majesty's Government's evaluation of the BAC Three-Eleven. In order to provide a balanced view of the merits of the project, the chapter concludes by analysing scenarios of potentially negative outcomes of a Three-Eleven launch for the UK and European aerospace industries.

Chapter 4

This chapter analyses civil aircraft developments in Europe following the UK's decision not to back the Three-Eleven. Covered here is the evolution of Britain's commercial airliner policies, from the decision to re-join the Airbus Industrie consortium in 1978, to the present day. This historical excursus will show how France's leadership, established on the original A.300 Airbus, was reiterated and reinforced with each consecutive European project, despite several British attempts at getting back into the driving seat. This chapter also provides a broad estimate of the opportunity cost to the UK economy of the loss of European leadership, measured in terms of foregone revenues in civil aerospace over the period 1970–2004 and over the next thirty years.[6]

Chapter 5

This chapter focuses on the basic reasons why the UK, in what appears to be an attack of masochism, decided to forego leadership in a sector of the aerospace industry where the country had a distinctive and substantial comparative advantage (at least at European level). After reviewing the different factors at play at the time in the UK aircraft industry and in the wider world, we conclude that the main reasons behind the British Government's deleterious decisions boil down to political expediency and to the loss of nerve by Britain's elite during a period when the country was in transition from relatively unchallenged world power to the much more limited role of regional power.

Although this book focuses specifically on one civil aircraft project and on a relatively short but momentous period in the history of the British aerospace industry, it has been written with a wide readership in mind, including: industry professionals who are interested in the historical evolution of the aircraft industry in the UK; politicians and civil servants in charge of industrial policy decisions, including Trade & Industry officials; academics and students whose areas of interest cover Industrial Economics and/or Economic History; strategy consultants and industrial policy advisers; the layman with an interest in the above topics, and civil aircraft industry enthusiasts.

We hope that this book will appeal to all of the above people and provide some pointers (in terms of a cautionary tale) for those whose task is to influence or direct the future industrial strategy of their countries.

1   Of course the Concorde programme was a 50/50 joint venture between Britain and France, the two countries sharing equally in the development costs and industrial workshare. However, since the engine selected for the aircraft was the Bristol Siddeley Olympus turbojet, Britain was given the lead on the development and production of the Concorde's engine and propulsion systems, with 60 per cent of the work going to Bristol Siddeley (with the support of BAC) and 40 per cent to France's SNECMA. Therefore, under the principle of *le juste retour*, Sud Aviation was given the lead on the airframe and a 60 per cent share of the development and industrial workshare, with the balance (40 per cent) going to BAC. In practice, Sud's 'leadership' on the Concorde airframe was more theoretical than real, and it can be safely argued that BAC contributed at least as much as Sud Aviation to the conception and development of the aircraft.

2   We must recognise, however, that British and German engineers together with their French colleagues, make a substantial contribution to these tasks on the Airbus projects. The same is true of the British contribution to the Boeing range of airliners. See later comments in Note 6.

3   As British Aviation historians are too painfully aware, the cancellation of the BAC Three-Eleven project followed a well-established pattern of British Government 'stop-go-stop' policies towards the aircraft industry since the end of the Second World War. From the mid-1950s onwards several myopic Government decisions were taken, including the cancellation of the Vickers V-1000/VC-7 military transport/long-range jet airliner in 1955 and the infamous Duncan Sandys White Paper in 1957 which advocated a policy of 'no more manned aircraft' and which resulted in the cancellation of several promising military aircraft projects. The industry was further damaged in the 1960s during Harold Wilson's '100 days', which led to the cancellation of the BAC TSR2 fighter/bomber, the Hawker Siddeley HS.1154 Supersonic Harrier and the Hawker Siddeley (AW) HS.681 STOL military jet transport. Promising civil aircraft projects also suffered under the Wilson Government in the mid-1960s, and examples of this included the shelving of the BAC DB.264 derivative of the Vickers VC-10 and of the BAC Two-Eleven (see chapters 1 and 2).

4   The Society of British Aerospace Companies (SBAC) 2002 UK Aerospace Industry Statistics publication estimates that the UK's share of the commercial aerospace market is approximately 12 per cent for the decade 2000–2010. Based on the UK's share of Airbus, Britain has 10 per cent of the large airliner market worldwide, compared to French and German shares of 20 per cent each (Airbus currently has a 53 per cent share of the large airliner market).

5   In the many eulogistic books and articles that have been written on the history of the European Airbus the BAC 3-11 project, when mentioned at all, is given short shrift and is usually dismissed as being a hopeless programme compared to the A.300B. One of the tenets of the Airbus mythology is that no single European country would have been capable of developing a wide-body twinjet airliner on its own. In the case of the UK this is patently false as BAC would have been well able to produce the Three-Eleven had Government financial backing been forthcoming. Exploding the myth of the inevitability of European cooperation on an airbus-class aircraft (at least as far as the UK industry is concerned) is amongst the aims of this book.

6   Several senior British insiders to the Airbus programmes have pointed out to the author that the UK contribution to aircraft design and specification is much greater than the 20 per cent minority stake in Airbus would lead one to believe, and that it extends beyond the UK responsibility for the wing to include overall aircraft definition. While the author acknowledges this fact and recognises the contribution of hundreds of British engineers working for Airbus in Toulouse, the fact remains that overall project leadership, systems integration, final assembly, flight-testing and aircraft certification rest firmly with the French in Toulouse. To paraphrase Sir George Edwards, the UK gets no medals for providing a major design input from 'behind the curtain': the technological, industrial and economic benefits of project leadership accrue to France, not the UK.

I

European Commercial Airliner Developments from the Second World War to 1970

Introduction

In the years following the Second World War it was Britain that took the lead in Europe on the design, development and production of civil airliners. Indeed in 1942, in the middle of the war, the British Government set up a committee to advise on development of a range of commercial aircraft that would complement military aircraft production once peace was restored. France under de Gaulle also set about reconstructing its aircraft industry with a wide-ranging military and civil aircraft development plan, although initially France's effort was less ambitious than Britain's in both scope and technology. Thus in the immediate post-war years it was Britain and, to a lesser degree, France that spearheaded commercial airliner development in Europe. The reason for Britain and France taking the lead in Europe was in no small measure due to the moratorium imposed by the Allies on the aircraft industry of defeated Germany after the termination of the hostilities (Germany had arguably the most advanced aeronautical research base at the end of the war). The moratorium on German aircraft design and production was not lifted until 1955.

Major advances in airliner technology had already been achieved before the war in the USA. We can mention here the Boeing 247 (the first all-metal monoplane with retractable undercarriage), the Boeing 307 Stratoliner (the world's first pressurised airliner), and, of course, the Douglas DC-2 and DC-3 as outstanding examples of leaps forward in airliner 'state-of-the-art'.

The demands of the Second World War prompted a massive expansion in military aircraft output, as Britain and the Commonwealth countries on the one side (later to be joined by the USA) and Germany, Italy and Japan on the other, escalated their military operations. Notable developments in aerospace technology that took place during the war years include the introduction of radar, the jet engine and advances in the science of aerodynamics. Radar was essentially a British invention whereas German scientists proved to be masters in forwarding the science of aerodynamics. The credit for the invention of the jet engine must be shared between the British and the Germans, while a small isolated contribution came from Italy in the shape of the Caproni-Campini experimental jet aircraft.

In the remainder of this chapter we shall analyse European commercial aircraft development policies between the war and 1970, and the airliner programmes which resulted from these policies. Our review will cover principally Britain and France, but we shall also record the steps that Germany, Italy and the Netherlands took from the mid-1950s onwards in order to re-establish their civil aircraft industry.

Britain – The Brabazon Committee Programmes

Of all the major European countries, Britain was the one that suffered the least destruction to its industrial infrastructure. Also, despite the costly war effort, the country was still by and large Europe's biggest economy. In addition, the immense war effort that the country had embarked upon from 1939 onwards resulted in the Continent's largest aerospace capability. Not only that, the mass production of military planes had endowed the UK with a powerful if relatively inefficient production infrastructure, with manufacturing and assembly plants scattered throughout its territory. British politicians and industrialists realised as early as 1942 that this capability was a national asset that was worth preserving. In order to achieve this objective a strategic plan was formulated by Government to develop a series of civil aircraft that would complement a much-reduced output of military aircraft.

On the technology side, Britain was far ahead of other nations (with the notable exception of Germany) in jet engine and turbine power for aircraft applications. Sir Frank Whittle had first patented his jet engine design in 1931. Also advanced, through the invention of radar, was British technology in the field of navigation – that is, the complex electro-mechanical systems that were to be the forebears of what is today's modern avionics equipment. Once Germany was occupied, Britain, together with the USA and the Soviet Union, benefited enormously from very advanced German research in the fields of aerodynamics and propulsion. In fact the Allies were astounded at the level of sophistication that German aeronautics research and development had reached towards the end of the Third Reich. Britain, the USA and the Soviet Union wasted no time in applying this advanced research to their post-war military and civil aircraft programmes. Indeed a large number of German scientists and engineers went to work in Britain and the USA once the hostilities were over, thus accelerating their host countries' technology acquisition process. German aerospace engineers in the Soviet-occupied East Germany, on the other hand, helped the Soviet Union in its aircraft programmes.

Towards the end of 1942, while the war effort was still in progress, the British Government set up a study committee under the chairmanship of Lord Brabazon of Tara (the former British pioneer aviator) to consider possible civil transport aircraft developments. The Brabazon Committee submitted its first report to the Cabinet in February 1943. The report outlined the need for Britain to develop commercial transports for introduction at the end of the war, without which the industry was not deemed to be in a position to maintain its high output and technological achievements. The report also outlined five broad airliner types that would form the basis of such a programme. The Government then instructed a second Brabazon Committee to draw up a more detailed set of specifications that, after consultation with industry, led to nine individual projects. These are summarised in the table below. Brabazon also recommended the development of interim aircraft types, based on derivatives of war bomber designs.

Table 1 – Brabazon Committee recommended aircraft types

Type	Definition	Model
Type 1	Long-range piston-engined transatlantic airliner	Bristol Brabazon
Type 2A	Short-range piston-engined airliner	Airspeed Ambassador
Type 2B	Short-range turboprop airliner	Vickers Viscount
Type 2B	Short-range turboprop airliner	Armstrong Whitworth Apollo
Type 3A	Medium-range turboprop airliner	Avro 693
Type 3B	Medium-range piston-engined airliner	Avro Tudor (replaced Avro 693)
Type 4	Transatlantic jet-powered 'mail carrier'	De Havilland Comet
Type 5A	Piston-engined feeder liner	Miles Marathon
Type 5B	Piston-engined feeder liner	De Havilland Dove

(Source: Keith Hayward, Government and British Civil Aerospace)

On 25 February 1943 the War Cabinet endorsed the Brabazon programme, accepting its recommendations that the UK should 'maintain a substantial aircraft industry after the war' and that 'British air transport after the war shall be on a scale and quality in keeping with our world position'.[1]

Of all the aircraft developed under the auspices of the Brabazon Committee, two in particular were to play a revolutionary role in the history of air transport and these were the Vickers Viscount turboprop airliner and the de Havilland Comet jet airliner. But, whereas the Viscount was commercially successful, the Comet failed to live up to its promise, due to several fatal accidents involving the early models and caused by a phenomenon known as 'metal fatigue'. Apart from the Viscount, out of the nine aircraft types planned by the Brabazon Committee only the de Havilland Dove feeder liner achieved substantial success in the market place, with over 540 produced between 1945 and 1967.

Ironically, the project that bore Brabazon's name, the Bristol Brabazon, turned out to be a total commercial flop. Easily the world's largest airliner at the time of its first flight in September 1949 (wingspan of 70m, length 54m, fuselage width of 5.10m, capacity for 100 transatlantic passengers), this eight-engined 'monster' was beset from the start by technical problems relating to the engine transmission systems and was eventually overtaken by the development of turboprop and pure jet aircraft. The result was that only the first prototype was flown, while the second prototype was dismantled before it had a chance to fly. No much better fate was to greet the other Brabazon types, with the AW Apollo being eventually dropped in favour of the Viscount, and the Avro Tudor and Airspeed Ambassador entering service in small numbers (total output of thirty-one and twenty-three aircraft respectively).

It is appropriate at this point to describe the Vickers Viscount and the de Havilland Comet in some detail. In fact these two programmes not only catapulted Britain to the forefront of airliner development worldwide, but were also the catalysts for the evolution of the design and engineering centres of Weybridge and Hatfield into world-class civil airliner development centres.

The Vickers Viscount

The Vickers Viscount, which has the distinction of being the world's first turboprop-powered airliner, had an inauspicious start when its sponsoring airline, British European Airways (BEA) initially rejected it on the grounds that it had insufficient capacity and range.

Mainly due to the availability of a more powerful version of the Rolls-Royce Dart turboprop engine, Vickers eventually found itself in a position to design a larger and longer-ranged version with a passenger capacity of forty-seven to sixty-five (the original prototype having flown in 1948). BEA finally accepted the improved aircraft, christened the 'Viscount 700 Series'. From that moment onwards the Viscount never looked back, offering as it did far superior performance on short-medium range routes than its contemporary slower, noisier and fuel inefficient piston-engined equivalents. In the end a grand total of 444 Viscounts were produced in the fourteen-year period from 1950 to 1964. All the major world airlines operated the aircraft and, perhaps more importantly, over 150 Viscounts were exported to North America, the world's most demanding and sophisticated aviation market, and these were operated by prestigious airlines such as Capital/United Airlines, Continental Airlines, Northeast Airlines and Trans Canadian Airlines.

The de Havilland Comet

The Comet also occupies a significant position in the history of commercial transport development. When the prototype took off from de Havilland's Hatfield, Hertfordshire, airfield on 27 July 1949 it heralded the arrival of the jet age. In fact the Comet was the world's first purpose-built jet airliner, beating Canada's Avro Jetliner by three weeks and the Boeing 367-Dash 80 by over five years (the Dash 80, which acted as the prototype for the Boeing 707, first flew in 1954 and was the second production airliner to fly[2]). The Comet was truly revolutionary for its day: with its cruising speed of 490mph (825km/h) and cruising height of 35,000ft (10,500m), the aircraft left all other transports of the time literally 'well behind'.

The Comet project was financed principally by Britain's Ministry of Aviation Supply, and the nationalised long-haul carrier British Overseas Airways Corporation (BOAC) was its launch customer. On 2 May 1952 the Comet 1 made history when it introduced the world's first scheduled jet service from London Heathrow to Johannesburg via Rome, Cairo, Khartoum, Entebbe and Livingstone. In addition to BOAC, other early Comet customers were Canadian Pacific, Air France and France's UAT.

At this stage it looked as though de Havilland and Britain had cornered the market for high-speed jetliners. Major airlines like Japan Airlines, Air India, LAV of Venezuela, Air France and Pan Air do Brazil flocked to Hatfield to order the higher capacity and longer-ranged Comet 2 and Comet 3. The crowning glory for the aircraft came in 1953 when Pan American Airways of the US, the major airline on the North Atlantic route, ordered three Comet 3s plus options on seven more.

Alas, as we all know, the dream for de Havilland and Britain came to an abrupt end in 1954 when two catastrophic crashes of BOAC Comets off the coast of Italy brought to the world's attention the problem of metal fatigue. The Comets were grounded and their Certificate of Airworthiness was withdrawn. After a painstaking investigation into the crashes, involving de Havilland and the RAE at Farnborough under the direction of Sir Arnold Hall (later chairman of Hawker Siddeley), metal fatigue was identified as the cause of the disasters. With typical British fairness, de Havilland and the RAE shared their findings with other manufacturers that were then developing jet-powered transport aircraft (Boeing and Douglas in the USA, Sud Aviation in France and Tupolev in the USSR).

The British Government, de Havilland and BOAC showed their faith in the basic soundness of the Comet design and went on to develop the larger, longer-ranged Comet 4 series. Together with the 4B shorter range and the 4C higher capacity derivatives, these structurally strengthened Comets went on to give sterling service with BOAC, BEA, Olympic Airways, Mexicana de Aviacion, Aerolineas Argentinas, Misrair/Egyptair, Malaysia-Singapore Airlines, Sudan Airways, East African Airways and MEA. Indeed in October 1958 a BOAC Comet 4 had the distinction of flying the first North Atlantic journey by jet airliner, from London to New York, beating Pan Am's Boeing 707-120 service in the opposite direction by more than three weeks.

However, by the time the Comet 4 was introduced into service, Boeing and Douglas of the US were ready to introduce the much larger and longer-ranged

Boeing 707 and Douglas DC-8. These two aircraft went on to capture the market that should have belonged to de Havilland. The final production tallies tell the story more starkly than anything else: total Comet production amounted to only 114 units, and this compares to 1,010 Boeing 707s/720s and 556 Douglas DC-8s of all marques. Britain had indeed lost the war on long-range airliners, despite having won the first battle!

Ironically, technical brilliance and commercial failure were to characterise a number of subsequent British-developed civil jetliners and it is to these developments that we now turn our attention. However, the Comet placed Hatfield firmly on the map of the world's centres of expertise in commercial jet transport aircraft, in much the same way as the Viscount had established Weybridge as a world-class centre for civil aircraft development. Prior to the emergence of Toulouse in the early 1970s on the back of the Concorde and Airbus programmes, we can state without a hint of doubt that Weybridge and Hatfield were the finest airliner design centres outside the US and the Soviet Union.

Britain – Post-Brabazon Airliner Developments

Despite the Comet setback, both the British Government and the manufacturers were keen to preserve the country's capabilities in large airliner development. This was achieved, as far as the Government is concerned, through 'launch aid' schemes and through encouraging (one may say forcing) the nationalised airlines, BEA and BOAC, to buy locally developed products. There has been ample analysis of the British Government's policy towards civil aerospace and we shall not dwell on the topic in this book.[3] What is interesting to observe, however, is that the policy of encouraging the nationalised airlines to 'buy British' had mixed results on the commercial success of the aircraft developed for them. Indeed, apart from the Viscount and the BAC One-Eleven, plus the Weybridge-originated projects that did not see production (and here we include the BAC Three-Eleven), it is fair to say that the British airlines' influence on general aircraft specification was to prove disastrous in terms of the commercial prospects for the aircraft concerned. We shall review several such cases in the following paragraphs.

The Government also encouraged the consolidation of the many British airframe producers. This process was completed by the early 1960s, by which time two major groupings had emerged.

The British Aircraft Corporation (BAC) was created in 1960 and incorporated Vickers-Armstrong, English Electric and Bristol Aircraft. It also acquired Hunting Aviation of Luton. The main civil design centres were Vickers' Weybridge facility and Bristol's Filton works. English Electric at Warton carried on its specialisation as a military aircraft development and production centre.

Hawker Siddeley Aviation (HSA) was also formed in 1960, but full integration took place three years later in 1963. This large group comprised the Hawker Siddeley Group (formed in 1935 and which included Hawker, Avro, Armstrong Withworth and Gloster), and the recently acquired de Havilland, Blackburn & General Aircraft and Folland. HSA's main civil aircraft design centre was de Havilland's Hatfield headquarters. Avro's Woodford facility was also an important commercial transport development centre, although it specialised in smaller feeder liner aircraft (what one would now call regional airliners).

We shall now describe the post-Brabazon programmes that emerged from BAC, HSA and their predecessors in the 1950s and 1960s. For consistency we shall review the main developments by design centre rather than chronologically.

Weybridge Programmes

The Vickers Vanguard

Vickers at Weybridge developed the Vanguard turboprop following an expression of interest from BEA and Trans Canadian Airlines for an aircraft larger than the Viscount. First flown in January 1959, the four-engined Vanguard could carry up to 139 passengers in its wide, six-abreast cabin (more than double the passenger capacity of the Viscount). Alas for Vickers, the Vanguard came to the market too late to make an impact. By then Air France and other airlines were introducing the twinjet Sud Aviation Caravelle to their short and medium-haul routes, and this aircraft made the slower Vanguard suddenly obsolete. Although turboprop aircraft such as the Vanguard and Lockheed's Electra had good operating economics, the low price of aviation kerosene fuel at the time made pure jets like the Caravelle more competitive in terms of the higher speed they offered. In the end BEA and TCA remained the Vanguard's only customers, and only forty-four examples of the aircraft were built, resulting in a loss-making venture for Vickers. Ironically Vanguard production terminated in 1962, two years earlier than that of the Viscount! The Vanguard can nonetheless be remembered as the first example of a European 'airbus' concept (high capacity, short-haul airliner).

The Vickers 1000/VC-7

Despite the Comet setbacks, Britain had another great chance to win a substantial share of the long-range jet airliner market, but a combination of a change of heart from the Government and indifference or hostility from main target customer BOAC put paid to that.

Industry insiders and followers alike will have guessed that we are talking here of the Vickers 1000 military transport for the RAF and its civil airliner equivalent, the Vickers VC-7. This programme emerged as a large four-jet-engined transport aircraft based on the Valiant bomber, but with an all-new much larger fuselage and a modified enlarged wing. The aircraft was to be powered by four new Rolls-Royce Conway turbojets buried in the wing root à la Comet. Actually in external appearance the V1000/VC-7 resembled an enlarged Comet, with the range and payload to carry 120 passengers across the Atlantic non-stop in a comfortable six-abreast cabin. The Ministry of Supply gave Vickers a contract to develop the aircraft in October 1952 and in June 1954 a further contract for six production V1000s was placed with Vickers. Had the programme been allowed to continue, the first prototype would have taken to the air in mid-1956, two years before the Douglas DC-8 (May 1958) and almost three years before the long-range Boeing 707. Unfortunately the RAF and the Government had a change of heart, and decided that the turboprop-powered Bristol Britannia was a better option for the RAF Transport Command. Among the factors weighing on the decision was the fact that the Britannia would have been built under licence by Shorts in Northern Ireland, an area of high unemployment.

Despite the RAF's change of heart, Vickers and the Ministry of Supply were still hoping to interest BOAC in the aircraft. Unfortunately the airline – possibly put off by the Comet groundings and the delay in getting the Britannias into service – showed no inclination to order the VC-7 and was positively against it, arguing that they doubted an appropriate engine would be available to power the aircraft. They also argued that the aircraft was too heavy. Despite a last ditch plea by Canada's TCA to the MoS and the strong backing for the project by the MoS itself, the British Government announced on 11 November 1955 that the Vickers V1000/VC-7 project had been cancelled. At the time of cancellation the prototype was 80 per cent complete and the British taxpayer had invested £4 million in the programme (over £100 million in today's money).

This was how, in one of its recurring acts of masochism, Britain, and its aerospace industry, handed over the long-range jet airliner market to the Americans on a plate. To this day the event is considered a turning point in the development of Britain's commercial aerospace industry. Sir George Edwards, Vickers' chairman at the time, was quoted in *The Times* of 12 November 1955 as saying: 'I think it is a national decision that we shall regret for many years to come.' Many years later Sir George was reported as saying: 'The V1000 cancellation was the biggest blunder of all.' Sir Arnold Hall, chairman of HSA, also in connection with the VC-7/V1000, said: 'I see as a major turning point in the history of British aerospace the decision not to go ahead with the V1000 airliner/military transport… the nation turned to this [nuclear power] from long range jet aviation, cancelling the V1000 at precisely the moment when it was about to grow and we were ahead of everybody.'[4] Alas, as we shall see in more depth with the BAC Three-Eleven programme, this was not the last time that myopic short-term considerations by Britain's ruling elite were to cost the country's aerospace industry dear.

The Vickers VC-10

Although the UK lost the race to compete with the Americans in the long-range jet airliner market, its industry did develop and produce a long-range jet transport aircraft. In fact, from the ashes of the VC-7/V1000, the Vickers VC-10 (Vickers Commercial 10) was to emerge in the early 1960s. Designed to a BOAC requirement for an aircraft able to operate from the short runways of the 'hot and high' airports on the Empire routes, development of the VC-10 started in 1957 with the prototype flying for the first time from Brooklands airfield, Weybridge, on 29 June 1962.

Unlike the Boeing 707 and Douglas DC-8 that preceded it, the VC-10's configuration sported a clean wing (that is, with no engines on it) and four Rolls-Royce Conway turbofans grouped at the back of the fuselage under a T-tail. This configuration, pioneered by the French Caravelle, was unique among the larger, long-range aircraft and was adopted by other British-designed transports, including the HS (de Havilland) Trident and BAC One-Eleven. Indeed the VC-10 configuration was, flatteringly for Vickers, copied by the Soviets for their own long-range jet airliner, the Ilyushin Il-62. The main advantages of the rear-engined configuration are a clean, more aerodynamically efficient, wing and a quieter passenger cabin. In actual fact, the VC-10's wing was very advanced for its time, benefiting from the aerodynamics research which had been carried out at RAE Farnborough (the 'peaky' wing profile developed by Pearce and others). The Vickers VC-10, and the stretched Super VC-10 that flew in 1964, emerged as extremely elegant and handsome airliners (in the author's opinion, *pace* Concorde, the VC-10/Super VC-10 are the most aesthetically pleasing airliners ever produced) and were to prove very popular with passengers and crew alike. The VC-10 was also the largest jet airliner ever developed in Europe at the time of its introduction. The aircraft still remains to this day the largest airliner developed by a single European country to enter production (the Super VC-10 was 52.3m long, had a wingspan of 44.6m, wing area of 272sq.m, height of over 12m and maximum take-off weight of 152 tonnes).

Unfortunately, in the world of commercial aerospace, technical excellence does not necessarily translate into commercial success. In the case of the 139-seat VC-10 (and the 174-seat Super VC-10 that followed it) a combination of a change in the environment in which the aircraft was to be operated, and the strong antagonism of its main operator BOAC sealed its fate as a commercially unsuccessful programme. In fact the runways around the world were in due course lengthened to allow operation of the Boeing 707 and Douglas DC-8, and BOAC ended up complaining publicly that the VC-10/Super VC-10 had higher operating costs than the Boeing 707, despite the fact that the VC-10's higher passenger loads made the aircraft profitable. BOAC's damning of the aircraft cost Vickers/BAC several overseas sales, and total VC-10/Super VC-10 production amounted to only fifty-four. In addition to recalcitrant BOAC and to the RAF Transport Command, the aircraft was sold in small numbers to British United Airways, Laker Airways, Ghana Airways and East African Airways. Second-hand examples operated for Nigeria Airways, MEA, Gulf Air and Air Malawi.

A possible reprieve for the VC-10 appeared briefly in 1972, when the People's Republic of China's national airline CAAC expressed an interest in ordering thirty Super VC-10s. BAC was very keen to conclude this deal but, since the assembly line had been dismantled after the delivery of the last aircraft in February 1970, reopening it worked out to be prohibitively expensive and would have resulted in unit prices which were not competitive. Therefore, to BAC's regret it was decided that the relatively small order for thirty did not warrant reopening production.

The BAC One-Eleven

While Vickers was busy developing the stillborn VC-7/V1000 and its successor the VC-10, thoughts were being given to the development of a jet-powered successor to the ubiquitous Viscount. The aircraft, that was eventually to emerge as the BAC One-Eleven, started life as the Hunting H107 regional airliner project at Luton. This was to be a thirty-two-seater, powered by two rear-mounted Bristol Siddeley BS75 turbojets. BAC's Weybridge division, as Vickers had become known after the 1960 merger, adopted the Hunting design but developed it into a larger aircraft, initially able to carry fifty-six passengers (BAC 107). Further market studies induced BAC to further increase the aircraft capacity to between seventy-four and eighty-nine passengers. As such the programme was launched in 1961 as the BAC 111 (later called the One-Eleven). As finalised, the One-Eleven was a rear-engined twinjet powered by two Rolls-Royce Spey turbofans. Like the VC-10, it sported a T-tail and, like the Caravelle, it had ventral air stairs for passenger access at the back. The prototype One-Eleven first flew from Hurn (Bournemouth) airport on 20 August 1963. Hurn was where most of the Vickers Viscounts had been assembled. Unlike other British commercial aircraft, the One-Eleven was immediately successful and, at the time of the aircraft's maiden flight, BAC had already booked sixty firm orders (including orders from the US's Braniff Airways, Mohawk Airlines and – importantly – a thirty aircraft order from American Airlines, in addition to Britain's BUA). Other major airlines including Aer Lingus, Philippine Airlines and Brazil's VASP also ordered the aircraft. The One-Eleven was the first of the new generation of short-haul jet airliners, following the lead of France's Sud Aviation Caravelle and preceding the equivalent American offerings by almost two years (Douglas DC-9, first flight in February 1965) and four years (Boeing 737, first flight in April 1967).

Again, like the Comet (and like the VC-7, had it been allowed to proceed), the BAC One-Eleven had a considerable time advantage over its American competitors. Unfortunately, though the One-Eleven did become one of Britain's most commercially successful airliners, it failed to achieve anything like the success of its American rivals. This can be put down to two main factors. Firstly, the crash of the prototype during stalling tests (which killed the flight test crew on board) caused major delays in the aircraft's certification process while a technical solution to the 'deep-stall' phenomenon was being studied. Eventually the aircraft entered service with BUA in April 1965, only eight months before the Douglas DC-9. Therefore the time to market advantage for the One-Eleven was almost totally dissipated. The second factor, and probably the most significant in reducing the aircraft's market appeal in the long run, was that BAC failed to develop larger versions of the aircraft early on in the programme's life. The stretched One-Eleven 500 series, launched by a BEA order in 1967 and capable of carrying between ninety-nine and 119 passengers, did not enter service until August 1968. At that stage both Boeing with its 737 and Douglas with its DC-9 had developed versions that could carry up to 130 passengers. These developments continued to the point where the largest developments of the DC-9 and 737 could carry up to 172 and 210 passengers respectively (MD-90 and Boeing 737-900X).

One of the key reasons for the lack of early growth of the One-Eleven was its complete dependence on the underpowered Rolls-Royce Spey engine: had BAC offered the aircraft with the Pratt & Whitney JT8D turbofan as an alternative, the One-Eleven could have easily grown in the same fashion as the DC-9/MD-80 family eventually grew. The mistake of relying on only one engine model has not been repeated by today's Airbus and Boeing, which offer a choice of engines for almost all their aircraft.

Another reason given for the One-Eleven's unspectacular sales performance was its relatively narrow five-abreast fuselage cross-section, which compared unfavourably with the Boeing 737's six-abreast layout. However, even the DC-9/MD-80 family sported a narrow five-abreast cabin, and this did not prevent it from achieving considerable market acceptance.

Altogether, between 1963 and 1982, BAC manufactured a total of 244 One-Elevens (including nine that were assembled in Romania under a licence agreement) and these found favour with some fifty airlines and private operators. This production total was respectable in the context of UK and European programmes at the time (it lagged the Viscount's total of 444 units, but it was not far behind France's Caravelle output of 282 units – up to then Europe's most successful jet airliner) but paled in comparison to the DC-9/MD-80/MD-90 family (total exceeding 2,450 examples) and the Boeing 737 family (over 6,400 ordered, and counting!).

In addition to the several 1970s projected developments of the One-Eleven which we shall review in Chapter 4, in the mid-1980s a number of brave and praiseworthy attempts were made to give the One-Eleven a new lease of life by using the Romanian production line for green airframes combined with the new, more powerful and 'greener' Rolls-Royce Tay turbofans and a modern 'glass' cockpit. Unfortunately these valiant efforts were thwarted by British Aerospace, who were by then promoting the BAe 146. The same lack of cooperation from

BAe hampered a potential One-Eleven joint-venture development programme with Japan. It is reasonable to assume, on the basis of the market success of the equivalent Fokker 100, that an upgraded Tay-powered One-Eleven could have added up to 300–400 sales to the total production tally.

In summary, it must be acknowledged that the One-Eleven confirmed the Weybridge team's ability to design efficient, sturdy and economical short-haul airliners to build on the Viscount's success. This enabled BAC to achieve the broadest customer base of any European commercial aircraft developer of the day. The success of the Viscount and the One-Eleven should have provided a sound building block on which to launch new aircraft projects. As we shall see, despite the best efforts of BAC, these projects (particularly the Three-Eleven) were to come to nothing.

Bristol Programmes

The Bristol 175 Britannia

The Bristol Aeroplane Co. at Filton followed up the false start of the giant Bristol Brabazon with another large propeller-driven aircraft, this time the Bristol 175 Britannia turboprop. Unlike the Vanguard and the Viscount, which addressed the short-to-medium-haul market, the Britannia was designed from the start as a long-range airliner. Developed to a 1947 BOAC requirement for a medium-range transport, the Britannia was designed as a four-engined turboprop powered by Bristol Proteus engines. The prototype first flew on 16 August 1952 but the early loss of the prototype and continuing problems with the Proteus engine (recurring flameouts due to dry ice accretion) meant that the Britannia entered airline service only in 1957, by which time the faster, jet-powered Boeing 707 and Douglas DC-8 were close to entering service.

The Britannia was produced in several versions with capacity for up to 139 passengers seated six-abreast in a wide cabin. In addition to BOAC and the RAF Transport Command, the Britannia found favour with Aeronaves de Mexico, Cubana, El Al of Israel, Ghana Airways and Canadian Pacific among others. Technically it was an excellent airliner, but was too late in reaching the market. In the end only eighty-five Britannias were produced, compared to hundreds of US long-range jets. Affectionately known as the 'Whispering Giant' by virtue of its relatively low external noise footprint, the Britannia was produced under licence in Canada as the Canadair CL-44. The CL-44 was further stretched to a total length of 46.3m and could carry up to a maximum of 214 passengers over a range of 5,635km. CL-44 production totalled thirty-nine. If we add this to the UK production tally, we have a total of 124 examples, a relatively small number for such an excellent aircraft.

Bristol 223 Supersonic Transport (SST)

The false start with the giant Brabazon and the disappointing sales perform-ance of the Britannia did not prevent the Filton, Bristol, team from building up considerable airliner design expertise. This expertise was eventually put to good use in the design of the Bristol 223 SST (later to be called the BAC 223). The Bristol 223 formed the basis of the Anglo-French SST agreement of 1962 which in due course gave birth to the most ambitious airliner project ever undertaken in Europe, the Concorde. But that is a different story.

Hatfield Developments

De Havilland at Hatfield built on their expertise as the developers of the world's first jet airliner and went on to produce a short- to-medium-range fast jetliner, the de Havilland DH (later HS) 121 Trident.

The HS.121 Trident

De Havilland's second jetliner project stemmed from a BEA requirement issued in July 1956 for a 100-seat 600mph-plus jet airliner capable of carrying a payload of 10 tonnes over a 1,000-mile sector. BEA was aware of the potential competi-tion represented by Air France's Caravelle fleet. As it was politically unacceptable at the time for a British airline to order a European (never mind a French!)-built aircraft, and imports from the US were unwelcome given the need to support the British aircraft industry, BEA was encouraged to turn to the local manufacturers for its requirement, with the Ministry of Supply committing to provide launch aid for the winning bid. BEA received three proposals, all of which involved a three-engined configuration, with two engines at the rear of the fuselage à la Caravelle and one on the tail under the fin. The three proposals were: the Bristol 200, the Avro 740, and the de Havilland DH.121. The MoS, following Government guidelines that were aimed at consolidating the aircraft industry, stipulated that each submission should include a consortium of manufacturers. Therefore Bristol signed an agreement with Hawker Siddeley on the Bristol 200 and de Havilland created the Airco consortium with Fairey and Hunting to produce the DH.121. The Bristol-Hawker Siddeley joint venture meant the demise of the Avro 740 proposal, as Avro at the time was already part of Hawker Siddeley. After a fought-out competition between the Airco consortium and the Bristol/HS consortium, BEA announced in February 1958 that it had selected the DH.121, which eventually became the HS.121 Trident trijet.

The Trident story is well known and we shall only summarise here the main events. The original DH.121 was about the same size and had the same range and engine thrust as the broadly equivalent and contemporary Boeing 727 trijet. Due to a temporary dip in traffic volume, launch customer BEA panicked and ordered de Havilland to reduce the 121's size and range. Amazingly de Havilland accepted BEA's revised aircraft, despite knowing full well that it was giving away a huge world market to Boeing and its 727. The first HS.121 Trident, called the 1C series, flew for the first time on 9 January 1962 and entered service with BEA in March 1964. Despite being over one year ahead of the Boeing 727, the Trident 1C's smaller capacity (maximum of 103 passengers) and shorter range made it an unattractive proposition to all of the world's airlines except BEA. Thus de Havilland and later Hawker Siddeley spent the rest of the Trident's career trying to make it bigger and longer-ranged again. The Trident 1E, 2E and the stretched-fuselage Trident 3B (the latter with an overall length of 40m and high density capacity for 180 passengers) were introduced into service during the 1960s, but by then it was too late as the Boeing 727 had captured most of the market that could have been at least partly a preserve of the Trident.

In the end only 117 Tridents of the various marques were produced between 1962 and 1978. In addition to BEA, the Trident was ordered in quantity only by China's CAAC, its order for thirty-three Trident 2Es and two Trident Super 3Bs in the early 1970s saving the programme from being a total commercial disaster. Other orders for small fleets of Tridents were received from Iraqi Airways, Kuwait Airways, Air Ceylon and Pakistan International Airways. By comparison the Boeing 727's sales in its various versions reached a staggering 1,832 examples and over 150 operators ordered the American trijet.

If the HS Trident was a commercial flop, in many respects it was also a technological pioneer. In fact the Trident was the first aircraft in the world to operate a fully automated landing in fog ('blind landing'). The world's first automatic landing on a passenger-carrying flight was completed on 16 May 1967 by a BEA Trident 1C. The Trident also introduced to commercial aviation the 'aft-loaded'/ supercritical wing design concept, which in due course Hawker Siddeley successfully developed for the A.300 European Airbus and which was instrumental in establishing Airbus as a successful aircraft.

The Hawker Siddeley HS.125

Immediately after the Trident, de Havilland's team at Hatfield produced a small jet-powered transport, the DH.125. The twin-engined DH.125 first flew from Hatfield in June 1962, and entered production at Chester as the Hawker Siddeley HS.125. In its various versions the HS.125 was developed into a very successful business jet. A highly developed, turbofan-powered version of the HS.125 is still in production to this day in the US, as the Raytheon Hawker 800XP, forty-three years after its first flight. In total over 1,200 HS.125s/Raytheon Hawkers have been delivered. Sadly in 1993 BAe sold the HS.125 programme to Raytheon, and therefore the current aircraft is no longer a British product, although Airbus UK at Chester supplies Raytheon in the US with 'green' airframes (fuselages, wings and empennage).

Woodford Programmes

The HS (Avro) 748

Via the old established Avro at Woodford, HSA in the late 1950s developed a forty-four to fifty-eight-seater twin turboprop feeder liner – the HS.748. First flown in June 1960, the HS.748 went on to achieve considerable market success with a large number of airlines and air forces worldwide. It was also produced under licence in India by HAL for the Indian Air Force and Indian Airlines. Many flag carriers including Varig of Brazil, Aerolineas Argentinas, Lan Chile, Philippine Airlines, Thai Airways, Royal Nepal Airlines, Austrian Airlines, and most of Africa's flag carriers, operated HS.748s. Total production amounted to 382 units, which made it Britain's most successful airliner after the Viscount, until the arrival of the later BAe 146/Avro RJ regional jet. It also kept the Woodford factory busy for a remarkable twenty-seven years.

France – Post-war Civil Aircraft Developments

France's commercial aircraft developments after the Second World War did not match the UK programmes either in number of models launched or in ambition and technical innovation, with the notable exception of the Sud Aviation Caravelle. France's aircraft factories had been either destroyed by the German invading armies or converted to production of German aircraft, but design offices and technical expertise survived the German invasion, ready to be exploited again once the hostilities were over. Unlike the British programmes launched by the Brabazon Committee, France's immediate post-war airliner efforts were either designed before the war or finalised during the war on the basis of pre-war designs.

The greatest part of the French airframe industry had been nationalised in 1936. In the nationalised segment of the industry three groups played a key role in the renaissance of the French aircraft industry. These groups were Societé Nationale des Constructions Aéronautiques du Sud-Est ('SNCASE', commonly known as Sud-Est Aviation) based in Toulouse, Societé Nationale des Constructions Aéronautiques du Sud-Ouest ('SNCASO', known as Sud-Ouest Aviation) and Societé Nationale des Constructions Aéronautiques du Nord ('SNCAN' or Nord Aviation). These companies had, at the time of nationalisation, absorbed the most famous names of French aviation, including Farman, Louis Bleriot, Dewoitine, Loiré et Olivier and Potez.

In the private sector and fiercely independent, we had Societé Louis Breguet and Avions Marcel Dassault (originally Avions Marcel Bloch). As we shall see, both Breguet and Dassault produced commercial transports, but it was from the nationalised companies that the most significant French efforts emerged. These efforts were encouraged and backed by the French Government which, under General de Gaulle, recognised early on the importance of a strong aerospace industry as a tool to enhance and promote France's technological progress and prestige abroad.

The Sud-Est SE-161 Languedoc

Among the immediate post-war designs, the most successful was the Sud-Est SE-161 Languedoc. The original design, the Marcel Bloch MB.161, was completed before the hostilities broke out in 1939. The first prototype eventually flew for the first time in September 1945 as the SE-161 Languedoc. The aircraft was a four-engine monoplane powered by four Gnome-Rhône 14N radial engines, and could carry between thirty-three and forty-four passengers. Air France ordered forty Languedocs, which remained in service with the airline up to the mid-1950s, serving domestic, European and North African destinations from Paris. The Languedoc was successfully exported and sixty were produced for such airlines as Poland's LOT, Tunis Air, Iberia, Egypt's Misrair, Atlas Air and the French Air Force. In total 100 Languedocs were produced.

The SE-2010 Armagnac

Sud-Est then developed a much larger aircraft, the SE-2010 Armagnac. Powered by four Pratt & Whitney R-4360-B13 radial piston engines, the Armagnac was slightly larger than the Bristol Britannia, boasting a wingspan of almost 49m and length of 39.7m. The Armagnac could carry up to 107 passengers in a single class, or up to 160 passengers in a high-density layout. First flight was achieved on 2 April 1949. Air France evaluated the Armagnac for its long-range operations but rejected the aircraft on the grounds of poor operating economics. Despite this, eight aircraft were produced and delivered to Société Auxiliaire de Gerence et des Transports Aériens (SAGETA). SAGETA operated the Armagnacs on troops, cargo and mail-carrying services between Paris and Saigon (via Beirut, Karachi and Calcutta) up to the late 1950s. With a total production of just nine units, the Armagnac was a total commercial failure. However, it enabled Sud-Est to gain large airliner experience that was put to good use in developing the Caravelle.

The SO-30 Bretagne

SNCASO in Cannes developed a small transport called the SO-30 Bretagne. Capable of carrying between thirty and forty-three passengers, the twin-engined Bretagne was designed during the war. Powered by two Pratt & Whitney R-2800 'Double Wasp' radial engines, the Bretagne flew for the first time in February 1945. Sud-Ouest produced a total of forty-five Bretagnes, which saw service with Air France, Air Algerie and a number of smaller operators in the French colonies.

The Breguet 763 Provence

Private sector Societé Louis Breguet designed the Breguet 763 Provence. Also called the 'Deux Ponts' for its distinctive two-deck fuselage (almost a precursor of today's Airbus A380 double-decker super-jumbo), the BR763 Provence flew for the first time in February 1949. It was a relatively large aircraft capable of carrying 117 passengers (fifty-nine on the upper deck, forty-eight on the lower deck), or a maximum of 135 in a high-density layout. It was powered by four Pratt & Whitney R-2800 'Double Wasp' radial engines. A total of twenty were produced, including the prototype, and the aircraft saw service with Air France and the Armée de L'Air from 1952 to the late 1960s. Although the Provence was not commercially successful, it did give sterling service to its operators.

The Sud Aviation SE-210 Caravelle

Without doubt the aircraft that established France's credentials as a major developer of civil airliners is the Sud Aviation SE-210 Caravelle. When launched in September 1952, it was not only France's first turbine-powered airliner to enter production, but also the world's first short-to-medium-range jetliner. It was also the first jet airliner to sport the widely copied fuselage-mounted, rear-engine layout. Originally planned as a trijet with three French-made SNECMA Atar turbojets mounted in pods at the rear of the fuselage, Sud later decided to adopt a twin-engined configuration by using the more powerful and more advanced Rolls-Royce Avon turbojets. The rear-engined configuration allowed for a clean wing, unobstructed by engines and engine pylons, and a much quieter passenger cabin compared to wing-mounted configurations.

The prototype Caravelle flew for the first time on 27 May 1955 from Sud's Toulouse-Blagnac airfield, having the distinction of being the fourth jet airliner to fly after the de Havilland Comet (July 1949), Avro Canada C-102 Jetliner (August 1949) and the Boeing 367-80/707 prototype (July 1954).

Interestingly the Caravelle represented the first example of Anglo-French collaboration in commercial aircraft. In fact, in order to save on development costs, Sud-Est adopted the Comet's nose and cockpit: the first few noses were delivered by de Havilland directly to Sud Aviation and after that Sud paid the British company a royalty on the licence production of the Comet nose and cockpit design. In other areas of the design Caravelle engineers Lucien Servanty and Pierre Satrè adopted a higher aspect ratio wing than the Comet, resulting in a lighter wing unencumbered by jet engines. Nevertheless the basic wing structure benefited to no small degree from de Havilland's experience. It is worth noting that this initial collaboration between Sud in Toulouse and de Havilland at Hatfield was to lay the foundations of Airbus, when the Hatfield and Toulouse design teams got together to design the original A.300 Airbus in 1966–1967. Indeed Airbus's first technical director Roger Betéille had worked on the Comet at Hatfield during a secondment to the British company, and then moved to lead the Caravelle certification programme at Sud Aviation. Other British elements on France's first jetliner included the Rolls-Royce Avon engines and the Dowty undercarriage, to name but the most obvious.

Unlike the Comet, the Caravelle was a substantial commercial success for its day. The original sixty-four to eighty-passenger Caravelle I and Caravelle III operated with all the European flag carriers bar Lufthansa, KLM and BEA (the latter did not order Caravelles only as a matter of *lèse-majesté*), as well as with international carriers like Aerolineas Argentinas, Varig, Lan Chile, Indian Airlines, China Airlines and Thai International. A sensational breakthrough for Sud Aviation came when United Airlines of the US ordered twenty Caravelle VIs, with more powerful Rolls-Royce Avon turbojets. This achievement was followed by an accord with Douglas Aircraft to produce a turbofan version of the Caravelle under licence (called the Caravelle VII 'Horizon'); this model attracted a preliminary order for twenty from TWA and another ten options from United, but this groundbreaking agreement fell through when Douglas decided to develop its own Caravelle equivalent, the Douglas DC-9.

Undaunted by the US setback, Sud Aviation went on to develop other turbofan-powered versions of the Caravelle (using the successful P&W JT8D engine). These versions, called the 10R, 10B and 11R, consolidated the Caravelle's success in the marketplace. The last Caravelle model was the 12 Series, stretched to carry up to 140 passengers in a high-density layout. Altogether Sud Aviation/Aérospatiale produced 282 Caravelles over the period 1955–1973. Until the advent of the European Airbus A.300B, the Caravelle was Europe's most numerically successful jetliner and gave Sud Aviation the confidence to take the lead on the cooperative Concorde and Airbus programmes.

The Nord N-262

Nord Aviation has the distinction of having produced France's first turboprop airliner, the Nord N-262. It remains to this day the only civil turboprop that France has produced independently. In the process, however, it has formed the basis for the highly successful Franco-Italian ATR (Avions de Transport Régional) 42 and ATR72 family of regional turboprops, the result of a 50/50 joint venture between Aérospatiale and Alenia of Italy.

Based on an original design by Max Holste (the MH.260) and redesigned around a circular-section pressurised fuselage, the N-262 first flew on 24 December 1962. Powered by two Turbomeca Bastan turboprops, the N-262 could carry a maximum of twenty-nine passengers over a range of 1,000km. The Nord N-262 achieved moderate market acceptance, and total production numbered 111, with the last example being delivered in March 1977.

Dassault Aviation

In the early 1970s Dassault Aviation made a spectacularly unsuccessful attempt at entering the civil jet airliner market. Better known as a military aircraft producer, with its highly successful series of Mirage fighters, Dassault also successfully broke into the business jet market in 1963, with the launch of the twin-engined Mystère Falcon 20. Military jets and business jets are still to this day Dassault's mainstay products. However, the company's foray into the commercial airliner market with the Mercure proved an utter failure.

The Mercure

Back in the 1960s, Dassault studied regional airliner versions of the Mystère 20 business jet, and the thirty/forty-seat Mystère 30 and 40 were proposed, but never built. Eventually Dassault designed a twin-engined jet airliner called the Mercure, with seating capacity for 150 passengers six abreast, and up to 162 passengers in a high-density configuration. Launched in 1968 with the support of the French Government, which undertook to finance 56 per cent of the non-recurring development costs, and with only one single order for ten aircraft from French domestic carrier Air Inter, the prototype Dassault Mercure first flew in May 1971. Other risk-sharing partners in the project were Aeritalia of Italy, CASA of Spain, Belgium's SABCA, Canadair and Switzerland's Federal Aircraft Factory.

The Dassault Mercure, though technically sound, was basically a reinvention of the Boeing 737 but six years too late, and without the latter's operating economics, longer range and multi-stage short-haul capability. The result was that Air Inter's ten aircraft remained the only order, and Dassault closed the production line in November 1975 after only twelve aircraft (including the two prototypes) had been built. Dassault, the French Government, and its risk-sharing partners, lost a lot of money on the Mercure programme and to this day the aircraft has the dubious distinction of being the world's least successful jetliner. A French attempt to launch a stretched, longer-range Mercure in the mid-1970s in cooperation with Aérospatiale and McDonnell-Douglas of the US came to nothing (see Chapter 4).

Probably affected by the failure of the Dassault Mercure and of other national attempts at producing civil airliners, the French Government and the nation's industry came to realise that any further attempt in the field of civil jet airliners should be based on a wider pan-European cooperative effort. In particular France realised that cooperation should include Europe's most experienced industry – that of the UK – in order to have any chance of succeeding in the world marketplace. The realisation of the need for a pan-European joint effort in aerospace, as we shall see, was not as strong in the UK at the time. This resulted in France being able to position itself as the lead partner in the key joint European airliner projects, the Concorde and the European Airbus, despite the fact that the country's experience in developing modern jet airliners was not as advanced as that of the UK. However, there were other factors that played a major role in Britain's inability to take the lead on Europe's key civilian projects, such as stronger lobbying power in Government circles of aero-engine maker Rolls-Royce vis-à-vis the country's airframe manufacturers, and willingness on the part of various British Governments to appease French ambitions in order to gain access to the European Economic Community.

If that meant transferring technological know-how in civil aerospace to France, so the British decision-makers reasoned, this was a small price to pay for the wider economic and political benefits that the country would gain in return.

Anglo-French Cooperation: The Concorde Supersonic Airliner

The seeds of Anglo-French cooperation in the development of civil airliners had already been sown, as we have seen, with the French Caravelle short-range jet. This cooperative effort had been based, however, on a private agreement between two firms.

The Concorde programme, on the other hand, was the first instance that saw formal cooperation between the two countries, with direct Government involvement in addition to that of the industrial contractors. It was not surprising that Britain and France should decide to cooperate in the production of a supersonic transport: the Concorde was, and probably remains to this day, the most technically ambitious airliner ever developed. The costs involved in its development were considered prohibitive for either Britain or France to bear alone, and this was true even before the project had been launched, let alone when the development costs escalated out of control over the life of the programme.

Plans to develop a supersonic airliner emerged in the UK as far back as 1956, when a Supersonic Transport Advisory Committee (STAC) was set up with the purpose of studying the feasibility of a supersonic transport (SST) airliner. The STAC received submissions from Hawker Siddeley and Bristol Aircraft (later part of BAC). The STAC eventually selected the Bristol design, which evolved from the larger six-engine Bristol 198 into the four-engine Bristol 223, capable of carrying about 100 passengers across the Atlantic.

In France, from 1959 onwards Sud Aviation and Dassault studied a similar concept for a short- to-medium-range supersonic airliner to be used by Air France on European and African routes, and this project emerged as the Super Caravelle SST, presented in model form at the 1961 Paris Air Show.

The British Government meanwhile realised that the cost of developing a SST was too high for the country to bear alone, and efforts were made to find a partner in the venture. The USA was discarded on the grounds that at the time

their industry was evaluating the development of a much larger machine capable
of Mach 3, as opposed to the Bristol 223's Mach 2 maximum speed. This left
France as the only other country in a position to participate in the development
of such a complex programme. At the political level, the British Government
under Prime Minister Harold Macmillan hoped that France would see technological cooperation as an example of Britain's goodwill towards Europe. The
Government, therefore, reasoned that by agreeing to a joint aircraft project with
France it would ingratiate General de Gaulle and thus facilitate Britain's entry
into the European Economic Community. General de Gaulle was a strong advocate of the development of a SST as a means of challenging American supremacy
in commercial airliners, but was realistic enough to realise that France could not
go ahead without the financial backing and the technical expertise of its neigh-
bour across the Channel. Therefore, when BAC approached Sud Aviation with
a view to merging their respective projects, the reception from the French was
enthusiastic.

Negotiations between the two governments and their airframe and engine
companies ensued and eventually concluded with the signing of an Anglo-
French agreement in November 1962. This agreement stipulated that Britain
and France would share in equal proportions the development and production
of a SST. Since the engine selected for the aircraft was an advanced version of
the Bristol Siddeley Olympus turbojet, it was decided to split the engine work
60/40 in favour of Britain, with Bristol Siddeley and SNECMA of France sharing development and production. In observance of the principle of *le juste retour*,
work-share on the airframe was split 60/40 in favour of France, with Sud Aviation
and BAC being the main contractors. It was also decided to develop two versions
of the aircraft, a long-range version to be led by BAC, and a short/medium-range
version to be led by Sud. After many, sometimes acrimonious, meetings between
the French and the British, it was eventually decided to drop the short/medium-
range version. Interestingly, at the request of the British, the November 1962
agreement was given the force of an International Treaty, with a clause preventing
unilateral withdrawal by either country. Their insistence on this latter clause was
a reason for regret for successive British Governments when they later tried to
terminate the programme.

It is not our intention here to provide an exhaustive analysis of what became
the Concorde programme, as innumerable books have been written on the subject and we refer readers to that literature[5]. Suffice for us to make the following
observations:

Without doubt, Concorde was an outstanding technical success, enabling the
British and French aerospace industries to gain expertise at the very frontiers of
technology. By the same token, the programme was an unbelievable commercial and financial disaster, costing the UK and French taxpayers in the region of

£2 billion at 1978 prices, compared with an original estimate of close to £200 million.

The programme was managed by committees, which included representatives of each country's Government and industrialists. This made for costly and inefficient duplications and delays. Add to that the continuous rivalry between the British and French design teams and the need for every document to be produced in English and French and to get the *placet* of both parties, and it is hardly surprising that cost overruns and delays occurred.

It is fair to conclude that, of the two countries, Britain lost out more in the long run than France, for the following reasons:

The British were ahead of the French in SST airliner research and technology and, through Concorde, transferred a substantial amount of their know-how to France for little or no consideration.

Strengthened by the Concorde programme, the French were in a position to demand leadership on the development of the original European Airbus and subsequent variants. This promoted Toulouse instead of Weybridge, Hatfield or Filton, Bristol, as the master centre of European airliner development.

The enormous cost overruns on Concorde were without doubt one of the key reasons why Britain found itself short of cash when it came to launching less ambitious but more commercially sound projects like the BAC Three-Eleven wide-body airliner.

General de Gaulle in the end refused Britain entry into the EEC in 1963. It was only in 1973, following de Gaulle's death, that the UK was allowed in. A decade had elapsed.

The first Concorde prototype (001) eventually took off from Toulouse-Blagnac in March 1969 followed one month later by the first flight of the British prototype from Filton, Bristol. At one stage Aérospatiale and BAC held seventy-four options for Concorde from some of the world's top flag carriers, including Pan Am, TWA, Lufthansa, Air India and Japan Airlines, but by the time the Oil Crisis hit the world economy in 1973–1974, all those options had lapsed. In the end only the flag carriers of the sponsoring nations, BOAC (later British Airways) and Air France, ordered the Concorde, and only twenty aircraft (including the two prototypes and two pre-production aircraft) were rolled off the Bristol and Toulouse assembly lines. The final Concorde was delivered from BAe's Filton, Bristol, plant in April 1979.

Bar the tragic July 2000 Air France Concorde crash near Paris Charles de Gaulle airport, the Concorde gave many years of safe and successful service with British Airways and Air France until its final retirement from service in 2003. It is, however, in terms of the beneficial (or negative) effects on the two countries' civil aerospace industries that we must assess Concorde's legacy. In this respect we cannot fail to acknowledge that, whereas for France Concorde acted as the launch pad from which the world-beating Airbus organisation emerged in Toulouse, sadly for Britain the project turned into an albatross and reduced the financial support for other programmes, notably the BAC Three-Eleven, which could have done for Weybridge what Airbus eventually did for Toulouse.

Germany – Post-war Efforts in Civil Aerospace

As we have seen at the beginning of this chapter, German aerospace engineering was at the very leading edge at the end of the Second World War. Unfortunately for Germany, defeat in the war meant that the Allies imposed a very understandable embargo on development of aerospace technology in the immediate post-war years. This embargo was not lifted until 1955, and there again close scrutiny was retained in terms of military hardware development.

In view of the above, it is not surprising that Germany's aerospace renaissance was principally based on programmes developed within the framework of European cooperation, first with France (Nord Noratlas and Transall military transports, Breguet Atlantique maritime patrol aircraft and Dassault-Dornier Alphajet military trainer), then with the UK and Italy (Tornado fighter/bomber aircraft and Eurofighter), finally culminating in the Airbus partnership with France and the UK. The German industry also played the card of licence production of American and Italian designs (like the Lockheed F-104 and Fiat G-91 military aircraft). To this very day, German aerospace output is linked to international programmes, the principal of which are Airbus and Eurofighter.

However, Germany did make a brave attempt at flying 'solo' in civil airliners, developing what was arguably the first true regional jet. Unfortunately for them, the programme turned out to be a total commercial flop.

The VFW 614
This short-haul regional jet originated in 1962 as the Elbe Flugzeugbau E.614. The general layout of the aircraft was that of a twin-engined forty/forty-four-seat regional jet airliner with its two Rolls-Royce/SNECMA M45H turbofans placed on pylons above the wings. This novel and unique configuration had a number of advantages including low external noise footprint in flight and lower chance of debris ingestion when using unpaved runways. VFW (Vereinigte Flugtechnische

Werke), based in Bremen, which had absorbed three prestigious names in German aviation, namely Focke-Wulf, Weser and Heinkel (later Elbe Flugzeugbau), took over responsibility for the E.614 programme. In 1968 the VFW 614 was launched into development and production with the backing of the German Government. In line with the prevailing industrial policies at the time, VFW invited Fokker of the Netherlands and Northern Ireland's Short Bros to contribute to production as risk-sharing partners.

The prototype first flew at Bremen in July 1971. Initial market interest was good, with Cimber Air of Denmark and France's Air Alsace and TAT ordering or leasing the first examples off the production line. However, initial reliability problems with the M45H engines, the world economic recession following the 1973 Oil Crisis and, more significantly, the fact that the VFW 614 was ahead of its time counted against this pioneering aircraft. In order to stem mounting losses, VFW-Fokker decided to terminate the programme in 1977, after only nineteen aircraft had been flown.

Italy – Major Subcontractor and Joint Venture Partner

Like Germany, Italy's aerospace industry paid a heavy price as a consequence of the country's defeat in the war. In the early 1960s the industry developed a string of successful military aircraft (amongst them the Fiat G-91 jet fighter, the Aermacchi MB-326 light attack/trainer jet and the Fiat (Aeritalia) G-222 twin turboprop military transport). In the civilian field Aeritalia entered into major subcontract agreements for McDonnell Douglas and Boeing, producing fuselage panels for the Douglas DC-9/MD-80 families of twinjet airliners and the DC-10 wide-body trijet in the 1960s and 1970s, and then producing wing and tail sub-assemblies for the Boeing 767 from the late 1970s onwards. In the early 1970s Aeritalia was invited to join the Airbus consortium as a full partner, but in its wisdom decided to stick with the Americans (wrongly, as events were to prove, but it is always easy to say that in hindsight).

Netherlands – A Successful Player in the Regional Airliner Market

The Netherlands has a proud tradition in the production of commercial transports dating back to the pre-war years, when Fokker airliners were ubiquitous both in Europe and the United States. The core of the Dutch aerospace industry has always revolved around Fokker NV, the company established by Anthony

Fokker in the early part of the twentieth century. Unfortunately for Holland and their aerospace industry, the company went bankrupt in 1996. But that is a different story.

The Fokker F.27

Powered by two Rolls-Royce Dart engines (the same engines that powered the Vickers Viscount and the Hawker Siddeley HS.748), the Fokker F.27 first flew in 1955 and proved an instant hit with airlines around the world. Early on, a licence agreement was struck with Fairchild Aerospace of the US for the latter to produce the F.27 in North America, with the attached responsibility of marketing the aircraft to North American customers. Christened the 'Friendship', the F.27 remained in production until 1986, by which time 787 examples had been delivered to customers all over the world. To this day, the F.27 Friendship remains the Western world's most numerically successful turboprop airliner. A revised and developed version, the Fokker F.50 was first flown in 1986. Powered by new, fuel-efficient Pratt & Whitney Canada turboprops, the F.50 sold over 210 units worldwide although its life was sadly cut short by Fokker's bankruptcy in 1996. In total the Fokker turboprop family sold a remarkable 999 units over forty years.

The Fokker F.28

In the early 1960s Fokker identified a need to develop a jet successor to the F.27, to be positioned just below the BAC 1-11, Douglas DC-9 and Boeing 737 in terms of seating capacity. Christened the Fokker F.28 Fellowship, the company's first jet airliner made its maiden flight in May 1967. A twinjet powered by Rolls-Royce Spey-555 turbofans (a de-rated version of the powerplant that powered the BAC 1-11 and HS.121 Trident), the F.28's initial passenger capacity of sixty-five grew to eighty-five in the stretched '4000' model. Sales of the Fellowship were initially slow, but picked up from the late 1970s onwards. By the time production terminated in 1986, 243 F.28 Fellowships had been flown, of which 241 were delivered. Although it did not reach the totals of its stablemate F.27 Friendship, the F.28 attracted orders from major flag carriers and leading US airlines, including Air France, SAS, Iberia and THY Turkish Airlines in Europe and Piedmont and USAir in North America.

The Fokker F.100 and F.70

In 1983 Fokker launched a new regional jet family based on the Fokker F.28. First flown in November 1986, the F.100 was an extensively revised and stretched development of the F.28, powered by two new-technology Rolls-Royce Tay turbofans and with capacity for 100–110 passengers (up to 122 in high-density layout). Together with its shortened variant, the F.70 for seventy to eighty passengers, total production reached 327 examples at the time of the company's bankruptcy, of which 324 were delivered to customers. Therefore the F.100/F.70

outsold its progenitor by 40 per cent and was ordered in quantity by such prestigious operators as American Airlines, USAir and TAM of Brazil. In Europe, the aircraft found favour with Swissair, Alitalia, KLM and Austrian Airlines. It also sold to Malev of Hungary.

It is sad to reflect on the fact that Fokker's bankruptcy not only wiped out one of the world's premier airliner producers, but also cut short the potential of the F.100/F.70. Indeed the Fokker JetLine family, up to termination of the programme, was achieving good market penetration in the face of strong competition from British Aerospace's BAe 146 and the Boeing 737-500.

Summary Conclusion: Britain as the Established European Leader in Post-war Civil Aircraft Production

If one takes a snapshot of the European civil aircraft industry at the end of 1970, it will become apparent that Britain was the established European leader in civil aircraft. Indeed the UK had held this position in the field since the end of the war. British leadership in modern turbine-powered airliners in relation to the other European countries can be assessed from several angles:

Technology: Britain was the first country in the world to produce a jet airliner (Comet) and a turboprop airliner (Viscount). These aircraft were followed by the development of advanced second-generation jetliners (Hawker Siddeley Trident and Vickers VC-10 in particular).

Range of products: By the mid-1960s Britain had designed, developed and produced no fewer than four jetliners and six turboprop airliners. These aircraft covered the complete matrix of range and passenger-carrying capacity of the day, and included second-generation jetliners for short, medium and long-range operations (BAC One-Eleven, HS Trident and Vickers VC-10).

Complete capability: Britain was the only European country able to produce advanced airframes, the engines to power them and almost all the equipment (including the sophisticated avionics) that went into them.

Sales volume: By 1970 the UK had sold over 450 jet airliners, representing 60 per cent of total European output and 11 per cent of world production. In addition, 950 British turboprop airliners had been delivered or were on order, again accounting for 60 per cent of European production.[6]

France by comparison had only the Sud Aviation Caravelle twinjet in service. The Caravelle, a very successful design by European standards, gave France 37 per cent of total European jetliner production. In any case, the Caravelle had a substantial British element to it, comprising engines (Rolls-Royce Avon turbojets), equipment, and airframe (de Havilland Comet nose and cockpit). The Netherlands were just entering the small jet airliner market with their Fokker F.28 twinjet, having established a marked presence in the regional turboprop segment with the successful Fokker F.27. Lastly Germany was making a bid to enter civil aircraft production with their VFW 614 regional jet.

It can be rightly argued that the commercial success and market penetration of Britain's post-war airliners was poor compared to their US equivalents, with the notable exceptions of the Vickers Viscount, BAC One-Eleven and Hawker Siddeley HS.748. This argument is, however, valid also for France, whose only successful design was the Caravelle. Notwithstanding the poor commercial returns, the historical evidence of the transport aircraft industry shows that no other European country at the time had the same depth of technological skills, extensive product range and market penetration that Britain had. We shall see in the remainder of this book how Britain's European leadership in civil aircraft was squandered as a result of some ill-judged Government decisions in the late 1960s and in 1970, allowing France to take the mantle of European leader from Britain.

1   Quoted in Hayward, *The British Aerospace Industry*.

2   The Avro Jetliner, the second jet transport to fly, never achieved production.

3   The reader interested in this topic can consult: Hayward, *Government and British Civil Aerospace*; also, Hayward, *The British Aerospace Industry*.

4   The above quotes are taken from Henderson, *Silent, Swift, Superb: The Story of the Vickers VC-10*; Wood, *Project Cancelled*; Reed, *Britain's Aircraft Industry: What Went Right? What Went Wrong?*; Hayward, *The British Aircraft Industry*.

5   For a good analysis and review of the development history of Concorde, see Trubshaw, *Concorde: The Inside Story*.

6   See Appendices III to VIII for jetliner production totals and country market shares.

The European Airbus Project – From its Genesis to the First Flight of the Airbus A300B (1965–1972)

Introduction

The market requirements that gave birth to the European Airbus project were the same as those that prompted BAC to develop the Three-Eleven project. Indeed, the birth of the Three-Eleven is inextricably linked to the emergence of the European Airbus, as both projects competed for the same market and, as far as the UK was concerned, for the same Government launch aid. We cannot therefore understand the genesis of the Three-Eleven without first providing a fairly detailed history of the birth of the European Airbus. The European Airbus was eventually launched into full production, whereas the Three-Eleven was killed off by the UK Government's unwillingness to provide launch aid to BAC. Aviation historians agree that, had the Airbus programme been solely reliant on the British Government's backing, it too would have not seen the light of day. If this had been allowed to happen, it is most likely that today Europe would not be building large commercial airliners and would be wholly dependent on imports from the United States. Fortunately for Europe, the French and German Governments took a very different view of the Airbus programme from that of the UK Government, and firmly put their weight and funding behind the idea that Europe ought to have a competitive airliner manufacturing industry. The resulting foresight of Britain's two largest European partners means that currently Airbus leads the market ahead of Boeing of the US, having managed to push the other two great US powerhouses in commercial aerospace – McDonnell Douglas and Lockheed – out of the market altogether. This has been achieved through the technical excellence and market appeal of Airbus's products, to which Britain's aerospace industry has made a significant contribution, despite having a junior role in the overall project.

For the reasons outlined above it is therefore opportune to recall the fascinating history of the genesis of the European Airbus. Intertwined with this history are the two fatal decisions of the British Government in 1969 and 1970: first to pull out of the European Airbus programme and then to refuse funding for the BAC

Three-Eleven, its wholly British alternative. These unfortunate decisions allowed France, at a stroke, to overtake Britain as Europe's leader in commercial airliner development, and Germany to reach parity with Britain. As we have seen in Chapter 1, the British civil aerospace industry was way ahead of both France and Germany when these fatal decisions were taken. Our analysis, therefore, cannot ignore the dynamics of the geo-industrial and political games that brought about this reversal of roles, at a time when the major European countries were jockeying for position to lead the new post-war Europe. It is this very combination of politics, economics, technological and industrial leadership and geo-political balance of power that makes aerospace such a fascinating industry to study.

For clarity of exposition this chapter is divided into four parts:

Part One
Overview of the market requirements behind the opportunity to develop a large capacity airliner for short to medium-range operations, and of the discussions that took place among European airlines and aircraft manufacturers.

Part Two
Review of the Plowden Report and the effects that this Government-sponsored analysis of the aerospace industry had on the UK airframe industry and on the British Government's policy decisions in respect of the industry.

Part Three
Brief history of the stillborn BAC Two-Eleven project, a twinjet design for 190–210 passengers aimed principally at BEA's requirements for a Vanguard and Trident replacement. The project is important not only because it provided the blueprint from which the larger wide-bodied Three-Eleven emerged, but also because it was the first instance when the UK Government found itself facing a funding dilemma between a wholly national airliner and the Pan-European Airbus.

Part Four
The story of the troubled birth (only from a political perspective, we must emphasise) of the first European Airbus, the A300, the original launch in 1967 as an Anglo-French-German venture, its definitive launch in May 1969 as a Franco-German programme, and finally its first flight in October 1972.

A Market Opportunity is Identified

By the early 1960s it became apparent that air traffic in Europe was growing fast. The continent had by then enjoyed nearly twenty years of peace following the end of the war in 1945. The US aid packages under the Marshall Plan and, more importantly, the formation of the European Economic Community and the European Free Trade Area had triggered fast economic growth within Europe and a substantial increase in trade among the European countries. This in turn stimulated demand for air travel, both for business and for leisure purposes. The latter was the result of the rising disposable income of larger and larger strata of the European population. In brief, European air traffic volume was catching up fast with the larger and much more developed US air transport market.

We have seen in the previous chapter that the main European airlines responded to this increase in demand first by ordering turboprops and subsequently by backing the new generation of short to medium-haul jets. Thus in Britain BEA started operating Vickers Viscounts and Comet 4Bs, and then replaced these with higher capacity Vickers Vanguards and Hawker Siddeley Tridents. Air France and Lufthansa also started off in the 1950s and early 1960s with Vickers Viscounts. Air France subsequently replaced the Viscounts with home-grown Sud Aviation Caravelles and Lufthansa proceeded to order the new Boeing 727 trijet. In the mid-1960s the specialised short-haul airliner made its appearance: BEA ordered the domestically developed BAC One-Eleven, Air France introduced new versions of the Caravelle, followed by the Boeing 727, and Lufthansa became the launch customer for the Boeing 737. Many other European airlines became loyal operators of Douglas's new short-haul twinjet, the DC-9. Among DC-9 operators in the 1960s were KLM, Alitalia, Swissair, SAS, Iberia and Finnair.

While airlines were in the process of ordering the second-generation short-haul jets, their managements were thinking of the sort of plane that airlines would need by the early 1970s, when traffic was projected to more than treble compared with the early 1960s level. In June 1965 the principal European airlines met informally at the Paris Air Show to flesh out what, if any, common requirements in respect of such a plane could be agreed. The airline group comprised Air France, Alitalia, BEA, Lufthansa, Sabena and SAS. A further formal meeting was held in London in October 1965 but the airlines failed to reach any consensus. The meeting in London, however, led to the formation of an Anglo-French Ministerial Working Party whose task was to report on the prospects for the development of a high capacity short-haul jet airliner. This working party built on work originally done in Britain by the Lighthill Committee as far back as 1961, which addressed the requirement for a minimum-cost high-capacity short-haul airliner. The Lighthill Committee concluded that by the early 1970s an aircraft with a passenger capacity of 200–225 seats and a range 810 nautical miles would be needed to meet traffic demand. Lighthill had suggested that such an aircraft should offer seat-mile costs 30 per cent below those of the Boeing 727-100, at the time considered the benchmark aircraft for short-haul routes. The Anglo-French Working Party published its report in November 1965. Entitled 'An Outline Specification for a High-Capacity Short Haul Aircraft', the report formed the blueprint for the requirements that laid the foundations for the European Airbus.

While the airlines deliberated and Governments formally considered joint projects, Europe's aircraft manufacturers started independent studies of large-capacity aircraft. In particular BAC and Hawker Siddeley in Britain and Sud Aviation, Breguet and Nord Aviation in France studied various narrow bodies and wide bodies that would satisfy the airlines' needs for higher-capacity airliners. In the case of Europe's leading civil airframe companies – Sud, HSA and BAC – such studies were expected to provide successors to their Caravelle, Trident and BAC One-Eleven designs.

Encouraged by the respective Governments, British, French and German manufacturers explored the possibility of cooperation in developing and producing such an aircraft. As early as 1964 Sud Aviation and BAC (already partners on the Concorde supersonic airliner) had got together to study a joint project for a 200-seat aircraft, christened the Galion (French for Galleon) by Sud. However, the two allies/rivals soon fell out on the right aircraft size, with Sud preferring a larger 300-seat aircraft, and BAC believing that 200 seats would address the market better.

Meanwhile in Germany a consortium of the country's seven airframe manufacturers (ATG Siebelwerke, Bolkow, Dornier, Flugzueg-union Sud, HFB, Messerschmitt and VFW) established an airbus study group, Studiengruppe Airbus, on 2 July 1965. This was the first time that the term 'airbus' was officially used. The German companies had already held discussions about cooperation with the French industry at the Paris Air Show in June. By December 1965 the German group was formalised as the Arbeitsgemeinschaft (Arge) Airbus, to act as the German partner in any joint European development.

As these developments were taking place, Hawker Siddeley linked up with Breguet and Nord Aviation of France to form the HBN Group. Based at HSA's Hatfield, Hertfordshire, commercial aircraft headquarters, this Anglo-French joint venture studied five baseline proposals, dubbed sequentially the HBN.100 to HBN.104. The five proposals basically reflected the independent work done by HSA, Breguet and Nord. After further detailed evaluation, the HBN Group selected the Hatfield-designed HBN.100 as the project showing the greatest commercial promise. The HBN.100 design was a conventional wide-body airliner, to be powered by two wing-mounted high-bypass ratio Pratt & Whitney JT9D turbofans (then under development for Boeing's 747 Jumbo Jet) and capable of carrying between 225 and 261 passengers eight or nine-abreast in a 19ft-wide fuselage. Eventually the HBN.100 evolved into the design of the A300 European Airbus.

Not to be outdone Sud Aviation, now bereft of its partner BAC, refined its Galion project. Originally based on a series of studies codenamed Grosse Julie ('Fat Julie'), Sud joined with fellow French company Dassault to enable its Galion project to meet the Anglo–French Working Party specification. The Galion and HBN.100 had similar configurations, but while the HBN.100's new large high-bypass engines were hung on pylons jutting from the wing's leading edge, the Galion's engine layout resembled that of the Boeing 737 or Dassault Mercure (that is, they were attached on short stubs under the wing).

In January 1966 the first inter-Governmental official meeting was held, with Government officials from Britain, France and Germany. At that meeting the industrial partners from the three nations were announced as Hawker Siddeley for Britain, Sud Aviation for France and Arge Airbus (later Deutsche Airbus) for Germany. At the same time the HBN.100 was chosen as the baseline design. At this point it is worth opening a parenthesis to explain why the UK and France in particular chose the companies they did to be the partners in the joint programme. In fact, in the case of Britain, both HSA and BAC could have taken the role of British partner in the venture, as they were both highly experienced in the design and development of large civil jetliners. As far as France was concerned, Breguet and Nord, and not Sud Aviation, were the original members of the HBN partnership, whose HBN.100 design had been selected as the baseline project.

The reason for the British Government choosing Hawker Siddeley instead of BAC was twofold. Firstly, BAC was already partnering Sud Aviation on the Concorde programme, and therefore it was HSA's turn to be the partner in the UK's other major cooperative venture in civil airliners. This rationale, which BAC polemically branded as a case of 'Buggin's turn', was not the only consideration however. Hawker also had relevant technical skills, having developed the Trident airliner, arguably Europe's most advanced subsonic jet transport at the time. The second reason for the Government's choice of HSA was therefore the company's expertise in designing a modern 'second generation' subsonic jet airliner. Also, we must not forget that HSA's Hatfield team had led the design of the HBN.100, which was selected by the three partners as the baseline design. Track record and expertise was also the reason behind the French Government's choice of Sud Aviation as the French partner. Not only had the Toulouse-based company designed France's only modern jetliner, the Caravelle (the Mercure was still to emerge at this stage), but had been partnering Britain's BAC on the Concorde programme.

The first formal meeting at board level between HSA, Sud and Arge Airbus took place in September 1966. The three industrial partners quickly established a cordial working relationship based on mutual respect and by October of the same year a formal application for the necessary funding was made to the three Governments. With the application came a brochure outlining an aircraft called the Airbus A300 (which stood for Airbus 300 seats), although this was still the baseline HBN.100, revised upwards in terms of capacity and with some refinement in the aerodynamics and systems.

At this point it is worth opening another parenthesis to analyse why Britain and its Government chose the European cooperative route for the development of a relatively straightforward (from a technical standpoint) subsonic airliner. We may recall that in those days the UK had the most advanced civil airliner capability in Europe. Unlike France, or Germany for that matter, the UK could have easily developed an Airbus-type aircraft on its own. In the case of Concorde, the sheer technical complexity of the programme and especially its enormous development costs dictated the need for Britain to find a partner. The wide-body jetliner, on the other hand, was a fairly conventional aircraft, well within the capabilities of Britain, the only country in Europe that had experience of designing 'second generation' jet transports (Vickers VC-10, Hawker Siddeley Trident, BAC One-Eleven). In order to understand the country's reluctance in going it alone in this sector we must first review the industrial policy of the Labour Government of the time, and in particular the Government's policy towards aerospace. The letter was strongly influenced by a study carried out in 1965 by an ad hoc committee under the leadership of Lord Plowden. It is to the findings of this committee that we now turn.

The Plowden Committee and its Report on the UK Aerospace Industry

The Labour Government under Prime Minister Harold Wilson had come to power in October 1964 under a manifesto calling for industrial and technological regeneration as a spur for the country's economic growth. The new Government was positively interventionist in industry, encouraging the formation of larger industrial concerns as 'national champions' in order to improve their competitive position. 'The white heat of technology', as Wilson put it, was the Government's credo and one of its first acts was to create a new Ministry of Technology (MinTech) which absorbed the old Ministry of Aviation Supply. An Industrial Reorganisation Corporation (IRC) was also formed to encourage mergers and to provide another channel for state aid to industry.[1]

Despite the lofty principles summarised above, the aircraft industry was regarded with some hostility by the new Government. Roy Jenkins, the new Minister of Aviation, stated that the aerospace industry had 'been feather bedded for too long' and that it would be in 'for a few shocks'. His advisors had calculated that the industry had received from the state £1,350 per employee per annum – equivalent to 25 per cent of national R&D expenditure. A couple of years later, at the SBAC dinner of 1967 the new Minister of Technology Tony Benn gave an infamous address that ended up upsetting most industry members, when he said that: 'Ministers of Aviation had been the most hated and feared ministers in government. While their colleagues were grateful for anything they could wring from the Chancellor of the Exchequer, Ministers of Aviation ran off with sums of money that made the great train robbers look like schoolboys pinching money from a blind man's tin.'

The Government was not slow in following up its words with concrete actions. In 1965 Labour cancelled the three new military aircraft programmes that the industry was working on at the time. These were the Hawker Siddeley P1154 VTOL supersonic fighter (an advanced supersonic aircraft which was to build on the work done with the Harrier), the Hawker Siddeley HS.681 military four-jet transport, and the BAC TSR2 tactical, strike and reconnaissance fighter. These decisions wiped out all the indigenous military aircraft then under development, and these programmes were replaced with imports from the US. In the case of the TSR2 the decision to cancel the programme looked even more dubious, as the Government had already spent £250 million in developing the platform and five prototypes were either flying or completed. It was not until 1971, with the launch of the HS1182 Hawk trainer/light attack aircraft, that the UK again developed an indigenous military aircraft. For more complex platforms, the cancellations of 1965 signalled the end of UK independent development of military aircraft, as all subsequent aircraft (Jaguar, Tornado, AV-8B Harrier II and Eurofighter) were developed as cooperative ventures with other European countries or the USA.

In December 1964 Roy Jenkins announced that a Committee of Inquiry was to be set up under the chairmanship of Lord Plowden to consider the future place and organisation of the aircraft industry. One of the principal remits of the committee was to give special attention to the 'possibilities of international co-operation'. The work of the committee was contained in the Plowden Report, which was published in December 1965. Its conclusions, as we have said earlier, were not only to shape Government thinking on aerospace policy for the rest of its term in office, but were also to have a profound, and not too favourable, effect on the industry going forward. In particular, the report in all likelihood signalled the end of the belief that Britain could develop large and complex civil and military aircraft on its own and suggested that any future such programmes should be undertaken as part of – preferably European – international cooperation.

The report opened by outlining the difficulties involved in Britain maintaining an independent capability in aerospace in the face of fast and extensive technological change and ever-increasing development costs. Key constraints for the British aircraft industry were identified as being the relatively small size of its domestic market and its limited financial resources. These factors, in the report's view, made the scale of British manufacturers too small to be efficient when compared with their US counterparts. The small scale and limited domestic market in turn made for short and unprofitable production runs, which did not allow the companies to generate enough cash flow to finance their R&D on the next project. The only exception to this rule, according to Plowden, was Rolls-Royce, which had sufficient scale and financial resources to compete effectively in world markets. The main airframe companies, BAC and HSA, were instead perceived to be too small to compete effectively in the world markets dominated in the West by the US powerhouses.

The Plowden Report stopped short of saying that the UK could do without an aerospace industry altogether: it did recognise, amongst other things, the industry's contribution to technological windfalls for other sectors and its positive contribution to the country's balance of payments. The industry, however, needed, according to Plowden, to increase its efficiency, achieve competitive economies of scale and reduce aircraft development costs.

Its main recommendations included: a move towards international collaboration; an eventual merger of the two main airframe companies, BAC and HSA; some form of public ownership, either through nationalisation or though public shareholding. In respect of this last recommendation the ex-Conservative Minister of Supply, Mr Aubrey Jones, one of the committee members, attached a dissenting note to the report.

In terms of international collaboration, Plowden called for Britain to 'seek a comprehensive programme to include *most of the aircraft projects* [author's emphasis] on which the industry will be working'. This definition was to include all advanced combat aircraft and long-range, large and especially complex civil aircraft.

The Government accepted in principle most of the Plowden Report's recommendations. In February 1966 the new Minister of Aviation, Fred Mulley, informed the House of Commons that, although the overall level of Government support would fall, it endorsed the general case for retaining an aircraft industry with a comprehensive design and development capability. The Government recognised, Mr Mulley said, that 'the industry had to turn to collaboration as the principal means of improving the relationship between the size of the market and initial production costs and as the key to remaining a major force in aviation'. Of greatest relevance to our story is what Mr Mulley said next. In one of the best-remembered phrases of the day, Mulley stated that: 'Britain is unlikely to be justified again in embarking alone on an expensive new project.' Clearly this view, propounded by the Plowden Committee and accepted by the Government, was to have a profound effect on the country's aerospace policy from then on and contributed in no small measure to the demise of the BAC Two-Eleven project (described further on).

The aerospace industry, or at least the airframe side of it, did not take too well to Plowden's conclusions. In fact, the implied commitment of the UK to international collaboration in advance of clear agreement on specific programmes was perceived by the industry as placing a dangerous limitation on Britain's negotiating position with its prospective European partners. The SBAC in particular stated this point in the following terms:

[We need] a precise definition of the nature, extent and means of collaboration on joint programmes, bearing in mind that we must retain our national capability to design and manufacture to our own requirements in times of need… collaboration can be advantageous only if Britain can negotiate from a position of strength; we must therefore continue to undertake the basic research and development work to enable us to influence the choice of joint projects and, in the last resort, in individual cases, to carry them through independently.

The industry also expressed fears that industrial effectiveness would be compromised by politically determined work-sharing agreements which would have a particularly detrimental effect on the then far stronger British equipment industry. For example, Sir George Dowty was reported as saying at the time: 'the developing collaboration with countries such as France on new aircraft projects has brought about unfortunate decisions to parcel out this work [equipment supplies] on the basis of not what is best but what seems to be politically expedient.' The chairman of BAC, Sir George Edwards, commented that he did not 'recall a French minister saying that it would not be possible for France to undertake projects on her own any longer and that they could only start if she had a colleague country on which to lean. It is no good going to the table with one's own government openly professing inability or unwillingness to go it alone.'

What are our own conclusions on the Plowden Report and on its effect on the British aircraft industry? There is no denying that most of the analysis of the problems facing the British aircraft industry was correct. Limited size of the domestic market, dispersion and inefficiency of the R&D effort, the small scale of the UK companies vis-à-vis their American competitors and their inability to generate sufficient cash flow to finance their new programmes without major Government support: all these were valid points.

However, there is also no denying the fact that Plowden, by excluding *a priori* the idea that the UK should produce a major military aircraft or large civil airliners on its own fatally undermined the country's position at the negotiating table. As Sir George Edwards rightly pointed out, France did not go around saying that they were unable to 'go it alone'. While privately recognising that they too needed the help of other countries in funding major aerospace projects, France's Government officials and industrialists always demanded project leadership when negotiating to take part in a collaborative programme. France effectively achieved this goal on Concorde, Airbus, the Jaguar military aircraft and the three helicopters it developed with Britain. In the few cases where France did not gain project leadership, namely the Anglo-French Variable Geometry (AFVG) military fighter in 1967 and the European Fighter Aircraft (EFA, eventually Eurofighter), the country subsequently pulled out of these British-led consortia and developed its own indigenous alternative (Mirage IVG and Rafale respectively). Unfortunately for the British aerospace industry, its Government did not defend the industry's best interests in cooperative ventures. It also repeatedly showed its unwillingness to back purely national programmes when the market evidence pointed in that direction, as we shall see when we review the BAC Three-Eleven project in detail in the next chapter.

On balance, the Plowden Report had a major deleterious effect on the British airframe industry (not on Rolls-Royce, as we shall see), undermining the Government's confidence and belief that the industry could develop major programmes independently, and weakening its negotiating stance when agreeing collaborative projects. This was despite the fact that Britain was by some margin the most technically advanced European country in aerospace at the time. If we limit ourselves to civil aerospace, poor Government decisions influenced by the Plowden doctrine included:

Agreeing to France's design leadership claim on the European Airbus in return for Rolls-Royce having exclusivity on the engine. This position was agreed despite the fact that Hawker Siddeley was the most experienced of the three partners in the development of a modern second-generation subsonic jet airliner.

Refusing to fund the wholly national BAC Three-Eleven after having backed out of the European Airbus, in the belief that the UK could not afford to develop a successful purely national large airliner.[2]

Accepting a smaller stake than France and Germany in the Airbus consortium when Britain did rejoin in 1978.

Although in many respects the Plowden Report did achieve its aim of providing an analysis of Britain's position in the world and therefore of the smaller role its aircraft industry could realistically expect to play, in our opinion it went too far in its negative conclusions by overplaying the industry's limitations. These conclusions were reached at a time when the market for aerospace products, especially commercial airliners, was about to show 'explosive' growth. The overwhelmingly defeatist stance on the part of the UK decision-makers (backed by the Plowden Report) played into the hands of France and its political elite, who, given ammunition by Plowden's conclusions, formed the view that the British aerospace industry, like the rest of the country, was in terminal decline. France therefore cleverly forged the pan-European collaborative ventures in a way that would enable the country to wrest leadership from Britain.

Incidentally an Italian aerospace publication of the early 1970s commented along the following lines: 'France is taking the leadership in Europe in aerospace and toppling from the Number One spot the British industry, which has been progressively declining over the recent past.' This statement clearly indicates the negative perception of the state of health of UK aerospace that the Plowden Report encouraged throughout Europe. In an editorial published on the eve of the 1970 Farnborough Air Show, the leading American weekly, *Aviation*

Week & Space Technology, reiterated the perceived lack of dynamism of the British aerospace industry in relation to its French counterpart in the years following Plowden. While acknowledging that 'the British aerospace industry is not only the largest in the European sphere but also the most fully developed and the only one between the US and USSR that has fully integrated technological capability' the magazine went on to say that 'the French aerospace industry ranks next to the British in size and capability, but in our judgement it has outstripped it in enterprise and salesmanship.'[3] To back up these statements *AW&ST* mentioned not only French industry successes at exporting Mirage fighter aircraft and Caravelle airliners in quantity, but also the country's ability to wrest leadership from Britain on *every single* aerospace joint venture programme. The Plowden Report in the end reinforced the Labour Government's antipathy towards the industry and its perception that the British aerospace industry was in terminal decline. The combination of these two factors led the Labour Government to negotiate very poor aerospace deals with France.

In conclusion, the Plowden Report in many ways was a typical reflection of the defeatist and pessimistic outlook on the country's future which gripped Britain's elites in the 1960s and 1970s, and which was reversed only when Mrs Thatcher brought the Conservatives back to power in 1979.

The BAC Two-Eleven Project

Arguably the first victim of the Plowden doctrine was the BAC Two-Eleven airliner project. As we have seen earlier, BAC and Sud Aviation had originally joined forces to study a common project for the Airbus requirement. Thus in 1964 the two companies decided to work together on a 200 to 250-seater twinjet based largely on Sud's original Galion study. However, BAC and Sud soon fell out on the exact size of the aircraft. BAC, under the influence of BEA and through its own independent market studies, considered that the right aircraft size should be about 200 seats. Sud, on the other hand, was convinced that a plane with seating capacity nearer 300 better addressed the market needs, although Sud's views were in no small measure influenced by Air France's requirements. Therefore the two companies decided to terminate their joint venture and to continue their studies independently. Sud in due course was to join HSA and Arge Airbus on the European Airbus programme.

The official launch of the BAC Two-Eleven proposal was triggered by a 1966 BEA requirement for a larger aircraft aimed at the replacement of its short-haul fleet. In the summer of 1966 BEA requested permission from the Board of Trade to order a fleet of up to thirty-five Boeing 727s and Boeing 737s to replace its Viscounts, Vanguards and Comets. But in August 1966 the request was turned down on the grounds that it would represent a major US Dollar purchase and therefore weigh unfavourably on Britain's balance of payments. BEA was also informed by the minister that they had to buy British, with the proviso that the Government would ensure that the airline would not suffer financially as a consequence. This proviso implicitly meant that the Government would pay a subsidy to the airline if the operating costs of the British alternative were to be higher than the US equivalent aircraft.

In order to meet BEA's requirements, BAC proposed the One-Eleven 500 in lieu of the Boeing 737 and a new project, the Two-Eleven, as a substitute for the Boeing 727. Hawker Siddeley, for their part, proposed the minimum change Trident 3 as an alternative to the 727, as well as more radical Trident developments such as the HS132 and HS134.

The BAC Two-Eleven was designed around two rear-mounted Rolls-Royce RB211 turbofan engines of 30,000lb (13.3 tonnes) thrust each, giving the aircraft a range of about 1,500 nautical miles (2,800km).[4] The aircraft could carry between 192 and 208 passengers in a six-abreast configuration based on a circular fuselage of 3.86m diameter (larger than the 'narrow-bodies' of the time). In order to minimise development costs, scaled-up versions of the BAC One-Eleven's cockpit, wing and tail surfaces were adopted and the flight deck was based on that of the BAC One-Eleven 500.

BAC estimated total Two-Eleven development costs to be about £100 million, of which £50 million related to the airframe and £50 million to the engine. As soon as the programme was announced, it received BEA's enthusiastic backing. The airline's chairman, Sir Anthony Millward, went on record as saying that the Two-Eleven was a much better proposition than the Boeing 727 and that, had the project been offered earlier, BEA would have ordered it in preference to the US design. The airline followed up on this statement by signing a letter of intent, subject to project launch, for thirty firm orders and ten options for the Two-Eleven. Another two British independent airlines, Laker Airways and Autair, also signed letters of intent for the aircraft. The BoT gave its explicit backing to the project and BAC's development timetable envisaged a first flight in the autumn of 1970 and an in-service date of 1972, with twelve aircraft slotted for delivery to BEA by May of that year. In addition to a substantial domestic market, BAC's extensive market research and a survey of airlines worldwide showed that there was a market for over 1,500 Two-Eleven Class aircraft, of which BAC was conservatively estimating to win 20 per cent based on One-Eleven sales to date.

In terms of aircraft funding, BAC had most of its internal private funds tied up in the development of the One-Eleven and its new variant, the '500' stretched version, and was looking to the Government to provide most of the non-recurring costs funding. However, plans were also in place to find risk-sharing partners in the UK and Europe for up to 50 per cent of the non-recurring costs. Sud Aviation in France expressed an interest in taking on wing production (amounting to 35 per cent of the aircraft value), Shorts in Northern Ireland was earmarked to manufacture the front and rear fuselage sections and Fokker in the Netherlands and Italy's Aeritalia were also keen to risk-share on the programme.[5]

Unfortunately the Two-Eleven project emerged around the same time as discussions on the European Airbus were being formalised and therefore found itself competing for UK Government funds with the Airbus. Superficially at least, the two aircraft were not competitors in the marketplace, the Two-Eleven addressing a BEA need for a 200-seat aircraft, whereas the European Airbus was a somewhat larger aircraft, being planned to carry 300 passengers in wide-body twin-aisle configuration. BAC and the BoT repeatedly made this point to the Government, emphasising the fact that the two aircraft addressed distinct market segments. BEA, on its part, made it quite clear to the Government that it wanted the Two-Eleven, and that it considered the Airbus too big. However, this was not the way that the French regarded the project. On the one hand, they saw the BAC Two-Eleven as a potential diversion of British energies away from the Airbus, on the other hand they feared that the aircraft would eventually become a serious threat to the Airbus by way of subsequent 'stretches' during the programme's life. Therefore during the negotiations on the European Airbus that led to the Memorandum of Understanding of September 1967, the French put increasing pressure on the British Government to kill off the Two-Eleven project. The British Government refused to acknowledge that it would acquiesce to the strong French political pressure. However, on 15 December 1967 the Government announced in the House of Commons that there would be no funding for the BAC Two-Eleven because it was believed that there was an 'insufficient market' for the aircraft. The Government insisted that the decision not to proceed with the Two-Eleven had been dictated only by a stringent cost-benefit analysis.

Despite what the Government claimed at the time, there is no denying the fact that the decision not to back the Two-Eleven was at least in part political, and mainly driven by the desire to appease French concerns. Regardless of the fact that BAC had planned to subcontract a substantial amount of Two-Eleven work within Europe, the British-led Two-Eleven project was perceived to go against the Plowden dogma that large civil aircraft should be developed only within the framework of international (European) cooperation. The UK Government at that stage was whole-heartedly committed to European cooperation on large aircraft programmes, and backing the Two-Eleven was seen (wrongly) as a backward step.[5] There were also some criticisms within BEA of Sir Anthony Milward's enthusiasm for the aircraft. These criticisms hinged on the view that the Two-Eleven was the result of direct negotiations between Milward and BAC's chairman, Sir George Edwards, and that the design did not meet with the universal approval of BEA's technical staff.

Even allowing for the factors related above, an objective assessment of the BAC Two-Eleven project would conclude that in all likelihood the aircraft would have been a substantial commercial success. On a direct comparison with the aircraft available at the time, and with the Boeing 727 in particular, the Two-Eleven offered increased capacity with a larger degree of comfort, superior airfield performance, much quieter, environmentally friendly and economical engines and higher power-to-weight ratio on take-off and climb. We only need to consider the market success of the much later Boeing 757 (over 1,000 sold), Boeing 767 (over 950 sold) and Airbus A310 (over 250 sold) to see that the Two-Eleven and its further developments would have won a substantial share of the market. In addition, as others have pointed out, the Two-Eleven would have greatly reduced the appeal of the Boeing 727-200 and 727-200 Advanced and could, at the limit, have prevented McDonnell Douglas from developing the MD-80 and MD-90 series. In any case, we firmly believe that the aircraft would have helped preserve a viable independent British civil airliner industry, building on the success of the One-Eleven. In the end, political expediency and the desire to appease French concerns sacrificed a thoroughly commercial British aircraft project (we must not forget that in 1967 the British Government was still trying to gain admission to the European Economic Community). When the Two-Eleven was killed off, Sir Anthony Milward went on record as saying: 'The Two-Eleven was, in my view, the finest and most advanced aircraft that this country could produce, and incorporated the very latest in engine design, both as regards economy and, above all, quietness. It therefore grieves me very much that the government should shy away from this project like a startled horse because we cannot afford it. If we cannot afford the best, can we afford the second best?'[6]

A similar fate to that of the Two-Eleven was to befall another domestic proposal aimed at the same market, this time from Hawker Siddeley in the shape of the HS134. The HS134 study was launched in 1966 on the basis of a radical development of the Trident airliner. Unlike the rear-engined Trident trijet, the HS134 was to be powered by two Rolls-Royce RB178 high-bypass turbofans, mounted on pylons under the wing. The latter was based on a high aspect ratio, highly efficient supercritical design. The Trident's cockpit and fuselage width were retained, but the stretched fuselage and low tailplane mounted at the end of the fuselage gave the aircraft the general appearance of the much later Boeing 757. Passenger capacity was for 188 in two classes and for up to 210 in all-economy configuration. Again, nothing came of this promising and economical design; HSA could not afford to develop the aircraft from its own resources, and no overseas partner could be found to share the non-recurring costs. The only good that came out of Hawker Siddeley's effort on the HS134 was the know-how on advanced supercritical aerofoils and on the general aircraft configuration (large wing-mounted engines), knowledge that the company later put to good use in helping with the design of the Airbus A300.

In the end BEA was forced to settle for the 'third best' of the options on offer, and ordered the minimum-change stretched Hawker Siddeley Trident 3, capable of carrying 146 passengers in a two-class configuration or up to 180 in a high-density layout. Twenty-six Trident 3s (plus ten options, which were never exercised) were ordered on 6 August 1968 as an interim solution before the Airbus A300 became available in the mid-1970s. In addition to BEA, the Trident 3 sold only to China's CAAC (and the latter's order was for only two aircraft!), thus resulting in a total commercial fiasco. It is ironic to think that the Trident 3 operating subsidy agreed by the Government with BEA represented almost 40 per cent of the launch costs of the BAC Two-Eleven, an aircraft that would have had a much wider market appeal and that without doubt would have enabled the UK aircraft industry to remain in the 'Big League' of commercial airliner-producing nations.

Again, political expediency driven by the desire to appease French and German anxieties resulted in the UK electing to forego development of an aircraft that would have built on, and most likely exceeded, the success of the One-Eleven. Indeed both BAC and HSA, with the Two-Eleven and HS134 respectively, offered thoroughly commercial and competitive large airliner designs that would have kept the country at the forefront of civil airliner development and, more importantly, kept control of the project in UK hands.

The Development of the Airbus A300

With the domestic alternatives out of the way, the British Government put all its energies into launching the three-nation European Airbus. The first official meeting at Government level took place in Paris on 9 May 1967. The meeting launched the project definition stage of a large-capacity short-haul aircraft able to carry 300 passengers, to be powered by two Rolls-Royce RB207 high-bypass turbofans each rated at 50,000lb (23 tonnes). The meeting was attended by John Stonehouse, UK Minister of State for Technology, André Bettencourt, French Minister of State for Foreign Affairs, and Dr Johann Schollhorn, West German State Secretary at the Economics Ministry.

The total market potential for the aircraft was estimated at 250 units. It was also expected that the three national carriers of the sponsoring nations, BEA, Air France and Lufthansa, would provide the launch orders. Total airframe development costs were estimated at £190 million, with HSA of Britain and Sud Aviation of France each having a 37.5 per cent share of the research, development and production. Arge Airbus of Germany was to receive the balance (25 per cent). Engine development costs were estimated at £60 million, with the UK's Rolls-Royce receiving 75 per cent of the development funding, while SNECMA of France and MTU of Germany were to receive 12.5 per cent each of the balance of funds.

In return for the higher proportion of engine work assigned to Britain, the British Government agreed to cede design leadership on the airframe to Sud

Aviation of France. This decision, as later events were to prove, represented very poor bargaining by the UK Government and industry. In fact, overall leadership on the airframe side of the programme eventually entitled France to renege on the exclusivity of Rolls-Royce, and to opt instead for American engines. Ironically, despite the fact that the chosen baseline design for the A300 European Airbus was the HBN100 principally developed at Hatfield by HSA, in the end project leadership went to Sud Aviation, meaning that an essentially British design became a French-led programme. Finally, agreeing to Sud's leadership did not reflect the expertise of the three partners at that time: Hawker Siddeley was the only one of the three to have developed a modern second-generation jetliner in the shape of the HS121 Trident (Sud Aviation's Caravelle was a first-generation jet airliner). Thus, on technical grounds alone, one would have expected that leadership should have gone to the most experienced design team. However, as is always the case in collaborative programmes in aerospace, the work-share decision on the A300 Airbus was intensely political. We shall see, however, that Hawker Siddeley was to play a key role in the development of the first Airbus, sharing its extensive expertise of modern jet airliners with its French and German partners.

By the summer of 1967 the Airbus definition study was completed and the delegates of the three Governments and industrial partners met at Lancaster House, London, on 25 July. At this meeting Stonehouse and Schollhorn were joined by the French transport minister Jean Chamant to sign a mission statement. This read: 'For the purpose of strengthening European cooperation in the field of aviation technology and thereby promoting economic and technological progress in Europe, to take appropriate measures for the joint development and production of an air bus.' The project received its formal go-ahead on 26 September 1967, with the signing of an intergovernmental Memorandum of Understanding (MoU). The MoU established that detailed design of the Airbus would begin in June 1968. The MoU also established that the A300 would not be launched unless the three flag carriers of the sponsoring nations had agreed to buy a minimum of seventy-five aircraft. Of the three Governments, it was the British who insisted on this clause: as we shall see, the fact that the original A300 and its derivative A300B did not achieve this sales target would have a major bearing on the UK Government's decision to pull out of Airbus two years later.

With the September 1967 MoU launching the detailed design phase of the European Airbus, the A300 project grew and grew in size, fostered by promises of ever increasing thrust from Rolls-Royce for its RB207 turbofans. The aircraft's capacity grew in this period from the 225–260 seats of the original HBN100 to 320 seats, fuselage width grew to 21ft (slightly larger than the Boeing 747 Jumbo) and fuselage length from 160ft to 177ft.

Tellingly, the larger the aircraft grew, the less interest the airlines – including those of the sponsoring nations – showed in the programme. To the great concern of the project team, by the time the June 1968 deadline arrived, there was not a single order to the A300's name.

In the meantime, in the United States, Douglas Aircraft and Lockheed had launched their own wide-body trijets, the DC-10 and L-1011 respectively. These were aimed at an American Airlines requirement for a short to medium-haul large capacity airliner for transcontinental US routes. The specification for this aircraft was drawn up by American Airlines' technical director Frank Kolk, who had originally envisaged a wide-body twin-engined aircraft. Kolk's 'book of requirements' was to play a major role in the refinement of the Airbus A300, but in the US it gave birth to the DC-10 and L-1011. After considering twin-engined designs, both Douglas and Lockheed decided that only a trijet configuration gave the plane the reliability and safety margins to fly over the Rockies in the central part of the United States. The choice of three engines by Airbus's US competitors was eventually to prove a blessing in disguise for the European fledging organisation, as it resulted in much heavier and fuel-thirsty aircraft than the emerging A300. When the fuel crisis hit the world's airlines in 1973, suddenly the A300 found itself in a category of its own among large-capacity short-haul airliners.

One more immediate – and disastrous – effect that the launch of the American programmes had on the European Airbus and Britain's commitment to it was that it distracted Rolls-Royce from developing the RB207 for the Airbus; in fact all of the famous British aero-engine group's energies went into achieving a presence on one or both of the new American wide-bodies. Rolls-Royce management's view at the time was that the very survival of the company as a major aero-engine manufacturer was dependent on getting exclusivity on American airframes. Rolls's management were privately sceptical of Airbus's chances of success, given the poor sales record of the UK and European airliner designs produced up to then. Another reason for Rolls-Royce's doubts, and British scepticism in general about the Airbus, was the fact that the project was led by France, a nation which British businessmen perceived – rightly or wrongly – to be more interested in aerospace programmes for the national prestige that they would bequeath on France than for their economic and financial viability.[7]

Rolls Royce, with a guarantee of financial backing from the British Government, mounted a strong campaign in the US to convince both Douglas and Lockheed to adopt its novel three-shaft high bypass turbofan engine, the RB211, for their new trijets. Douglas eventually turned down Rolls-Royce's design in favour of General Electric's new CF-6 turbofan, a development of the military TF-39 for the Lockheed C-5 Galaxy military transport. However, after a long and tough sales campaign by Rolls-Royce and hard negotiations by Lockheed's chairman Dan Haughton, in July 1968 the British company struck a fixed price deal to supply RB211 engines for the L-1011 TriStar on an exclusivity basis. The signing of the Rolls-Royce contract, valued then at US$250 million, was hailed as an enormous success for the British aerospace industry. The country's press was full of eulogies on the technological prowess of Rolls, and the Labour Government fully backed the deal, hailing it as an example of successful public-private partnership in leading-edge technology and fully consistent with the Government's objectives of creating successful technology-driven national champions.

The Lockheed deal, however, had hidden within it two time-bombs that were to eventually undermine the UK's position on Airbus, and by reflection the country's standing in civil aircraft development.

Firstly, it distracted Rolls Royce's energies away from the European Airbus. Rolls started to pour almost all its energies into the RB211 for the TriStar and, as the programme proved over time more technically complex than was at first envisaged, the RB207 engine development quietly fell by the side, forcing the Airbus partners to look for an alternative.

Secondly, the fixed price nature of the Lockheed/Rolls-Royce contract, with no provision for cost escalation, eventually brought the UK company to its knees, to the point that it had to file for bankruptcy in February 1971. The escalating costs of the RB211 development over time called for more and more Government funding, to the point where it starved airframe projects like the BAC Three-Eleven and the A300, of any spare Government cash.

As the Rolls crisis became apparent, the Airbus partners, HSA, Sud Aviation, and Deutsche Airbus, under the leadership of Roger Beteille of Sud, started looking for alternative engines for the A300. Sir Arnold Hall of HSA is generally credited with calling Beteille and Sud president Henri Ziegler to inform them that he had got wind that Rolls-Royce was not going to deliver on the RB207, and that they had better look for US-built alternatives. In addition airline interest was progressively waning as the A300 got bigger. It was then that Roger Beteille assembled a small team of top Sud Aviation engineers to scale down the A300 from a 300-plus-seat aircraft to a 250-seater, basically returning to the original HBN100 specification. In its new guise the aircraft would not only cost less to develop, but could use the lower thrust of the existing American high bypass turbofans, Pratt & Whitney's JT9-D (adopted by Boeing for the 747) and General Electric's GE CF-6, both rated at approximately 50,000lb of thrust. The revised design was christened internally the A250, although when it was announced to the public the aircraft was called the A300B.

It is interesting to point out that at the time of the original HBN100/A300 discussions, the partners had considered the JT9-D of Pratt & Whitney as the favoured engine. The adoption of an American engine was then particularly favoured by the French and the Germans, on the not unreasonable grounds that an American engine would improve the saleability of the Airbus A300 in the American market, the world's largest. Another strong point for the adoption of the JT9-D was that the engine was already in development for the Boeing 747s ordered by Pan-Am and that therefore the A300 would benefit from a more proven engine and engine commonality with the long-haul wide-body fleet. Things progressed as far as the signing of a MoU between Pratt & Whitney and Bristol Siddeley and SNECMA for the licence production of the JT9-D in Europe for the Airbus.

This scenario was, of course, anathema to Rolls-Royce, who saw the deal as a US Trojan Horse in its 'home' market. Rolls-Royce proceeded to purchase Bristol Siddeley outright in October 1966, in a deal valued then at £67 million. The take-over of Bristol Siddeley by Rolls meant that the MoU with Pratt & Whitney was allowed to lapse. In the longer term the Bristol Siddeley take-over deprived Rolls of much-needed cash, which would be required later at the peak of the RB211 development. All said, the adoption of the JT9-D would not have been looked on with favour by the British Government who, under strong lobbying from Rolls-Royce, in 1967 had negotiated that the Airbus should be powered by Rolls-Royce engines exclusively.

On 11 December 1968 Sud Aviation and Hawker Siddeley announced that they had scaled down the Airbus A300. The revised aircraft, called A300B, would now seat approximately 250 passengers, and could be powered by Pratt & Whitney JT9-Ds, General Electric CF-6s or Rolls Royce RB211s.[8] In revealing the revised aircraft the two companies pointed out that, as the aircraft was now smaller, development costs on the airframe would be reduced to £130 million from £190 million. Also, the aircraft's smaller size and choice of engines would broaden its market appeal, particularly in the US market, the world's largest. Sud and HSA acknowledged that the first A300B would most likely fly with American engines, as the 50,000lb version of the RR RB211 would not be available on time for the first flight. As we have seen, Rolls was first introducing the RB211 with a 40,000lb thrust for the L-1011 TriStar.

It is clear that the change in the status of Rolls-Royce from being the exclusive supplier of Airbus engines to being one of three suppliers competing for Airbus orders with its two American rivals did nothing to endear the Airbus project to the British Government. In actual fact the British Government's disenchant-ment with the European Airbus had been growing soon after the ink had dried on the September 1967 MoU. A series of developments since the signing of the MoU had contrived to cool the British Government's commitment towards the European project. These developments included:

France's pulling out of the AFVG military aircraft programme in 1967, citing budget constraints, and then going ahead to develop a domestic alternative. This was the only Anglo-French aircraft programme where Britain (in the shape of BAC) had design leadership on the airframe, the others providing for French airframe leadership. France's backing out of this programme left a sour taste in British industry and in Government circles, highlighting the perceived 'treachery' of the French when an arrangement did not suit their political goals.

Rolls Royce's master deal with Lockheed me⬛t, in the UK Government's eyes, that the company was now far less dependent on the Airbus as a means to remain at the forefront of civil aero-engine development.

The A300 programme had been around for almost two years, and not a single order had been received from any of the three flag carriers of the project's sponsoring nations, let alone from foreign airlines.

BEA, the UK short-haul national carrier, had repeatedly stated that they were not interested in the A300 and were instead getting more and more interested in the wholly national alternative, the wide-bodied BAC Three-Eleven, which BAC had announced in July 1968 as a response to BEA's requirements.

Another Anglo-French civil airliner, Concorde, was absorbing larger and larger amounts of UK Government development cash, and its commercial prospects did not look sound. In addition, the relationship with the French on the project was proving difficult and various disagreements were contributing to cost escalation.

Britain had a fully national alternative to the European Airbus in the shape of the BAC Three-Eleven. Not only did this project have the full backing of BEA, Europe's largest short-haul airline, but the UK Government was also aware that BAC was by far the most experienced developer of airliners in Europe, having sold by then over 850 Viscounts, Vanguards, Britannias, VC-10s and BAC One-Elevens to airlines the world over, including several US airlines. These facts suggested that the BAC Three-Eleven would be a more robust commercial proposition than the European Airbus.

The British Government had strong reservations about Sud Aviation's ability to carry the A300B project to successful completion, both on technical grounds and in terms of management resources.[9]

It did not come as a complete surprise, therefore, when Anthony Wedgwood-Benn, the then Minister of Technology, announced in the House of Commons on 10 April 1969 that Britain was withdrawing from the European Airbus. The main reasons cited for the withdrawal were that the conditions laid out in the 1967 MoU, namely the achievement of seventy-five sales to the three flag carriers and the exclusivity of Rolls-Royce as engine supplier, were not met by the new A300B proposal. But of course other reasons, as outlined above, played their part. In the first quarter of 1969, sensing the British Government's progressive detachment from the Airbus venture, strong diplomatic efforts from the Germans and the French were made to keep the Wilson Government involved. But last-ditch attempts by the German Chancellor in February 1969 to convince Harold

Wilson of the viability of the European Airbus project were to no avail. As Wilson himself commented at the time: 'the deserts are littered with the whitening bones of failed European attempts at industrial cooperation.'

At this stage the British Government expected that its withdrawal would lead to the collapse of the Airbus programme. Instead the French and German Governments vowed that they would proceed with development of the A300B, 'with or without the UK's involvement'. Little more than one month later, on 29 May 1969, on the eve of the Paris Air Show, France and Germany signed the definitive agreement for the launch of the Airbus A300B. The programme was to be developed on a 50/50 joint venture basis between the two countries.

Needless to say, the British Government's decision was a massive blow for HSA. At the time of the 1967 MoU it was decided that HSA, as part of its 37.5 per cent share of the airframe, would design, develop and manufacture the A300's entire wings, with all their moving surfaces, as well as the engine pylons, the nacelles and the landing gear. Sud Aviation, also with 37.5 per cent, was given responsibility for overall aircraft design and systems integration, the nose section, including the cockpit/flight deck, the lower-mid fuselage including the wing centre section torsion box, final assembly, flight testing and aircraft certification. Arge Airbus, with 25 per cent of the airframe, was responsible for most of the fuselage, the fin/rudder and the horizontal stabilisers. At the time of the British Government's withdrawal, HSA had basically completed the detailed design of the wing and its moving surfaces, and was preparing to tool up for manufacture. The Airbus was expected to represent the key commercial programme for the British group, and a means to recover the heavy development costs that had gone into the HS121 Trident airliner.[10] On the Airbus reaching full production, it was expected that some 10,000 people would work full time on it in HSA alone, with another 30,000 among the subcontractors. Now the Government's withdrawal left the company out on a limb, or as its chairman Sir Arnold Hall said at the time, 'holding the baby'.

The French and German partners in Airbus were also facing a crisis as a result of the British Government's withdrawal: now there was the very real risk that HSA would also be forced to withdraw from the programme, suddenly depriving the consortium of its wing designer and manufacturer. Hawker Siddeley had spent over two years developing the advanced supercritical wing for the A300, and the French and German industrial partners were aware that there was no real expertise outside Britain to develop a complex subsonic wing. Also the two partners did not have the industrial resources (plant and machinery) to manufacture such a large and key element of the airframe. Some consideration was given to the possibility of Deutsche Airbus developing an alternative wing in Germany, with the help from Sud Aviation and Dassault Aviation in France, and from Hawker engineers who would have gone freelance to Germany, but this scenario entailed delaying programme development by anything from one year to up to two years, depending on how optimistic one was about the outcome of an alternative German-led wing development programme. Such delay could have fatally wounded the commercial, if not technical, prospects of the A300 Airbus.

In the wake of the British Government's withdrawal announcement, the Hawker Siddeley Board proceeded to evaluate the options open to the group, and decided that it still wanted to be part of the Airbus programme, although for financial and risk management reasons the Board decided that it could only finance 40 per cent of the development costs of the wing (equating to about 7.5 per cent of total programme costs). Who would then finance the remaining 60 per cent of the development costs? Fortunately for the Airbus programme, the Bavarian Minister for Aviation, Franz Joseph Strauss, was able to convince the Finance Ministry of the German Federal Government to step in and finance the 60 per cent share of HSA's development costs. The indirect subsidy of some US$70 million from the German Government to a British industrial company appeared *prima facie* an unlikely act of generosity, as some commentators have said. However, the true reason behind the German Government's subsidy deal with HSA has emerged only recently, when a senior British civil servant revealed that an arrangement was agreed between the German and British Governments whereby the Germans would finance British private involvement (at company level) in the European Airbus as an offset for the cost of keeping British troops stationed in West Germany.

In any case, the German Government's financial intervention and HSA's own decision to stay with the Airbus proved to be the only means of keeping the A300B programme alive, as most observers agree that without Hawker Siddeley's wing expertise it is unlikely that the European Airbus would have been successfully developed. For his enormous contribution to saving the Airbus programme, Franz Joseph Strauss was rewarded with the chairmanship of the Airbus supervisory board.

Once the financial arrangements with the German Federal Government had been agreed, in July 1969 Hawker Siddeley signed a binding agreement with Sud Aviation of France and Deutsche Airbus of Germany to continue with the design and development of the A300 wings, the manufacture of the structural wing boxes for the four prototypes and the eventual production aircraft, as well as continued wing development for future variants. HSA also agreed to fulfil a consultancy role on the overall aircraft design, as well as seconding staff to the marketing department. But the British group's relationship with its French and German counterparts was now that of a subcontractor, not of a full partner. It was invited to the consortium's Board meetings, but had no vote in Board decisions. Also, its workload was now reduced from 37.5 per cent to approximately 18 per cent, and HSA had to forego the production of the wing's slats, flaps and other moving surfaces (which went to Deutsche Airbus) and the design and production of the engine pylon (which went to Sud Aviation). Final assembly of the complete wing – including moveable surfaces - also went to Germany (to Bremen, to be precise), and this arrangement lasts to this day as far as the wide-body Airbus families are concerned.

More importantly, the decision by the British Government to withdraw had enormous negative implications for the British equipment industry, which at the time was by far the most advanced in Europe. The contract for the A300's landing gear, for example, originally assigned to Dowty, went to France's Messier, who built the Dowty design under licence. Even more serious was the loss to the British avionics companies such as Smiths Industries and Elliott Automation, which were expected to play a major part in equipping the Airbus cockpit. Instead it was mainly French companies such as Sfena that got the lucrative Airbus cockpit contracts, allowing them to build expertise first via licence manufacture of American equipment, and later via in-house designs. Ironically, the British avionics companies who had led the world in autopilot and automatic landing technology, found themselves playing a marginal role on the A300 Airbus programme. In 1969 it was the Hawker Siddeley Trident and Vickers VC-10 cockpits that were the most advanced in Europe. This situation for British equipment suppliers to Airbus was never fully reversed, and as Airbus cockpit technology evolved over the years to the standard-setting fly-by-wire suite, it was French and not British companies that took hold of the high-value-added elements of the cockpit.

Following the Franco-German agreement to go ahead with the project at the 1969 Paris Air Show, the A300 European Airbus development programme proceeded smoothly. The shares of the partners, split 50/50 between Deutsche Airbus and Sud Aviation, were eventually conferred into Airbus Industrie, a special purpose company established as a Groupement d'Interet Économique (GIE) on 18 December 1970 with headquarters in Paris. In 1974 the Airbus Industrie HQ was transferred to Toulouse in South-West France, where the main design offices and the Airbus final assembly plant were located. It was at the insistence of the Germans that Airbus Industrie was set up, as they wanted to prevent Sud Aviation from becoming the dominant partner in the venture, in spite of the shares of the Airbus GIE being owned in equal proportions by Sud and Deutsche Airbus GmbH. The formation of Airbus Industrie as a separate marketing and aircraft development entity ensured a single interface with potential customers, and guaranteed an equal voice for the German partner, who was no doubt the junior partner on technical grounds.

The British Government was given a first chance to rejoin the Airbus consortium in late 1970, when the new Conservative Government under Edward Heath was tasked with deciding between backing the wholly British BAC Three-Eleven or rejoining the A300B European Airbus. We shall discuss this at length in the next chapter, but this opportunity was eventually turned down.

The year 1970 also saw the creation – in January – of the new French group Aérospatiale, born of the merger of Sud Aviation, Nord-Aviation and ballistic missile group SEREB, and the signing of a letter of intent by Air France for six A300Bs, plus ten options. This contract was firmed up in 1971. That it was Air France who committed first to the Airbus is highly indicative of the consistent strategy by the French Government to promote the interests of its aerospace industry (Air France was wholly Government-owned at the time).

In spite of the vast scepticism that surrounded Airbus in the United States and Britain at the time, the French-led consortium was able to develop the A300B on time and within the agreed cost parameters. In this regard we must recognise that the contribution of the British engineers of HSA to the development of the European Airbus was very significant, and much greater than their reduced status and share in the programme would lead people to believe.[11] It must also be recognised that the French partner, Aérospatiale, and its top management of Henri Ziegler and Roger Beteille, proved to be up to the challenge of coordinating the immensely complex task of designing and developing an aircraft on a multinational basis, with British, French, German and eventually Spanish engineers working together for the first time. As for the German contribution to the project, this was principally financial, by way of the Federal Government's commitment and Franz Joseph Strauss's unflinching support to the extent of subsidising HSA, although, to be fair, the Germans' technical input was also noteworthy. The very first Airbus, the prototype A300B1, was rolled out at Toulouse in late September 1972 and made its first flight from Toulouse-Blagnac Airport on 28 October 1972, three months ahead of schedule. This was the beginning of an incredible European renaissance in the production of large civil aircraft. However, very few people at the time believed that a multinational team from three disparate European countries would go on to challenge the mighty Boeing for market supremacy in commercial airliners.

In the meantime Spain, via its national aerospace company Construcciones Aeronauticas SA (CASA), had joined the Airbus consortium in 1971, with a 4.2 per cent share and with responsibility for the production of the horizontal stabilisers, which had been designed by Deutsche Airbus. The shares of Aérospatiale and Deutsche Airbus in the consortium were therefore reduced to 47.9 per cent each. At the industrial level, Aérospatiale and Deutsche Airbus had 36.5 per cent of A300B production each, Hawker Siddeley 20 per cent, Fokker-VFW of the Netherlands 2.8 per cent (as an associate, not as a partner) and CASA the remainder.

1 For a comprehensive review of the 1964–1970 Labour Government's policies towards aerospace and the Plowden Report, see Hayward, *Government and British Civil Aerospace*; Hayward, *The British Aircraft Industry*.

2 In fact the BAC Three-Eleven would have been a multinational programme at the industrial level (see Chapter 3).

3 *Aviation Week & Space Technology* Editorial, 'The European Challenge', by Robert Holtz, 7 September 1970.

4 The technical description of the BAC Two-Eleven is based on Richard Anthony Payne's series of articles, which were published in *Air International* in three issues (September, October and November 1998).

5 See Hayward, *Government and British Civil Aerospace*, for an extensive review of considerations.

6 See Richard Anthony Payne, *Air Pictorial*, October 1998.

7 HMG files reveal that the Ministry of Aviation Supply, MinTech and the Board of Trade were highly sceptical of Sud Aviation's ability to lead and project-manage the A300 European Airbus and the subsequent A300B. As we know, in due course the facts proved them wrong.

8 Airbus's revision of the A300 into the smaller 250-seat A300B was strongly influenced by BAC's launch of the Three-Eleven wide-body proposal in July 1968.

9 Reported in HMG paper dated 24 February 1970 (MinTech note). However, this last point was not made public in order not to upset diplomatic relations with the French.

10 See Hayward, *Government and British Civil Aerospace*; Hayward, *The British Aircraft Industry*.

11 HSA, as part of the consultancy agreement entered into with Airbus in July 1969, contributed to the overall aircraft design and definition, in addition to designing the A300B's wing. This was another example of the British leading 'from behind the curtain' and, while this British contribution helped to make the A300B a technically and commercially successful aircraft, it represented yet another instance of the UK giving away intellectual property and know-how to its European partners for little or no consideration.

3

The BAC Three-Eleven Project

Project's Origins

The BAC Three-Eleven twinjet wide-body airliner was designed in response to a BEA requirement for an airbus–type aircraft with 200-250 seats and a 1,500 nautical mile range, which the British airline expected it would need in the early 1970s. This BEA requirement stemmed from projected traffic volume growth which indicated that by 1973 BEA's HS Tridents and Vickers Vanguards, the mainstay of its fleet, would be too small to cope with traffic on the carrier's high-density trunk routes, such as London–Paris or London–Amsterdam.

Around the same time Europe's other main carriers, including Air France and Lufthansa, identified a similar requirement for a large wide-body jet to be used on their high-density short-haul routes. Indeed the combined requirements of BEA, Air France and Lufthansa for a large short-haul airliner to be made available in the early 1970s were the catalyst for the launch of the Pan-European Airbus A300, whose project definition phase was officially approved in September 1967 by the British, French and German Governments. However, early on in the proceedings it became obvious that Air France's and BEA's requirements in particular diverged in no small measure. The French flag carrier leaned towards a 300-seater aircraft, whereas British European Airways was more interested in a 180/200-seat jet. In response to this specific BEA requirement the British Aircraft Corporation put forward a proposal dubbed the BAC Two-Eleven (see Chapter 2).

Following the cancellation of the Two-Eleven project in December 1967, BAC's designers at Weybridge concentrated their engineering efforts on an entirely new advanced technology wide-bodied twinjet airliner, still aimed at satisfying BEA's original requirements. BEA, from the early days of the Airbus project, had let it be known that it did not like the Airbus as it was deemed too big for its needs – the A.300 at the time being designed as a 300-plus-seat aircraft.

Preliminary design work on the new BAC aircraft, christened the BAC Three-Eleven, was completed in May 1968, and the general technical specification of the project was made public in the summer of the same year.

3

General Description of the Aircraft

The BAC Three-Eleven was an advanced technology wide-body airliner powered by twin rear-mounted Rolls-Royce RB211 high bypass turbofans. The Three-Eleven's general layout followed the rear-mounted engine configuration that Vickers and then BAC had successfully used in the VC-10 long-range jet airliner and the BAC One-Eleven short-haul twinjet. In this respect the Three-Eleven's configuration differed from the other wide-bodies being introduced or being developed at the time such as the Boeing 747, Airbus A.300, Lockheed TriStar and Douglas DC-10. In all of the above cases, the engines were mounted on pylons under the wings, although in the case of the trijet TriStar and DC-10 out of necessity the third engine was positioned at the back, at the bottom of the fin. BAC engineers said that the Three-Eleven's rear-engined configuration was decided upon after several design studies of under-wing and fuselage-mounted engine layouts. BAC listed several 'significant' advantages of the rear-engine layout, including: superior cross-wind landing capability; better directional control with asymmetric thrust; negligible trim changes with power adjustment; powerplants being less prone to bird and debris ingestion during take-off and landing; greater safety in wheels-up landing; lower risk of engine casing damage from servicing vehicles on the ramp; the aircraft's lower height allowing a high degree of compatibility with existing hangars and current and new generation ground equipment; quieter cabin.

However, aerospace engineers know that the rear-engined configuration also gives rise to some disadvantages, which BAC took care not to highlight in its marketing literature. The principal disadvantages include:

Lack of wing bending relief, this being one of the main benefits for an aircraft when the engines are mounted under the wing. The lack of bending relief usually requires the wing to be strengthened structurally, resulting in a higher weight penalty.

The presence of the engines at the rear of the fuselage also requires the tail structure of the aircraft (the area aft of the rear pressure bulkhead, and which includes the tailcone, fin, rudder, tailplane and elevators) to be strengthened, and this again incurs an extra weight penalty.

Rear-engined aircraft present centre of gravity (CG) issues, which are addressed with having the greater length of the fuselage (and any significant fuselage stretches) ahead of the wing.

T-tailed aircraft have a tendency to enter a 'deep stall' under certain conditions (when the wing reaches very high angles of attack and the resulting turbulent air nullifies the efficacy of the tailplane and elevators). The 'deep stall' phenomenon emerged in accidents during early flight-testing of the Boeing 727, HS Trident and BAC 1-11, with tragically fatal consequences for the test crews involved.

On large aircraft like the Three-Eleven, the rear-engine configuration makes engine inspection and maintenance more difficult than in an underwing configuration, as the engines are higher up from the ground level.

Notwithstanding the limitations of the rear-mounted engine layout mentioned above, BAC had considerable experience of airliner development, having produced airliners with both wing-mounted engine configurations (Viscount, Vanguard, Britannia and Concorde) and tail-mounted configurations (VC-10, One-Eleven). It is therefore reasonable to conclude that the company thoroughly evaluated all the 'pros and cons' of each configuration. In the end BAC came out in favour of the rear-engine configuration for the Three-Eleven, once the trade-offs of the two configurations had been balanced against each other. Indeed, on the 'deep stall' risk front, BAC had sufficient experience with the VC-10 and One-Eleven to design flight control systems that would prevent the aircraft from reaching that condition. As far as the weight penalties were concerned, BAC managed to achieve an empty weight for the 'final' Three-Eleven proposal which was not dissimilar from the broadly equivalent (in terms of payload) A300B Airbus, as we shall see further on.

In terms of cabin cross-section, BAC gave the Three-Eleven a generous wide-body fuselage of 19ft 9in (6.02m) width, providing an internal cabin trim-to-trim width of 18ft 11in (5.77m). The fuselage diameter and cabin width were identical to those of the wide-body trijets being developed in America, namely the Lockheed TriStar and Douglas DC-10, but notably wider than those of the European Airbus A300B. The Airbus A300B's fuselage and cabin width were in fact 18ft 6in (5.64m) and 17ft 4in (5.28m) respectively, resulting in a cabin width some 1ft 7in (0.5m) narrower than the Three-Eleven. The Three-Eleven's generous cabin width allowed therefore not only standard twin-aisle eight-abreast seating arrangements, but also high-density nine-abreast for operators serving the inclusive tour (IT) market.

As a result of feedback from all the major world airlines approached by BAC, the Three-Eleven grew in size and capacity (payload) over the project definition period: the latter lasted from the preliminary design 'freeze' in May 1968 up to the days when a final launch decision was due to be taken (summer of 1970). The table overleaf sets out the principal parameters of the Three-Eleven project when first disclosed (July 1968), and in August 1970, prior to BEA's conditional launch order announced at Farnborough 1970.

Table 3.1   BAC Three-Eleven general specifications

BAC 3-11 parameters	July 1968 specification	August 1970 specification
Overall length	173ft (52.7m)	183ft 7in (55.95m)
Wing span	140ft (42.7m)	147ft 0in (44.80m)
Overall height	41ft 6in (12.6m)	43ft 4in (13.20m)
Wing area	2,450sq.ft (227.6m²)	2,713sq.ft (251m²)
Wing sweep	25° at quarter chord	25° at quarter chord
Ramp weight	269,000lb (122,110kg)	305,000lb (138,500kg)
Max take off weight	267,000lb (121,100kg)	303,000lb (137,500kg)
Landing weight	242,000lb (109,770kg)	273,000lb (124,000kg)
Operating empty weight	165,646lb (75,135kg)	185,127lb (84,000kg)
Maximum payload	49,354lb (22,390kg)	69,873lb (31,700kg)
Maximum range	3,625 miles (5,800km)	2,500 nm (5,800km)
Max. payload range	1,730 miles (2,785km)	1,360 miles (2,180km)
Max. level speed (25,000ft)	593mph (954km/h)	593mph (954km/h)
Maximum operating speed	0.84 Mach	562mph (905km/h)
Power plant	2 x Rolls-Royce RB211-24 turbofans of 43,040lb (19,500kg) thrust each	2 x Rolls-Royce RB211-61 turbofans of 50,000lb (22,680kg) thrust each

(Source: *Flight International*, July 1968; BAC Technical Sales Department, August 1970)

Technical Description

BAC incorporated into the Three-Eleven project the substantial aerodynamics, structural and systems experience that the company had acquired in the development and production of the Vickers Viscount, Vanguard, VC-10 and BAC One-Eleven, as well as the experience on the Concorde (which at the time was still under development in cooperation with Aérospatiale of France). We outline briefly below the principal design philosophies applied to the Three-Eleven.

Wing

The wing design was based on an aerofoil that used the 'rear loading' concept, with the greater lift being generated by the rear of the aerofoil and moderate lift by means of suction peaks near the leading edge. Based on advanced aerodynamic studies conducted by Vickers/BAC in conjunction with the Government-sponsored Royal Aircraft Establishment (RAE) at Farnborough and the National Physical Laboratory (NPL) at Teddington, the Three-Eleven's wing was at least as advanced as that which Hawker Siddeley was designing at the time for the Airbus A300B and provided the same (or perhaps a higher) degree of operational efficiency to the aircraft in the different flight regimes.[1]

The wing's aspect ratio was 8 and the sweep 25° at the quarter chord. The moving surfaces included powered ailerons outboard of the flaps, powerful wide-chord Fowler flaps and full-span, hydraulically operated leading edge slats which enabled excellent take-off performance and effective low-speed control characteristics. In addition, hydraulically operated spoilers in three sections on each wing, and lift dumpers ahead of inboard flap sections, provided ample control for the aircraft during descent and landing.

Fuselage

The fuselage was of conventional circular-section all-metal fail-safe structure, with continuous frames and stringers. However, major load-bearing structures such as the fuselage centre-section frames in proximity to the wing interface and the rear-pressure bulkhead frames were to be built of titanium, and carbon-fibre reinforcing was to be employed for structural components such as the cabin floor. Titanium/carbon-fibre alloys were also to be used for several stress-critical components in other areas of the aircraft.

Cockpit/flight deck

The Three-Eleven flight deck was designed from the beginning for two-crew operation (captain and first officer), plus seats for an optional third crew-member and an observer. In this respect the Three-Eleven would have been the first wide-body aircraft to be certificated for two-crew operations. The big American trijets and the Airbus A300B were originally designed for three-crew operations (two pilots, plus flight engineer), and it was not before the early 1980s that Airbus introduced the two-crew flight deck with an Airbus A300B4 delivered to Indonesia's Garuda.

The cockpit would have incorporated the latest automatic flight control systems suitable for Cat IIIa operation. Provision was also being made for the installation of head-up display units. BAC was, at the time, also beginning studies of the so-called 'glass' cockpits, and the Three-Eleven would have in due course benefited from such advanced cockpit displays, as subsequent Airbus and Boeing aircraft did.

Systems

The aircraft's main systems were designed with multiple redundancy in mind. Fully duplicated air conditioning and pressurisation systems used air tapped from the IP and HP stages of each engine. Additional air supply was available from the tail-cone-mounted APU on the ground, during take-off and approach. Three independent hydraulic systems powered by pumps on each engine and the APU operated flaps, ailerons, spoilers, lift dumpers, variable incidence tailplane, elevators, rudders and brakes. All services could be operated by any two of the three systems. The electrical system utilised three generators, one on each engine driven through a constant-speed drive and one on the APU. All services could be operated by any two of the three generators. Finally, two separate DC systems were supplied by transformers-rectifiers.

As part of HMG's evaluation of the Three-Eleven the Ministry of Technology instructed the RAE at Farnborough to carry out a full technical audit of the BAC Three-Eleven and the rival European Airbus A300B. This audit was performed between 1969 and 1970 and showed that the Three-Eleven in its original form had an 8.5 per cent Direct Operating Cost (DOC) advantage over the A300B. Boeing, who had studied the Three-Eleven as part of a possible joint venture deal with BAC, estimated the aircraft's DOC to be some 10 per cent better than the A300B. When the project grew in size to its final August 1970 specification, the Three-Eleven still showed a 5 per cent DOC advantage over the A300B. BEA's own evaluation of the Three-Eleven indicated that the aircraft had 3 per cent to 4 per cent better DOC than the European Airbus.[2]

In the opinion of the RAE the BAC Three-Eleven was a well-balanced design. With regard to the aircraft's aerodynamics the technical staff at the RAE reported that impressive progress had been made in the aerodynamic design of the 'clean' wing and that the aircraft would achieve the take-off and landing performance estimated by BAC. Concluding on aerodynamics, the RAE said that there was no obvious way of improving the aerodynamics of the aircraft within the *then* state of the art. The RAE's estimate of structure weight was in close agreement with BAC's own calculations and on structures generally the RAE concluded that BAC had saved as much weight as they could do without compromising their standards of structural integrity or accepting unreasonable risks. Overall the RAE regarded the BAC Three-Eleven as a superior aircraft to the Airbus A300B in terms of operating performance and design philosophy.

Addressable Markets

BAC envisaged that the Three-Eleven would initially cater for three distinct market segments: European scheduled services; European inclusive tour (IT) market;

and US trunk operations. Seating arrangements for these three markets evolved over time as follows:

Table 3.2   BAC Three-Eleven cabin layout

Cabin layout	July 1968 specification	August 1970 specification
European scheduled services	220 passengers eight-abreast at 34in (0.86m) pitch	245 passengers eight-abreast at 34in (0.86m) pitch
European IT services (high density)	270 passengers nine-abreast at 30in (0.76m) pitch	300 passengers nine-abreast at 30in (0.76m) pitch
US trunk routes	36 first class (six-abreast at 38in (0.965m) pitch), plus 152 coach class (eight-abreast at 36in (0.914m) pitch), for a total of 188 passengers	36 first class (six-abreast at 38in (0.965m) pitch), plus 168 coach class (eight-abreast at 36in (0.914m) pitch), for a total of 204 passengers

For avoidance of doubt we must point out, however, that BAC did not narrowly tailor the Three-Eleven specification to fit only the three market segments outlined above, but gave the aircraft sufficient flexibility to cater for the global market, including Latin America, Australia and the then emerging Asian market. In fact the views of such carriers as All Nippon, Japan Airlines, Thai International, Indian Airlines, Philippine Airlines and Australia's Ansett and TAA were fed back into the final specification.

Depending on the chosen layout and passenger density, the Three-Eleven's amenities would have included one bar and five galleys, or three bars and three galleys. Toilets numbered five for the standard layout (of which four at the rear of the cabin) or six for the high-density layout. Generous stowage facilities of up to four wardrobes were also to be provided, depending again on cabin layout.

Market Research and Internal 'Launch'

As soon as the details of the Three-Eleven were first made public in the summer of 1968, BAC launched a substantial marketing campaign, firstly to get confirmation from the world's airlines that the projected aircraft responded to their needs, and secondly to incorporate into the design key suggestions and required modifications. The campaign used a combination of detailed market surveys carried out by BAC's market research department, the results of specific questionnaires handed in to the airlines, and direct interviews with the carriers' fleet planning and operational management. In October 1968 three carefully selected sales teams from BAC's Weybridge Division, each led by a director, embarked upon a series of presentations to airlines throughout the world. Over the next six months BAC sales teams visited over forty airlines worldwide. The airlines visited included all the major European flag carriers, the US 'majors' (United, American Airlines, Eastern, Continental, Delta), US regional carriers, and the key Asian and Australasian airlines (Japan Airlines, All Nippon, Indian Airlines, Thai International, Pakistan International, MSA, Philippine Airlines, Ansett and TAA).

BAC originally estimated the total market for Three-Eleven Class wide-body twins to comprise 800 deliveries by 1985, and that competition to the Three-Eleven would come from the Airbus A300B and eventually from a newly launched American twin.[3] In the early months of 1970 the total market over the period to 1985 was revised upwards to 1,150. In each case BAC forecast that the Three-Eleven would capture at least a 22 per cent share of this market (the same market share that the One-Eleven had at the time), resulting in 240 to 280 Three-Eleven aircraft delivered by 1985. Company break-even for the project was put at 200 units. We now know, with the benefit of hindsight, that BAC was quite conservative in estimating the size of the 200/300-seat twinjet market. As it turned out, over 2,800 airliners of this class have been sold since the Airbus A300B's first flight in 1972.[4]

On the assumption of a favourable reaction from the airlines to the baseline aircraft, BAC was hoping to give a formal internal 'go-ahead' to the project in April 1969 with a first flight slotted for September 1972 and certification to be achieved by late 1973. Six aircraft were to be used in the certification process and deliveries of the first forty aircraft would take place throughout 1974. In this programme timetable BAC factored in the feedback on product improvements and design changes to the aircraft that the airlines suggested. As we shall see, the schedule was to slip by several months as lengthy negotiations on project financing arrangements with the Government, BAC shareholders and the City, together with the British Government's indecision on launching aid, took longer than BAC had at first envisaged.

At the time of making the first public announcement of the new airliner programme, BAC's Commercial Aircraft Division declared that the Three-Eleven would not be launched into production unless the company could secure at least fifty preliminary launch orders from three or four major airlines. This pre-condition to launch stemmed from BAC's painful awareness of the commercial failure of the Vickers Vanguard turboprop and the VC-10 long-range jetliner, which had been launched into production without the number and spread of orders likely to assure a profitable programme. The corporation was determined to make the Three-Eleven a fully commercial proposition, responsive to worldwide market needs and unhindered by politically driven compromises and national flag carriers' diktats such as those that had strangled the market prospects of the Vickers VC-10 and de Havilland Trident.

BAC also stated that higher-capacity and longer-range versions of the Three-Eleven would be made available within a couple of years of the aircraft's introduction into service. In addition BAC studied a lighter 200-seat version at the behest of Eastern Airlines of the US.

If the target launch orders were achieved, then BAC would approach Her Majesty's Government with a request for launch aid.

Preliminary Order Book and Positive Response from the Airlines

In the wake of the worldwide tour by BAC's marketing teams, BAC at Weybridge built a fully furnished cabin mock-up, as well as a cockpit mock-up, which were visited over the next several months by key representatives of most of the world's major airlines. The operational management of almost all these airlines left Weybridge suitably impressed by the Three-Eleven's potential to provide cost-effective economics of operation and strong passenger appeal.

The Three-Eleven's provisional order book built up gradually, and BAC was in a position in February 1969 to announce that it had collected twenty-nine conditional orders for the aircraft from six airlines.[5] Shortly before this announcement, Sir Freddie Laker's Laker Airways said that it had signed a letter of intent for four Three-Elevens. At the Farnborough Airshow in September 1970, BEA announced an order, subject to project launch, for twenty aircraft. At that point BAC held conditional orders and commitments for forty-three aircraft from eight airlines, including BEA. The order book is summarised below:

Table 3.3 BAC Three-Eleven preliminary order book

Airline	Number of aircraft
BEA (UK)	20
Laker Airways (UK)	4
Britannia Airways (UK)	4
Tarom (Romania)	3
Paninternational (Germany)	3
Bavaria Flug (Germany)	3
Court Line (UK)	3
Austral (Argentina)	3
Total	43

(Source: BAC – The Market Assessment Programme and Results, June 1970)

Although this total fell seven units short of BAC's self-imposed goal of fifty firm commitments before launch, the importance of BEA's strong commitment and the geographical spread of the orders compared very favourably with the Airbus A300B's total of six firm plus ten options, resulting from an MoU signed by Air France at the same Farnborough Air Show.

It was estimated that future Three-Eleven requirements from the eight airlines that had signed the forty-three preliminary orders would total close to 100 aircraft by the mid-1980s, with BEA's requirements alone projected to reach as many as fifty aircraft by 1985. In addition, American Airlines (already a BAC One-Eleven operator) and Eastern Airlines in the US expressed considerable interest in the aircraft, to the point that BAC was making firm proposals of a lower capacity 200-seat version of the Three-Eleven to Eastern. As it is well known, Eastern would eventually launch the A300B Airbus in the USA in 1977, opening the floodgates of market success and widespread acceptance of the Airbus family worldwide, but that is another story. Closer to home both BUA and Caledonian Airways (soon to merge to form British Caledonian Airways) expressed strong interest in the British wide-body aircraft, with an initial potential requirement for ten. In June 1970 BAC also published a list of Three-Eleven early sales prospects (airlines with which BAC had a high chance of sales success). This is set out in Table 3.4 below:

Table 3.4 BAC Three-Eleven early sales prospects

Airline	Number of aircraft
Eastern Airlines (USA)	70
American Airlines (USA)	50
Mohawk (USA)	16
JAT Yugoslavian Airlines (Yugoslavia)	10
Aer Lingus (Ireland)	8
SABENA Belgian World Airlines	10
South African Airways	10
LOT Polish Airlines	5
Total	179

(Source: BAC – The Market Assessment Programme and Results, June 1970)

At this stage all boded well for the future of this new British aircraft, which had to its credit:

Substantial market interest, underpinned by a forty-three-aircraft order book from eight airlines and sales potential for an additional 180 aircraft to other airlines.

The strong support of BEA, Europe's largest short-haul airline.

The backup of BAC's exhaustive market research and its considerable experience in producing successful short-to-medium-haul airliners.[6]

In the wake of the positive market reaction to the Three-Eleven programme and of the establishment of a preliminary order book for the aircraft, BAC approached HMG with a request for launch aid.

Project Financing and Industrial Arrangements

BAC estimated total Three-Eleven development costs at some £150 million, plus £25–£30 million to finance a new production line for the aircraft. Engine development costs for the Rolls-Royce RB211-61 turbofan engine were put at £60 million. BAC expected the UK Government to provide about half of the non-recurring costs through the 'Launch Aid' scheme, with the company bearing all cost overruns. This in practice translated into a proposal that the UK Government would provide around £75 million in financing to BAC, together with a £25–£30 million loan guarantee to set up the production line and fund prototype development.

Meanwhile, with overwhelmingly positive feedback from seventy-two airlines worldwide, BAC had refined the Three-Eleven proposal, and this refinement had resulted in a larger aircraft with a higher payload and increased range, as we have seen earlier. After having kept the Government informed of progress on the Three-Eleven project at the marketing and industrial levels, on 25 November 1969 BAC's chairman Sir Reginald Verdon-Smith wrote to the Minister of Technology, Tony Benn, with a firm proposal for joint financing of the development of the aircraft. The letter stated that the BAC board had given the project a preliminary go-ahead, subject to Government financial support.[7] The proposal was that the Government would take a 50 per cent share in financing the project, with recovery of its monies through a levy (royalty) of 6.25 per cent on each aircraft sold, plus a similar royalty on spares.

We shall recall at this point of the story that the British Government had pulled out of the European Airbus project in April of 1969. At the time of the withdrawal from the Airbus Tony Benn said: 'in this new situation [i.e. the fact that the original RB207-powered A300 Airbus had been dropped in favour of the smaller American-powered A300B] we shall judge these or any other proposals on their merits against the stringent economic criteria which we apply when government launching aid is sought, including the assurance of a firm market, and against the need to control the aggregate level of public expenditure'.[8] There was an implicit understanding in BAC and the industry at large that the reference to 'any other proposals' in Benn's statement was a tacit acknowledgement of the Government's

willingness to consider financing the Three-Eleven. Indeed, from private soundings of the minister himself and of officials from MinTech, it was clear to BAC
that the Three-Eleven proposal was well received and that Benn himself was sympathetic to seeing the project go ahead.[9] This apparent reversal of the Plowden
doctrine[10] on the part of the Wilson Government was understandable, as the
recent experience of Anglo-European and particularly Anglo-French cooperation had not delivered the benefits first envisaged. In fact in 1967 the French had
unilaterally pulled out of the AFVG fighter (Anglo-French Variable Geometry
aircraft, which BAC would have led) on cost grounds, and ever-rising Concorde
development costs were proving to be a bottomless pit for the Treasury.

MinTech responded to BAC's proposals with the counter-proposal that it
would be prepared to increase its launch aid contribution to 60 per cent of total
development costs if BAC were to increase its share capital from £30 million to
£50 million and if the company were responsible for financing of the production
line. This, in the ministry's view, would demonstrate the commitment of BAC
(and the private sector) to the project, and would therefore underpin the market's
support for the Three-Eleven as a commercially viable project.

The Financing Package

Eventually discussions between BAC and the Government centred around a
complex financing package for the Three-Eleven project, whose main elements
are summarised below:

HM Government would provide £84 million of launch aid, equivalent to 60 per
cent of the project's non-recurring costs. The money would be interest-free, and
the Government would recover it through royalties on the sales of the aircraft and
related spares.

In order to fund its £56 million share of the development costs plus £20 million
for setting up the production line, BAC would: increase its share capital from
£30 million to £50 million through a rights issue of £8 million to be subscribed
by its two shareholders GEC and Vickers, and the underwriting of Convertible
Subordinated Unsecured Loan Stock (CSULS) of £12 million with maturity in
1986–90 to be raised in the City, in all probability before the spring of 1971; sign
'work and risk sharing' deals with airframe subcontractors and systems contractors
worth another £20 million; finance the remainder through internally generated
annual operating cash flow of £5 million.

Finally BAC would be responsible for any cost overruns on the programme.

The break-even point for BAC was set at 200 aircraft sold whereas HMG calculated that it would recover its monies on 240 deliveries plus spares. BAC instructed

merchant bankers Lazard Bros & Co. to find City underwriters for a major proportion of the £12 million CSULS (about £4 million of which was to be underwritten
by BAC's shareholders). Initial reactions and interest from City investors were positive, and Lazards wrote to BAC on 29 September 1970 confirming that it had
received institutional commitment in the City indicating full subscription of the
loan. This proved that the Three-Eleven project was perceived to be a commercially
viable proposition by the notoriously risk-averse investor community.

Industrial workshare

It was understood from the start that BAC would be looking for risk-sharing
partners to help finance the development and production of the Three-Eleven.
These partners would include both subcontractors on the airframe and systems
contractors. The risk-sharing scheme entailed that these companies would finance
their tooling and any research and development spend from their own resources
for the relevant airframe assembly or piece of equipment for which they would
bid. In return they would be assured long-term contracts over the life of the programme, thus giving them an effective monopoly over that particular assembly
or component(s). The subcontractors would then amortise their non-recurring
costs over 200 production aircraft sets: should sales of the aircraft not reach 200,
the subcontractors would absorb any unrecovered costs. As we know, this system
has become commonplace in today's internationalised aerospace industry and is
widely used on the Airbus programmes, but at the time of the Three-Eleven discussions the risk-and-reward-sharing scheme was relatively novel.

However, BAC made it clear from the start that project leadership and overall
programme management would rest firmly in BAC's hands, thus ensuring that
the UK industry would retain full control of large aircraft development and production. This approach contrasted with the Airbus A300B arrangements, where
Sud Aviation of France had been given programme leadership. The British Airbus
partner HSA was given the important role of developing the aircraft's wings and
also acted in a consultancy capacity on the overall definition of the aircraft, but
did not have the last say on systems selection and systems integration. Eventually
Airbus embraced a more collegial decision-making scheme that somewhat
reduced Aérospatiale's role of project leader but, notwithstanding this, the UK did
not recover its leading role in Europe on large civil airliner development.

BAC at once approached several companies in the UK, Europe, Japan and
the US with a view to finalising contracts for major airframe sub-assemblies.
Advanced talks were held with a number of potential partners such as Fokker in
the Netherlands, Aeritalia in Italy and Boeing in the US and preliminary agreements were signed with Shorts and Scottish Aviation in the UK. Work packages
in return for launch orders were also discussed with the aerospace industries of
Yugoslavia, Romania and Poland. In fact in November 1970 BAC and Preduzece
Soko Mostar of Yugoslavia signed a MoU for the detailed design and production

of the Three-Eleven's fin, rudder and tailplane, to BAC's overall design specifications, a package valued at £25 million over the life of the programme.

This approach to international risk-sharing indicated BAC's willingness to make
the Three-Eleven an international project along the lines then favoured by the
British Government, although the aircraft was to remain a BAC product, unlike
the A300B which was sold by the multinational (initially Franco-German) Airbus
Industrie consortium. In those days the latter was an untested entity, whereas
BAC had a very good track record and strong reputation in the market for short-
to-medium-range aircraft addressed by the Three-Eleven. BAC's reputation was
strong both in terms of product quality and of product support and was based on
almost twenty years of sales and support of the Vickers Viscount, Vickers Vanguard
and later the BAC One-Eleven, for airline customers worldwide.

Table 3.5 sets out the preliminary deals in respect of work-share packages
between BAC and risk-sharing partners at the end of April 1970.

Table 3.5 Outline work-share on BAC Three-Eleven with risk-sharing partners

Package	Dev. Cost (£ million)	Probable supplier	Alternative
Nose fuselage	3.8	Scottish Aviation	
Forward fuselage	5.3	Short Bros & Harland	Poland (sub-assemblies only)
Six cabin doors	0.7	Fairey (Belgium)	Poland
Two freight doors	0.7	Fairey (Belgium)	Poland; Valmet (Finland)
Nose & main gear doors	0.35	Romania	Poland
Centre fuselage top panel	0.15	Romania	
Wing rib assemblies	0.8	Romania	Westland Helicopters
Machined wing ribs	0.8	DIAC Engineering Ltd	Kawasaki Heavy Industries
Wing leading edge & slats	3.1	Vickers Ltd	Canadair
Flaps	1.4	Canadair	Poland
Flap beams & fairings	1.4	Canadair	
Wing trailing edge, spoilers and lift dumpers	1.3	Romania	
Wing tips	0.05	Romania	Valmet, Finland
Ailerons	0.15	Romania	Poland; Kawasaki Heavy Ind.
Empennage	4.55	Soko Mostar, Yugoslavia	
Nacelle pods	2.45	Short Bros	

Centre fuselage subassemblies	0.82	E. Hillier & Son Ltd E. Henshall & Sons Universal Equipment Ltd	
Centre and rear fuselage large machined items	0.65	Morfax Ltd DIAC Engineering Ltd	
Cabin floors & misc. furnishing	0.2	William Mallinson	Palmer Aero Products
Wing spar assemblies	1.3	Kawasaki Heavy Ind.	
Engine stubs	1.6	Fairey, SA (Belgium)	Swiss Federal Factory Kawasaki Heavy Ind.
Main landing gear and hydraulic components	0.75	Dowty Rotol	Menasco (USA) Lockheed Precision Products
Large machined items in centre and rear fuselage	0.5	Cramic Industries	
Freight Handling System	0.12	Aviation Traders Ltd	
Pressure system ducting	1.5	C.F. Taylor	
Total	34.6		

(Source: HMG, Ministry of Aviation Supply file, 9 July 1970)

In terms of distribution of the work within BAC's own commercial aircraft plants, Weybridge was the overall design centre and would have been responsible for the production of major sub-assemblies. This latter function was to be shared with Filton, Bristol. However, final assembly of the Three-Eleven would have taken place on a new production line to be set up at the company's Bournemouth (Hurn) facilities, where the Viscount, and later the One-Eleven, assembly line was located. Flight-testing would have taken place at Fairford in Gloucestershire, where the Concorde flight-test team was based. The reason for choosing Hurn for final assembly and Fairford for flight-testing was that these sites provided much greater scope for expansion than space-constricted Weybridge, had longer runways and a larger amount of airspace around them for flight-testing (Weybridge being very close to Heathrow's international airport).

It was estimated that Three-Eleven employment at BAC would grow to 2,500 by 1971, with a peak of 9,000 by the mid-1970s. The number of design staff on the project would grow from 500 in 1970 to a peak of 1,000 prior to entry into service and the programme would employ 250 design engineers for many years thereafter. Overall UK employment on the aircraft programme was expected to exceed 60,000, including work at Rolls-Royce, Shorts and Scottish Aviation and at nearly 800 other airframe and equipment suppliers.

Table 3.6 BAC Three-Eleven forecast direct employment in the UK (peak years)

Company/Industry	Numbers employed
BAC – Weybridge	6,360
BAC – Hurn	4,720
UK Airframe subcontractors	
Shorts – Belfast	2,270
Scottish Aviation – Prestwick	940
Dowty Rotol – Cheltenham	550
Others – mainly South East England	9,560
Subtotal	24,400
Others – Aero Engine Industry	9,500
Miscellaneous Metal Goods Industry	3,130
Radio and Telecommunications Industry	2,900
Electrical Industry	2,400
Other Mechanical (i.e. Hydraulic) Engineering	2,150
Iron & Steel Trades	2,000
Light Metals Industry	1,800
Other Supply Industries, Trades, etc.	17,610
Grand total	65,890

(Source: British Aircraft Corporation, 'The case for the BAC 3-11', taken from the econometric study carried out by Economic Models Ltd)

Following on from the very positive reaction of the airlines to the Three-Eleven concept and from the discussions of financing arrangements related above, in February 1970 the BAC board decided in principle to launch the Three-Eleven project internally and authorised continuous private funding of engineering development and marketing costs. Full launch of the project was subject to government approval of its share of the development costs, but the company was confident that such approval would be forthcoming.

Political Lobbying and Government Indecision

From the time of its approach to the British Government with a request for launch aid on 25 November 1969, BAC mounted a strong campaign to sway the Government's decision in favour of the Three-Eleven. In this campaign the company was supported by BEA's energetic commitment to the aircraft, and by the specialist press, with renowned weekly aerospace magazine *Flight International* being particularly vocal in its support for the Three-Eleven.

Countering this effort in favour of the Three-Eleven was Hawker Siddeley, which was still a member of the Airbus consortium, although on a private subcontractor basis after the British Government had withdrawn its financial support in April 1969. HSA was supported in its lobbying efforts by the French and German Governments and by the Foreign Office, which was trying to promote Britain's entry into the EEC. Basically the arguments of the HSA management and its Continental partners revolved around the absurdity of Britain launching a go-it-alone competitor to the A300B European Airbus, with the potential result of spoiling the market for both aircraft and of repeating the past mistakes of intra-European competition, with the predictable outcome that the Americans would win again. Hawker Siddeley also cast doubts over BAC's estimates of Three-Eleven development costs, and suggested a much higher figure than the £150 million estimated by BAC. The lobbying by the French and German Governments and by HSA was also a clear indication that the Airbus consortium regarded the Three-Eleven proposal as a serious threat to their aim of establishing Airbus.

BAC's main arguments in support of its Three-Eleven project were that:[11]

a) The company was Europe's most experienced developer of civil airliners, and the only one to have succeeded with two successive generations of short-haul aircraft (Viscount and BAC One-Eleven) in exporting substantial numbers of airliners to the US, the world's most important and most sophisticated market.[12]

b) BAC was the only non-US airliner manufacturer to be regarded technically and commercially able to stand side-by-side with Boeing and Douglas as suppliers of new equipment. This was a national asset.

c) In the period 1950–70 BAC civil aircraft had contributed an overall benefit of £800 million to the UK balance of payments. This contribution was set against a total HMG investment of £25 million, the latter still being reduced by continuing royalty payments on One-Eleven sales.

d) The peak HMG annual investment in the Three-Eleven project would be only £23 million, and this would be later offset by a peak annual tax yield of £28 million.

e) BAC was a recognised 'brand name' in the civil aircraft market, whereas the Pan-European Airbus consortium was not, and airlines were reluctant to buy from an untested manufacturer.

f) The Three-Eleven business case was backed by the most extensive market survey and analysis ever undertaken by BAC. Indeed the Three-Eleven was the most thoroughly researched UK commercial aircraft project. In addition the aircraft specifications were driven purely by market requirements, and airline reaction had been positive enough to warrant forty-three firm commitments *even before* project launch.

g) BAC was prepared to assume all project cost overruns – the Government's commitment being capped at £84 million. In addition a significant share of the development costs was to be funded by risk-sharing partners.

h) The project had full City backing, in terms of City investors being prepared to underwrite all of the £12 million CSULS.

i) BAC had a number of industrial partners in Europe and elsewhere who were willing to invest their own money in the Three-Eleven after having independently assessed the commercial rationale of the investment.

j) Significantly and importantly, the Three-Eleven would ensure that Britain retained project leadership and programme management, which had instead been traded away to France in the A300B deal. This would guarantee and sustain substantial high technology, quality work for the UK's equipment and engine suppliers for many years to come, with related revenue and employment benefits.

BAC concluded its business case for the project by stating that without the Three-Eleven the country's leading technological industry would have no new British airliner or even British-design-led airliner under development and that it was a fallacy to assume that the industry could opt out from a generation of aircraft development and then stage a revival from weak and depleted resources.

That the British Government was now prepared to seriously consider an all-British large airliner project showed how much had changed in Government thinking since it had enthusiastically embraced the Plowden dictum of European cooperation in the mid-1960s. The reasons for this mood change were several, and included: the French *volte-face* on development of the AFVG fighter aircraft when it emerged that it did not suit them in strategic terms; the costs of the Concorde, which were growing at an alarming rate; the French revision of the Anglo-French helicopter package which tilted the procurement in favour of the Aérospatiale helicopters and to the detriment of the Westland Lynx; and last but not least, the decision to drop Rolls-Royce as the exclusive Airbus A300 powerplant supplier in favour of American engines for the smaller A300B. The latter decision was indeed in breach of the original 1967 MoU between the British,

French and German Governments, and put the British Government in the awkward position of being asked to support the aircraft when its main conditions for participation (Rolls-Royce engines as sole powerplant, seventy-five orders from the three sponsoring airlines) had not been met.

Government thinking had also changed in the wake of the publication in 1969 of the St John Elstub report on the British aircraft industry.[13] In his report St John Elstub cast considerable doubt on the effectiveness of international collaboration. The requirements of *le juste retour* principle (whereby work-shares directly related to the national contributions to costs) were wrought with potential inefficiencies, prolonged negotiations could lead to delay, and the need in collaborative programmes to compromise on specifications introduced further sources of intrinsic inefficiency. St John Elstub also pointed to another disadvantage inherent in European or international cooperation, namely the transfer of British technology, *for little or no consideration*, creating for British firms 'competitors of tomorrow when they have fortified themselves technically through contact with the most experienced aircraft industry in Europe'. The Elstub report's conclusion was that collaboration could only work effectively 'if the initiative in seeking opportunities and negotiating partnerships is taken by industry'.

Serious questioning of the advantages to the British aerospace industry of collaboration with France and Europe had already emerged in 1968, when a senior UK industry executive was reported as saying that: 'France has, in three years of collaboration, gained ten years of technology free of charge from British airframe, engine, equipment and research establishments, paid for by the British taxpayer.'[14] An editorial published by *Flight International* on 13 November 1969 reiterated the perceived imbalance of collaborative ventures with France as far as the UK was concerned, by stating: 'nobody blames France for being ruthless in the interests of France. The real gremlins of collaboration are those who appease this ruthlessness at the expense of the British aircraft industry.'

Some may regard these lamentations as the bleating of an industry that had been outfoxed by the nimble negotiating skills of a combined French industry and Government 'front' in each single one of its collaborative ventures with British industry. It is therefore easy to merely read in these statements the British industry's envy and frustration at French success at twisting collaborative projects to France's advantage. However, it is an inescapable fact that British Governments *did* sacrifice the airframe side of the industry in cooperative ventures, as an expedient to achieve larger political goals (Common Market membership *in primis*) and that in general they put the interests of Rolls-Royce above those of either BAC or HSA. We shall analyse these issues further in our final chapter.

As said before, *Flight International* magazine was a vocal supporter of the BAC Three-Eleven throughout the period during which the project was being evaluated for launch aid financing by the British Government.[15] In its editorials the prestigious magazine argued that: the British aircraft industry was too priceless a national asset to be traded away for membership of the Common Market; it was imperative for Britain to retain its hard-earned position as the world's most successful airliner producer outside the USA (and thus to retain design leadership on a major airliner); already the country had given away technology to France for nothing in return; subcontracting to Europe might have been advantageous for a particular company (i.e. Hawker Siddeley) but was not in the best interests of the British aircraft industry as a whole, including its engine and its equipment suppliers.

The influential American journal, *Aviation Week & Space Technology*, also joined the debate in favour of the Three-Eleven, with a prescient editorial published during the 1970 Farnborough Airshow.[16] It is worth reporting here a large extract from that article:

> The key decision [on the airbus programs] rests not with the airline customers but with the British government in one of the most momentous techno-political decisions the industry has ever faced. From the Exchequer's point of view support of the HSA portion of the Airbus consortium would cost the government less.
>
> But without the BAC 3-11 the British Industry faces the future without a single completely British aerospace program – a prospect that will certainly make it difficult, if not impossible, to maintain the unique European asset of its fully integrated industry. If the British Industry faces the future only as a bidder for bits and pieces of joint European programs it cannot avoid degrading its present technical capabilities.
>
> The big decision now facing the British aerospace Industry and the new Conservative government is whether Britain will continue to develop its very tangible assets in aerospace from a position of technical strength and leadership or whether it will settle for lesser roles in future partnerships and thus abandon its hopes and capabilities for developing complete aerospace systems within the framework of its own specific resources and requirements.

With the benefit of hindsight, we can now see how spot-on this analysis was, at least as far as the status of the civil airframe side of the industry is concerned. As we shall see in Chapter 4, never again was Britain to regain design leadership on a major civil aircraft project.

A strong advocate of the aircraft (and a vocal one at that) during the Three-Eleven debate was BEA in the person of its chairman Sir Anthony Milward. BEA had consistently expressed its preference for the Three-Eleven since the programme's inception,[17] stating at the same time that it was not interested in the Airbus A300B. In September 1970, at the Farnborough Air Show, BEA announced a preliminary order for twenty Three-Elevens. In August Sir Anthony, writing in *BEA Magazine*, had said that the airline's most vital task was to get the go-ahead for the BAC Three-Eleven. This, he added, was 'certainly the major and the most urgent decision for our new government [Edward Heath's Conservatives having won the June 1970 election] to make as it affects our competitive capability from 1975 onwards and will also virtually decide whether Britain is still to remain a producer of civil aircraft, engines and components, or whether we buy abroad in the future'.

For his part, BAC's chairman Sir George Edwards went public in supporting the Three-Eleven. In a letter published in *The Times* in August 1970 Sir George wrote that: 'because the arguments in favour of collaboration with Europe are undeniable, we have so far been prepared to accept the role of junior partner. It is not right for this country, and not right long-term for Europe for Britain to accept this junior position permanently. Britain cannot retain its technological strength if she continues to accept a subordinate role.' On the aspect of the commercial viability of the Three-Eleven Sir George added that the fullest market survey ever undertaken by BAC showed that the company could expect to make the venture profitable and to contribute £1,550 million to the balance of payments. Sir George Edwards' letter to *The Times* was reiterating the views he had expressed in the 1970 Lubbock Lecture, where he argued convincingly for a more equitable distribution (as far as Britain was concerned) of the benefits of collaboration.[18]

We have already commented earlier that the Minister of Technology himself, Tony Benn, was sympathetic to the Three-Eleven and to BAC's business case. More generally, the civil servants at MinTech and the Board of Trade supported BAC's commercial assessment of the Three-Eleven's prospects. Although they expressed some concern at the effects of intra-European competition, they believed that the BAC Three-Eleven was a sounder proposition than the Airbus A300B.[19] Earlier, at the time of the BAC application for launch aid, a Government spokesman gave it a cautious welcome, saying that the application would be studied 'very carefully'. Subsequent discussions were described as a 'very good example' of industry-Government cooperation.[20] In the wake of Britain's withdrawal from the A300B European Airbus, Tony Benn and his ministerial officials tried to involve France and Germany in considering the BAC Three-Eleven as the basis of an alternative 'European Airbus' development to the A300B but both countries rejected this proposal. Germany and France in particular saw no reason why they should participate as junior partners in a BAC (British)-led project, when they had design leadership on the Airbus.

The intense political lobbying by both BAC for the Three-Eleven and HSA and its Airbus partners for the A300B eventually became a 'dour struggle' as one BAC supporter put it, and turned into 'competition for the esteem of the British government' as an HSA executive elegantly described it.

Despite the promising overtures in favour of the project, Harold Wilson's Labour Government was in no hurry to provide launch aid for the Three-Eleven, in the light also of the French and German refusal to share in its development. The project required a large financial commitment from the Government, and there was no intention of granting aid before a 'strict economic analysis' of the project's costs and benefits could be undertaken. We shall extensively review the Government's evaluation of the project further on in this chapter.

Also, as we observed earlier, the Government was not entirely insensitive to the likely reaction of the French and Germans to an immediate decision to support the Three-Eleven. Despite de Gaulle's rejection of British membership of the Common Market in 1963 and 1967, technological cooperation had a wider political value. Consequently the Government did not wish to needlessly antagonise the French and the Germans, who could still be partners in other ventures.[21] Therefore it is no surprise to find an entry in Tony Benn's diary dated 18 May 1970 to the effect that a final decision on the BAC Three-Eleven would be postponed until after the General Election.[22]

The June 1970 General Election and Airbus's Renewed Lobbying Efforts

To the surprise of many political observers and even the party itself, Labour lost the June 1970 General Election to Edward Heath's Conservatives. The change of Government created a predictable loss of momentum as far as a speedy Government decision on providing launch aid for the Three-Eleven was concerned.

During 1970 BAC continued to finance engineering and marketing development costs on the Three-Eleven from its own resources, spending over £3 million of its money on the project by the late summer of 1970. In addition to the cabin and cockpit mock-ups, BAC was completing the engineering mock up of the aircraft. A 9.75m (32ft) front fuselage section of the Three-Eleven was also being assembled in jigs at Weybridge, and engineering drawings were ready to be issued to the shop floor. BAC also started metal cutting on a small scale, on the expectation that a Government go-ahead would come soon. First flight was now scheduled for the summer of 1973 and entry into service with BEA for early 1975. Unfortunately the change of Government put a spanner in the works of BAC's schedule. A whole new set of ministers and civil servants now had to be briefed almost from scratch on the project. BAC made representations to the new Government at the highest level, stressing the urgency of a positive decision if the project was to reach its target market on time. BAC also made it clear to the Government that it had already spent a sizeable amount of shareholder money on the project and was not prepared to finance the Three-Eleven for much longer without Government support. BAC's key shareholder GEC and its chairman Lord Weinstock were particularly keen to limit BAC's exposure to the civil sector and were not prepared to wait for too long.

The new Government, through its Minister of Technology (first Geoffrey Rippon, then John Davies) and Minister of Aviation Supply (Frederick Corfield) promised that it would give the Three-Eleven application its urgent attention.

An additional complication that was to muddy the waters further for the new Government was a renewed proposal from the Airbus consortium, the Governments backing it, and Hawker Siddeley, for the British Government to abandon the BAC Three-Eleven and to rejoin the European Airbus A300B instead. Ironically, the appearance of the BAC Three-Eleven in the summer of 1968 had had a major bearing on Airbus thinking, convincing the consortium to abandon the original, larger, A300 and to develop the smaller, 250-seat, A300B instead. In all truth the main Airbus backers, France and Germany, regarded the BAC Three-Eleven as a very serious challenge to the market prospects for the A300B and looked upon the possibility that the British Government may actually back a wholly indigenous 'airbus-class' aircraft with real fear.

The new Airbus proposals, backed by the French, German and Dutch Governments, and tabled by Hawker Siddeley on the consortium's behalf, superficially had several attractions for the British Government:

Hawker Siddeley would rejoin Airbus as a full partner with a share of between 27 per cent and 30 per cent of the airframe, the same as France and Germany.[23]

A new larger version of the A300B, the B7, would be developed to suit BEA's needs. This version of the aircraft would be powered by Rolls-Royce RB211-61 engines (the same model as the one earmarked for the Three-Eleven). In addition Hawker Siddeley would have design liaison leadership on the A300B7, thus dispelling BEA's concerns about operating an aircraft produced by a consortium. The Airbus A300B7 would be over 50 per cent British by value and content.

Total Government investment in the B7 airframe could amount to as little as £18 million or a maximum of £30 million, as compared to £144 million (airframe and engine) in the case of the all-British Three-Eleven.

The German Government might be prepared to finance up to £20 million of the projected £60 million costs of developing the '61' version of the RB211 engine.

In more general political terms, Britain's re-entry into the Airbus consortium would no doubt enhance its prospects of gaining admission to the Common Market. Admission to the EEC was one of the Heath Government's electoral pledges and anything that might help the achievement of that objective would be welcome.

Despite the obvious financial attractiveness of the proposals from Hawker Siddeley and its Airbus partners, the Conservative Government did not wish to make a rushed decision. As it happened, many Conservative backbenchers were strongly in favour of backing the Three-Eleven. In fact over 100 Conservative MPs openly lobbied for the Government to back the Three-Eleven project.[24]

When Aviation Minister Frederick Corfield returned from a meeting with his German, French and Dutch counterparts to discuss the Airbus proposals, he stated that these needed to be investigated further, adding that the Government was not going to 'drop the Three-Eleven just like that'.[25]

Meanwhile BAC, conscious that the total cost to the Government of developing the Three-Eleven airframe and associated RB211-61 engine would now amount to £144 million (£84 million for the airframe and £60 million for the engine), proposed that a more economical solution would be to launch the Three-Eleven initially with American GE CF6-50 turbofans (the engine selected for the Airbus A300B). BAC could then subsequently provide an RB211-61-engined version when that engine found other applications. For its part, BEA stated that they would be happy to take the Three-Eleven with CF6-50 engines, which actually gave the aircraft slightly better performance than with the RB211-61s.[26]

Table 3.7 Comparison of BAC Three-Eleven and Airbus A300B key details (December 1970)

Parameter	BAC Three-Eleven	Airbus A300B
Length	55.95m	51.60m (B1) 53.75m (B2/B4)
Wing span	44.80m	44.84m
Wing sweep	25° at ¼ chord	28° at ¼ chord
Wing area	251m²	260m²
Height	13.20m	16.60m
Fuselage width	6.02m	5.64m
Cabin width	5.77m	5.28m
Max. TO weight	137,500kg	132,000kg
Zero fuel weight	111,550kg	109,000kg
Max. payload	31,700kg	28,000kg
Max. cruise speed	905km/h	935km/h
Range with max payload	2,510km	2,200km
Max. range (payload restricted)	5,210km	5,300km
Powerplant	2 x Rolls-Royce RB211-61 turbofans each rated at 22,680kg thrust	2 x General Electric CF6-50A turbofans each rated at 22,270kg thrust

(Source: *Flight International* Commercial Aircraft Survey, 19 November 1970)

1. BAC Three-Eleven cockpit mock-up. (© BAE SYSTEMS via Brooklands Museum)

2. BAC Three-Eleven cabin mock-up. (© BAE SYSTEMS via Brooklands Museum)

3. BAC Three-Eleven engineering mock-up under construction at Weybridge. (© BAE SYSTEMS via Brooklands Museum)

5. *Opposite below:* Artist's impression of BAC Three-Eleven flying over a US city. (© BAE SYSTEMS via Brooklands Museum)

4. *Above:* An artist's impression of BAC Three-Eleven in BEA livery. (© BAE SYSTEMS/ Richard Payne Collection)

6. The aircraft in the livery of launch customer BEA. (© BAE SYSTEMS via Brooklands Museum)

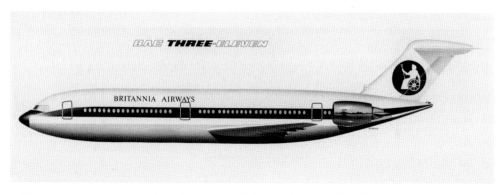

7. The aircraft in the livery of launch customer Britannia Airways. (© BAE SYSTEMS via Brooklands Museum)

8. The aircraft in the livery of launch customer Caledonian Airways. (© BAE SYSTEMS via Brooklands Museum)

9. The aircraft in the livery of launch customer Court Line. (© BAE SYSTEMS via Brooklands Museum)

10. The aircraft in the livery of launch customer Laker Airways. (© BAE SYSTEMS via Brooklands Museum)

11. The aircraft in the livery of launch customer Bavaria. (© BAE SYSTEMS via Brooklands Museum)

12. The aircraft in the livery of launch customer Paninternational. (© BAE SYSTEMS via Brooklands Museum)

13. The aircraft in the livery of launch customer Tarom. (© BAE SYSTEMS via Brooklands Museum)

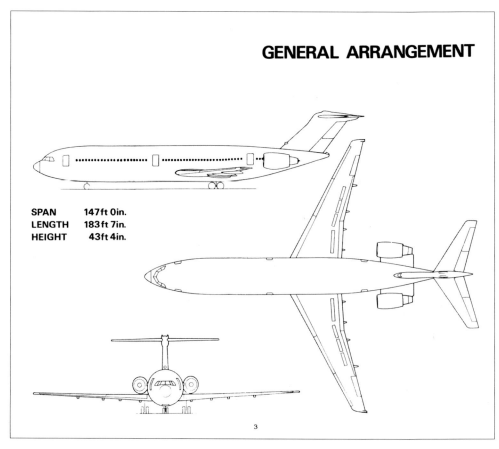

GENERAL ARRANGEMENT

SPAN   147ft 0in.
LENGTH   183ft 7in.
HEIGHT   43ft 4in.

3

14. BAC Three-Eleven general layout. (© BAE SYSTEMS)

15. *Opposite above:* BAC Three-Eleven seating layouts for three specific markets. (© BAE SYSTEMS via Brooklands Museum)

16. *Opposite below:* Three-Eleven cabin dimensions six-abreast. (© BAE SYSTEMS)

BAC THREE-ELEVEN

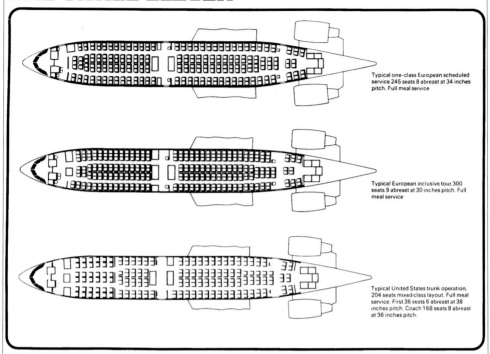

Typical one-class European scheduled service 245 seats 8 abreast at 34 inches pitch. Full meal service

Typical European inclusive tour. 300 seats 9 abreast at 30 inches pitch. Full meal service

Typical United States trunk operation. 204 seats mixed-class layout. Full meal service. First 36 seats 6 abreast at 38 inches pitch. Coach 168 seats 8 abreast at 36 inches pitch.

BRITISH AIRCRAFT CORPORATION
the most powerful aerospace company in Europe

6 ABREAST SEATING

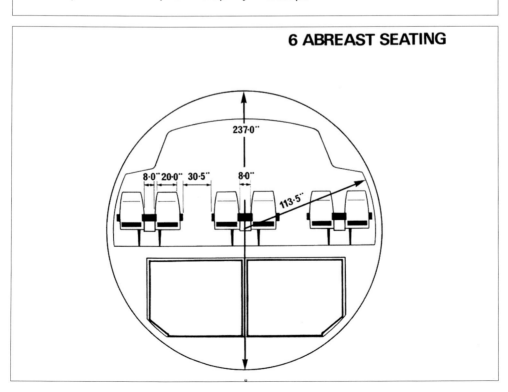

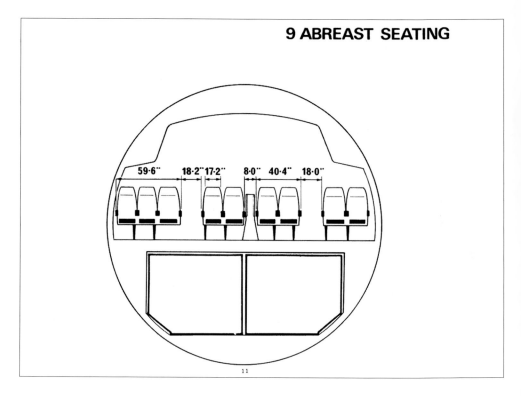

17. Three-Eleven cabin dimensions nine-abreast. (© BAE SYSTEMS)

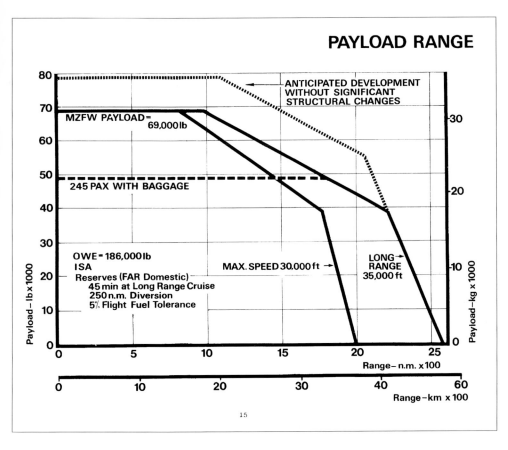

18. Three-Eleven payload range graph. (© BAE SYSTEMS)

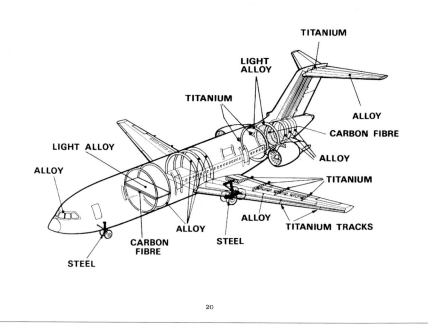

STRUCTURAL MATERIALS

TITANIUM

LIGHT ALLOY

TITANIUM

ALLOY

CARBON FIBRE

ALLOY

LIGHT ALLOY

TITANIUM

ALLOY

ALLOY

TITANIUM

ALLOY

TITANIUM TRACKS

CARBON FIBRE

STEEL

STEEL

19. *Above:* Materials planned for the Three-Eleven's load-bearing structures. (© BAE SYSTEMS)

20. *Left:* Three-Eleven front fuselage frames under construction at Weybridge at the end of 1970. (© BAE SYSTEMS via Derek Wood)

21. BAC Three-Eleven model at 1969 Paris Airshow. (© Royal Aeronautical Society)

22. Three-Eleven engineering mock-up under construction at Weybridge. (© BAE SYSTEMS via Brooklands Museum)

23. *Opposite above:* Artist's impression of BAC Three-Eleven in BEA livery. (© BAE SYSTEMS/ Richard Payne Collection)

24. *Opposite below:* BAC Three-Eleven general layout with Imperial and Metric measures. (© BAE SYSTEMS/Richard Payne Collection)

BAC *THREE-ELEVEN*

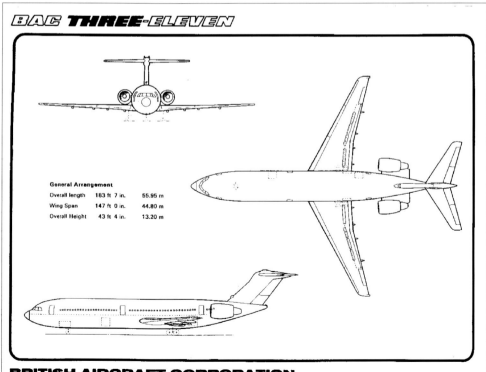

General Arrangement

Overall length	183 ft 7 in.	55.95 m
Wing Span	147 ft 0 in.	44.80 m
Overall Height	43 ft 4 in.	13.20 m

BRITISH AIRCRAFT CORPORATION
the most powerful aerospace company in Europe

25. BAC Three-Eleven over water at dawn. (© BAE SYSTEMS/Richard Payne Collection)

By November 1970 the BAC board was approving the financing of Three-Eleven development on a week-by-week basis and was growing increasingly impatient with the Government's indecision. It was thus that on 13 November 1970 BAC's most senior people, Sir George Edwards and Sir Reginald Verdon-Smith, decided to meet Prime Minister Edward Heath in person at 10 Downing Street, in order to stress to him the importance of going ahead with the BAC Three-Eleven. At that meeting Sir Reginald told the Prime Minister that a decision not to go ahead with the project would be disastrous and that BAC should either continue in the civil aircraft market or stand aside and leave the market to other people. Sir George on the other hand warned Mr Heath that the Weybridge design team that he had built up with the Viking, Viscount, Vanguard, VC-10 and BAC One-Eleven would be lost without the Three-Eleven. Sir George added that the Three-Eleven would give BAC a position of strength in negotiations with European companies. Alas, as we know, all these efforts were to prove fruitless.

As part of its efforts to lobby the Government, BAC also commissioned an independent study of the macroeconomic benefits for Britain of a Three-Eleven launch. The report was made public in late October 1970. It is to this study that we now turn.

Macroeconomic 'Cost-Benefit' Analysis of BAC Three-Eleven Project

On 23 October 1970 an independent study of the macroeconomic impact of a positive Government decision to support the BAC Three-Eleven (vis-à-vis the Airbus A300B and Lockheed TriStar) was made public at BAC's request. The highly detailed econometric study used an input/output model for the entire UK economy, and estimated three key parameters (balance of payments benefit, total employment and tax yield to HMG) in connection with the alternative invest- ment opportunities represented by the BAC Three-Eleven, Airbus A300B and Lockheed L1011 TriStar. A summary of the study's findings, prepared by Douglas C. Hague, director of Economic Models Ltd (a firm of econometric consultants) and professor of Managerial Economics at the Manchester Business School, was published in *Flight International*.[27]

The study started by analysing the returns the Government would make by lend- ing £75 million to BAC for Three-Eleven development. BAC would repay this sum over twelve years but with no interest. At the time Whitehall normally expected Government money to yield 10 per cent, so even if BAC sold the expected 240 to 280 aircraft by 1982, the Government would have foregone £20 million in yields otherwise available from other investments. If, on the other hand, only half the sales forecast were attained, the Government's shortfall would be £40 million.

Professor Hague's study, however, argued that if the Three-Eleven investment had little to recommend it on conventional investment criteria, other advantages of the project far outweighed the short-term disadvantages.

On the assumption of a production rate of thirty-six aircraft per annum, and of all Three-Elevens and half of the Airbus A300Bs having Rolls-Royce powerplants, the study showed that the former would generate 44,000 more jobs, £18 million more tax revenue and £105 million more net exports per annum. Comparing the Three-Eleven and the A300B, with both powered by non-British engines, the Three-Eleven would still provide 36,000 more jobs, £16 million more tax revenue and about £90 million more for the balance of payments than the A300B in a full production year.[28]

The study then compared returns from producing the Three-Eleven with those from buying US-built Lockheed TriStars and concluded that the former would generate 57,000 more jobs and £24 million more tax revenue. Buying the TriStar and dropping out of both Three-Eleven and A300B would allow money to be invested in other spheres but could leave the balance of payments £125 million a year worse off by the late 1970s.

Comparing all three aircraft, and assuming that the Three-Eleven and A300B were alternatives, with the TriStar a necessary import should neither the Three-Eleven nor the A300B receive British Government backing, the study indicated that between 1971 and 1975 the British balance of payments would be £8 million better off with the European Airbus. But, and this was where the Three-Eleven scored heavily, for some eight years after 1975 the annual contribution of the Three-Eleven to the balance of payments would be no less than £90 million, and employment numbers and tax returns would also be much greater.

Table 3.8 Comparative benefits to the British economy

Annual output of aircraft	Employment	Tax yield (£ million)	Balance of payments (£ million)
36 BAC Three-Elevens			
With Rolls-Royce engines	66,000	28	+93
Without Rolls-Royce engines	51,000	22	+63
36 A300Bs			
With Rolls-Royce engines	30,000	12	+1
Without Rolls-Royce engines	22,000	10	-14
Lockheed TriStars			
With Rolls-Royce engines	9,000	4	-34

(Source: D.C. Hague, Economic Models Ltd)

The study concluded that if the TriStar were bought, the £75 million investment saved by dropping the Three-Eleven would have to be used to increase exports in another field, and the social services – schools and hospitals – would not benefit. Having lost a major source of exports with the Three-Eleven, Britain would be doubling its difficulties by creating an unnecessary flow of imports. On balance Professor Hague's study made a clear case for backing the BAC Three-Eleven on economic and employment grounds.[29]

Her Majesty's Government's Evaluation of the Three-Eleven

It is now time for us to review how the British Government, via MinTech and the Ministry of Aviation Supply, evaluated the Three-Eleven project from the date of BAC's original launch aid application (25 November 1969) to the time when the decision was taken not to give the project Government financial backing. Tellingly, as we shall see in the following paragraphs, there was consistent and continued broad support for the project in both the Labour and Conservative administrations.

A document by the Labour Minister of Aviation, Lord Delacourt-Smith, dated 17 February 1970, stated that: '[Aerospace] is a field of technology where the [UK] have been and to a large extent still are in a leading position and [it] ought to exploit that for economic betterment.' Lord Delacourt-Smith then went on to argue that even if BAC's shareholders were unable to back the project financially, the Government should not wash its hands of the Three-Eleven:

> the [British] government should resist pressure to drop the [BAC 3-11] from the Airbus governments. BAC has a world reputation to a greater degree than HSA and the scrapping of the 3-11 would mean that either BAC would reduce activities or turn to subcontracting. If reduction of the aircraft industry and of design capacity has to take place, it would not necessarily be best for the reduction to take place in this way. It would reduce the UK's ability to take the lead in future international projects and so would reduce our bargaining power.[30]

Another paper from the Ministry of Aviation, also dated February 1970, makes as strong a case for the Three-Eleven, by arguing that:

> The BAC 3-11 is important to the future not only of BAC but of the aircraft industry as a whole and should be considered in relation to our broad policies for the industry and for the advance of British technology generally. The importance of continuing in business as designers and builders of large civil aircraft (an objective shared by all the large leading industrial countries) turns on the fact that this is a rapidly expanding business with a big export earning/import saving potential, and a total world market of £3 to £4 billion per annum by the 1980s. Since we have already opted out of the long haul

field (apart from Concorde), a decision not to undertake the BAC 3-11 would imply concentration on small short haul aircraft since it will be difficult to re-enter the field of larger and more sophisticated aircraft once this field has been abandoned…If the [BAC 3-11] does not go ahead, BAC will either sharply reduce their present scale of activity or undertake sub-contracts…though sub-contracting to Lockheed or Boeing might be commercially profitable in the short term, these would hardly offer long term future to BAC and they would probably drop out of the civil field altogether.

This will leave only Hawker Siddeley. Though technically competent, as the Trident shows, HSA have not established the same reputation as BAC among world airlines. Their role as sub-contractor to French and German industry on the A300B, for which they are designing and building the wing, will be likely to push them further into the background, with the French company Sud Aviation acting as the established leader…[31]

The paper concluded by stating that the Three-Eleven, far from damaging the country, would provide the UK with the essential foundation for collaboration on equal terms in the long term. However, around the same date, a memorandum from the Aviation Ministry's Permanent Secretary clearly stated that the top priority for the Government was to keep Rolls-Royce in the world league, thus assuring its presence in the US market.[32]

A paper by MinTech dated 24 February 1970 reiterated the department's support of the BAC Three-Eleven by affirming:

We regard the BAC 3-11 as potentially an excellent aircraft; in price and performance it is similar to the A300B, but BAC (with the Viscount, VC-10 and BAC 1-11) have a better standing with world airlines than the Airbus consortium, and a better organisation for world sales and servicing.

In the longer term, the BAC 3-11 should provide us with the foundation for collaboration as equals. Without it, we may well be able to participate in future civil projects on terms largely dictated by the French, who are anxious to stake a claim as leaders in European design and manufacture, but about whose capability in this role we have strong reservations…

The same paper stated that one of the reasons for the Government's withdrawal from the A300B project was that it had serious reservations about the adequacy of Sud Aviation's competence and resources to carry the project through to a successful conclusion. As we all know, such reservations were to prove totally unfounded in due course![33]

At the behest of Prime Minister Harold Wilson, a meeting to discuss the 'Airbus' options was held on 17 March 1970 at the Ministry of Technology. Senior officials of the Board of Trade, the Foreign Office, the Treasury and MinTech itself were present at the meeting.[34] Presiding at the meeting, the Minister of Technology Tony Benn stated, in relation to the BAC Three-Eleven, that the aircraft was recognised to be a good one technically and that BAC's reputation in this field was an obvious advantage commercially. Nevertheless, he was aware that it would be an expensive project for the Government in that there would be no other Governments to assist with the launch aid. The Chief Secretary (Aviation) added that one of the attractions of a solution based on the development of the BAC Three-Eleven, if financially feasible, was that it maintained in the British airframe industry a design capability that would be capable of meeting a continuing demand worldwide for civil aircraft.

Lord Chalfont of the Foreign & Commonwealth Office (FCO) said that the FCO's main concern was with the presentational aspects of any decision to support the BAC Three-Eleven project. If there were good industrial, technical and commercial reasons for UK Government support of the project, the FCO would not oppose such support. Since such decision, however, would be certainly described by the French and Germans as a case of the UK following its own national interest in conflict with the aim of European technological integration, the timing of any announcement and its presentation would need to be very carefully considered.

Sir Solly Zuckerman, the Government's Chief Scientific Adviser, sounded the only discordant note to the broad support the Three-Eleven received in that meeting. Sir Solly argued that in ten years' time there would either be one European aircraft company or no European aircraft industry to speak of. In his view the best course of action for the UK was to establish Rolls-Royce as the European aero-engine industry core, and to help build up a truly European airframe industry. As it happened, the A300B European Airbus already existed. Sir Solly concluded that the BAC Three-Eleven should be dropped and the UK should rejoin the A300B consortium, on condition that the plane would be exclusively powered by Rolls-Royce RB211 engines. In the end a consensus emerged that no immediate decision should be taken in respect of either the Three-Eleven or the A300B, and that the Three-Eleven option should be kept alive as a 'bargaining counter' while talks continued with the Europeans.

When Labour was replaced by the Conservatives following the June 1970 General Election, continued support for the case of going ahead with launch aid for the BAC Three-Eleven was evident both in MinTech and in the Ministry of Aviation.

A Cabinet paper by the Minister of Technology Geoffrey Rippon, presented on 20 July 1970, stated that he believed the Three-Eleven to be 'a sound and worthwhile economic project quite apart from its importance for other reasons'. Mr Rippon went on to say:

> I appreciate the difficulties of an immediate decision to support the BAC 3-11 before we have decided what savings are possible elsewhere, but I hope that the Cabinet will agree that I should discuss these proposals with the Chief Secretary, Treasury, and other colleagues with a view to decisions being taken as soon as possible... We withdrew from

the A300B because there was at the time no assurance of airline interest, insufficient financial participation by industry and doubts about the effectiveness of French project management. These objections remain valid…

Despite the competition from the A300B, based on Airbus's own market predictions (1,200–1,400 units), there is room for both projects, and if we consider that the BAC 3-11 is in the national interest, it would be wrong to abandon it in the face of pressure from foreign competitors. Whatever we decide about the BAC 3-11, it need not be regarded as a major factor in our approach to Europe or in the longer term prospects of aircraft collaboration, for which we should continue to work.[35]

Mr Rippon's note then listed the arguments for and against the Three-Eleven project as follows:

In Favour of Three-Eleven

Best remaining chance to avoid total dependence on America for subsonic commercial aircraft

Allows to exploit the very good reputation of BAC and Rolls-Royce worldwide for civil aircraft

Reduces industrial difficulties in the case of Concorde cancellation

[UK] cannot afford to become subservient to French and German industries in collaborative projects

BEA wants it

A major aircraft operating in world markets is a good demonstration of our technological abilities and can help other engineering industries

Helps the equipment industry to achieve sales on foreign aircraft[36]

Large subcontract packages for Shorts in Northern Ireland and Scottish Aviation in Scotland

Technical failure is unlikely since the design of the aircraft is already well established as a result of the last two years of work at BAC. They have a very experienced civil aircraft team and have proved themselves with their BAC One-Eleven as with the Viscount earlier, able to sell aircraft throughout the world

Against the Three-Eleven

Angering the French and Germans (but should not be afraid of doing so, as HMG could not find a basis for collaboration on the European Airbus) '…though it is disappointing that we did not find a basis for collaboration on Airbus, it was not for want of trying and we should earn no respect for a show of weakness now in the face of their protest'

Civil aircraft financing has been a constant drain on the Exchequer. Since 1960 we spent and committed £120 million and recovered only £6 million so far

Unfortunately, the BAC Three-Eleven did not enjoy the same support in the Treasury. On 21 July 1970, just one day after Mr Rippon's Cabinet paper supporting the project, a Cabinet paper presented by the Chief Secretary to the Treasury cast doubt on the projected aircraft's market potential, saying that:

> The Ministry of Technology's analysis of the market prospects suggests that sales might be in the range 150 to 240. Apart from the BAC 1-11, there is nothing in the recent history of the UK aircraft industry to suggest that these forecasts are likely to be achieved…

It concluded with the recommendation not to support the project, suggesting that:

> Unless [the project] were abnormally and improbably successful, the prospective foreign exchange benefits would not be sufficient to justify its high cost in national resources. Even in the unlikely event of selling 240 aircraft [sic!] the government would not, in discounted terms, recover its investment.[37]

A later report prepared by Mr R.A. Lloyd Jones of the Ministry of Aviation Supply for presentation to the Cabinet in the week beginning 12 October 1970 made the following points:

> The wide body twinjet market was estimated at 1,100 aircraft by 1984. The BAC 3-11/ European Airbus A300B segment was the sole remaining worthwhile market which [the UK] could bid for if, either alone or in collaboration with other countries, it wished to retain a significant place in the civil subsonic aircraft business.

> Since 1960 HMG had spent or committed £74 million in launch aid for civil aircraft (excluding Concorde and the RB211) and had so far recovered £6 million, and hoped to recover a further £22 million mainly on the BAC 1-11 and Spey engine. Therefore it could not be claimed that the civil activities of either the airframe or the aero-engine firms had paid their way by commercial standards.

To drop out now would mean sacrificing the best chance of sharing in one of the world's larger growth industries of the next ten or twenty years.

Without the BAC 3-11, [the UK's] national capacity to design and market major civil aircraft, now well established with the BAC 1-11, was likely to disappear, and on the airframe side at least [the UK] would rank only as junior partners in the future European industry, particularly in view of current French ambitions to dominate it.

BAC 3-11: this 250 passenger aircraft would fly in 1973 and come into service in 1975. It was devised by the BAC team at Weybridge who designed the BAC 1-11 and have achieved with that aircraft, as with the Viscount before it, a substantial world reputation. Its sales would probably lie between 150 and 240, assuming that the A300B also goes ahead, but this estimate has deliberately been pitched on the cautious side.

The sums involved (£144 million contribution from HMG) would be far larger than those required for earlier projects apart from Concorde.

The financial outlook of Rolls-Royce, who are already contributing massively to the costs of the RB211-22, has deteriorated still further since July [1970]…

Table 3.9. Estimated Three-Eleven and RB211-61 launch costs and Government share

	Total launch costs (£ million)	HMG share (£ million)
Aircraft	140	84 (60 per cent)
Engine (RB211-61)	60	60 (100 per cent)
Total	200	144

(Source: HMG, Ministry of Aviation files, 20 July 1970)

Attached to the report was a table of net economic benefits to the Exchequer and to the UK economy as a whole which showed that, in the base case scenario of 240 Three-Elevens sold, the British taxpayer would lose £53 million, and the UK economy would be £25 million worse off. The output of these calculations is set out in table 3.10 below.

Table 3.10 Output values of HMG's Economic Assessment of BAC Three-Eleven project

Three-Eleven units sold over life of programme	150 sales	240 sales
Government loss/gain (NPV in brackets)	-£60 million (-£72 million)	-£5 million (-£53 million)
Forex benefits (NPV in brackets)	£750 million (£335 million)	£1,300 million (£500 million)
NPV of net resources gains/losses to UK economy	(-£60 million)	(-£25 million)

Note: NPV = Net Present Value of cash-flows
(Source: HMG, Ministry of Aviation files, 8 October 1970)

Table 3.11 MinTech general provision contingently earmarked against new projects (£ million)

Financial Year	70/71	71/72	72/73	73/74	74/75	75/76	Total
Total provision	16	27.5	35	40	40	N/A	
RB211-22	12.5	12.5					25
BAC 3-11/RB211-61	4	22	34	38	27	19	144
L1011/RB211-61		0.5	2	5	3	0.5	11

(Source: HMG, Ministry of Aviation files, 12 October 1970)

On 9 October 1970 the new Conservative Minister of Technology John Davies presented a Cabinet paper in which, like his predecessor Geoffrey Rippon, he argued in favour of a BAC Three-Eleven launch. Acknowledging that Britain had then the most powerful aerospace industry in Europe and that BAC and Rolls-Royce were the most experienced companies in Europe in civil aircraft development, Mr Davies did not believe that re-joining the Airbus consortium, despite Hawker Siddeley's private involvement in it, could compensate for the loss of the Three-Eleven and for the consequent dispersal of BAC's key expertise. While recognising the fact that Three-Eleven financing would make it very difficult for him to meet his department's 1974/75 public expenditure limit, Mr Davies concluded his paper thus: 'In my judgment the BAC 3-11 should be supported both on its own merits and as an essential foundation for the future. Success cannot be guaranteed, but the potential prizes are great and in a much wider context than the projects themselves.'

A paper dated 2 November 1970 (exactly one month before the Three-Eleven cancellation announcement) and prepared by the Minister of Aviation Supply Frederick Corfield made the following points regarding the Three-Eleven versus A300B European Airbus:

If [HMG] could afford it and could weather the European reactions, the BAC 3-11/ RB211-61 is the best overall solution for all the reasons we have already advanced. I [Frederick Corfield] am not clear whether on present evidence we must regard this option as dead, except as a bargaining counter.

The BAC 3-11/GE engine combination would produce the best aircraft from almost every point of view. This would also save our design team, but would be anti-Europe and anti-Lockheed: in any event, Rolls-Royce said it would not participate, thus this option must be discarded.

To drop the BAC 3-11 and the RB211-61 would be the worst option for our aero-space industry.

I find it hard to accept a negotiating position based on the premise that in order to be good Europeans we must give up our leading European position in both the airframe and engine fields... I suspect the Consortium countries believe we have decided to cancel the 3-11 and that we are not saying so in order to keep the pressure on them.

By rejoining the Consortium and renouncing the BAC 3-11 [HMG] are serving notice that, having sacrificed Weybridge, HSA is now our nominated firm for major subsonic civil projects in the future and next time round, having been in a position of equality in the partnership on the A300B, we would expect HSA to assume the mantle at present being worn by Sud Aviation.

Three weeks earlier, on 12 October 1970, the Secretary to the Cabinet Sir Burke Trend had written a memo highlighting the substantial cost to HMG of backing the Three-Eleven/RB211-61 option. In his memo Sir Burke said:

the major question is whether the Cabinet regard it as essential to maintain, even at a high price, an independent British airframe and aero-engine industry capable of making large civil aircraft. And the direct price of maintaining it with the BAC 3-11 and RB211-61 is high, even on optimistic assumptions about costs and sales. Support for [the aircraft and engine] will only keep us in major civil aircraft for a few more years until the next, even costlier project comes along... to refuse to support the continuance of design and production capacity in the Big League is clearly difficult and will be unpopular in certain quarters. But can we really afford to continue with pensioners on this scale?

Concluding, Sir Burke Trend argued that HMG should not back either the BAC Three-Eleven or the Airbus consortium, but should allow BEA to buy the Lockheed TriStar. He considered the cost to UK plc of either the Three-Eleven or the A300B too high to bear. On the same date Sir Solly Zuckerman, the Government's chief scientific adviser, reiterated his support for rejoining the European Airbus consortium on the A300B, arguing against the 'absurdity' of a BAC 3-11 launch which would wreck the possibilities of future cooperation with the French and the Germans.

The Minister of Aviation Supply Frederick Corfield presented his last memorandum to the Cabinet on the 'airbus' choices facing HMG on 26 November 1970 (less than a week before the Three-Eleven cancellation announcement). In his paper Mr Corfield analysed the different alternatives (re-entry into the European Airbus consortium, backing the Three-Eleven, or doing neither) and again came out in favour of the British airbus, arguing that: 'the balance of national advantage lies in supporting the BAC 3-11. This should preferably be with the RB211-61 engines, but the GE engine represents a useful fall-back position if we wish to avoid a full commitment to the RB211-61 now…'[38] To be frank, Mr Corfield's document was worded in a very balanced, almost neutral, way and did not really make a strong enough case for the BAC Three-Eleven in strategic terms. Overall the memorandum left the impression that preference for the project was a question of degree, and rather marginal at that.

As can be seen from our review of the Government papers, there was a consistent consensus throughout the period that, as far as the Government's technical and industry departments were concerned, the BAC Three-Eleven was the best option for the UK aerospace industry, and that it was a worthwhile project for HMG to back.[39]

Interestingly, rejoining the European Airbus consortium, as proposed by Hawker Siddeley and the European Governments backing the A300B, was never seen by HMG as an attractive option other than for its 'political leverage' value in Europe. However, any gain of goodwill in Europe was offset, in the ministers' view, by the perceived economic and financial risks of the project, and by the marginal technical gains for the UK aircraft industry over and above the wing design package that HSA had already negotiated as a private subcontractor.

However, despite the consistent backing the Three-Eleven received from MinTech, the MoA and the Board of Trade, it was clear that the Treasury would need to agree to a substantial investment of public funds for this programme at a time when the demands of backing Rolls-Royce and its RB211-22 engine, together with Concorde's commitments, were already stretching the resources available for investment.

During the period when HMG evaluated the Three-Eleven, MinTech and the Ministry of Aviation sought or received the views of BAC's senior management and those of BAC's shareholders. Amongst the many contacts between industry and Government, it is worth recording the summary content of one particular letter from BAC's chairman Sir George Edwards, and the opinion of GEC's top man, Lord Arnold Weinstock, in connection with the project (GEC of course being one of BAC's two main shareholders).

Sensing that storms were brewing ahead for Rolls-Royce, Sir George Edwards, on 6 March 1970, wrote to Sir Ronald Melville, Second Permanent Secretary at MinTech. In this letter he suggested that:

> HMG should divorce the decision on the BAC 3-11 from that of the RB211 development programme, and should authorise BAC to proceed with the 3-11 on the understanding that the aeroplane will be designed from the start for the RB211-50, but if this engine were not available by end of June 1970, BAC will be free to fit the most suitable version of the GE CF-6.

Sir George went on to say that the latter combination 'would be acceptable to BEA'. As we know, the Three-Eleven/GE CF-6 option, which would have saved the Three-Eleven while allowing significant savings for the Treasury, was not pursued as it was considered 'politically unfeasible'.[40]

Early on in the evaluation of the Three-Eleven project, MinTech sought the views of Lord Arnold Weinstock of GEC on the project. Arnold Weinstock was considered, in those days, one of the shrewdest investors in British industry and therefore his opinions carried enormous kudos. At a business dinner with Aviation Minister Lord Delacourt-Smith, Lord Weinstock said that he believed that the BAC Three-Eleven would be a success. Asked if the BAC shareholders would be prepared to give security on the £30 million production loan, Weinstock replied that there could be no security. He added that, if the project were to proceed, it would need to have a very large amount of Government finance. Lord Weinstock also said that GEC wanted to get out of BAC, that Rolls-Royce had no money and also wanted to get out, while Vickers were prepared to stay but had no money. Asked whether the BAC Three-Eleven proposition as a whole represented something that the Government ought to accept, Weinstock replied that this was not a question which he should be expected to answer.[41] It is clear that, as far as Lord Weinstock was concerned, the decision to back the Three-Eleven had to be one that the Government had to take, and not private industry. In this he confirmed the private sector's aversion to high-risk civil aerospace projects and his own well-known reluctance to back civil aircraft programmes. In spite of Lord Weinstock's comments, however, in due course GEC would support the internal 'go ahead' of the Three-Eleven, subject to Government backing.

In summary, what can be said of the British Government's evaluation of the BAC Three-Eleven project? Without doubt, a lot of detailed technical, economic and financial analysis went into the exercise. There is little or no doubt that this work was carried out very professionally. First the RAE provided a complete technical audit of the aircraft and of its competitor, the Airbus A300B. Then the ministerial economists thoroughly reviewed the market assumptions underpinning the Three-Eleven's business case, looking at total market potential, and then at the aircraft's likely market share airline by airline. Non-recurring costs assumptions and selling prices were tested using 'state of the art' financial appraisal techniques. In short the Three-Eleven investment opportunity was undoubtedly subjected to the 'stringent economic criteria' that Tony Benn mentioned in the early stages of HMG's evaluation of the project.

However, and this is a typical shortcoming of the British mindset, at no stage did the Cabinet take a strategic view of the project in terms of the future position of the UK aircraft industry in global terms. This lack of vision and strategic thinking was in sharp contrast to the approach taken by successive French Governments and their civil servants. Too much focus was put, and energy spent, on 'project-by-project' ad hoc evaluations (BAC Two-Eleven, followed by the European Airbus agreement, followed by withdrawal from the Airbus, followed by the BAC Three-Eleven and re-evaluation of the European Airbus, etc.) without considering at any stage an overall strategy for the civil aircraft industry. In addition, throughout the evaluation period the Government's main preoccupation (one might say obsession) was with the fortunes of Rolls-Royce. Reviewing the documentation, one is left with the overwhelming impression that the interests of the airframe and equipment sides of the industry are at best incidental or at worst marginal to the interests of this major aero-engine company. While this may have been understandable given the great market success of the Derby-based company at the time, it produced a myopic assessment of the welfare of the industry as a whole.

To be fair to the Government it must also be said that, unlike its French and German counterparts, it was faced with a series of complex and stark choices: it had to decide between two alternative 'airbus' programmes addressing the same market, while at the same time having to take into account the interests of a powerful British aero-engine manufacturer. The 'airbus' programmes pitted against each other Britain's two leading airframe companies: BAC and HSA. Therefore the Government had to balance the interests of three powerful constituencies (Rolls-Royce, BAC and HSA) against a backdrop of budget constraints set by the Treasury and wider political goals in relation to its stated intention of entering the European Common Market. By contrast, the French Government had only to worry about the interests of Aérospatiale, France's only major civil aircraft company, while for aero-engine maker SNECMA the licence-production of the GE CF-6 engine for the A300B sufficed.

Cancellation

Alas, BAC's strong lobbying, the obvious commercial viability of the Three-Eleven, the City's preparedness to back the project financially, the macroeconomic study by Economic Models and the support of MinTech, the Board of Trade, and BEA together with strong support from the Conservative backbenches, all proved insufficient to win the Heath Government's financial backing for the Three-Eleven programme.

On 2 December 1970 the Minister of Aviation Supply, Frederick Corfield, announced in the House of Commons that the Government would not back the BAC Three-Eleven, nor it would take up the option of rejoining the European Airbus consortium on the A300B. He justified this decision on the grounds that all available monies for civil aerospace had gone towards supporting Rolls-Royce in its struggle to produce the RB211 engine to Lockheed's tight contractual terms, and towards the continuous investment in the Concorde programme, and, therefore, no spare monies were available to support either the Three-Eleven or Britain's re-entry into the A300B programme.[42] Indeed the RB211 engine and Rolls-Royce had absorbed almost £100 million of Government money up to December 1970. Ultimately the RB211 programme would precipitate Rolls-Royce into bankruptcy in February 1971, only two months after Mr Corfield's Three-Eleven cancellation announcement. The RB211 would eventually require a total of over £170 million of Government money up to completion of its certification. It was the Treasury in the end which opposed any additional exposure to the civil aircraft industry, given the Government's already substantial commitments to the Concorde and the RB211 engine.

In the Parliamentary debate and at the press conference that followed the statement, Mr Corfield praised the Three-Eleven design and BAC's market research – the latter he thought perfectly honest – but added that in recent times the airbus market had become less buoyant. Even on reasonable predicted sales of 240 Three-Elevens, the Government, said Mr Corfield, would have ended up £50 million in the red because of discount or interest losses. BAC could have expected to start to get their money back on 200 aircraft plus spares. The Government was latterly being asked to finance the development costs on a 60/40 basis with BAC, making an £84 million Government total plus £60 million or so on the engine. These amounts, he said, were too much for the Government to bear. Mr Corfield also mentioned the direct conflict between the Three-Eleven and the A300B, the Airbus/American trijets overlap and the 'considerable' cash shortage of the American airlines, in justification for his decision.

The reaction of MPs to the announcement varied. The ex-minister of technology, Tony Benn, declared that the Three-Eleven cancellation was a 'watershed decision for the airframe industry'.[43] Labour's Douglas Jay MP added 'many of us deeply regret the government's decision not to support the 3-11 which, apparently for the sake of a short-term budget saving, is likely to be highly damaging in the long run for the aircraft industry and the British balance of payments'. Another Labour MP, Mr William Rodgers, said: 'Many MPs on both sides will have been deeply disturbed by the Minister's grave news. There will be an unhappy suspicion that the fate of what might have been a very fine aircraft with real export potential has been settled not on merit, but according to preconceptions on public expenditure and public intervention.'

The Conservative backbenchers on the other hand accused Labour of being the true culprits by letting the Rolls-Royce situation get out of hand, thus leaving no money for the Three-Eleven. The reactions of the two Conservative MPs whose constituencies were most affected by the Three-Eleven cancellation are worth recording. Mr Cranley Onslow, MP for Woking, said: 'Many Conservatives will know how much the Minister must regret having to make this statement. If anyone is to be held to blame for this disappointment… [it is] Mr Wedgwood Benn, because this government's policy of supporting the airframe industry has been gravely damaged by the disastrous cost resulting from the Rolls-Royce-Lockheed contract which the previous government underwrote.' Mr Carol Mather, MP for Esher, added: 'I sympathise with the Minister in the dilemma in which he finds himself as a result of the improvidence of the previous government. There will be dismay in my constituency at Weybridge not only because of the jeopardy of jobs and design teams but because we all firmly believe that Britain builds the best aircraft.' In replying to a comment made by another Conservative MP, Mr Temple, Fred Corfield said: 'One of the dilemmas which faced this, and no doubt the previous, administration is that BAC's application for launching aid would have involved the government in supporting a project in direct competition with another project for which Hawker Siddeley were engaged without public assistance.'

In any event, the Heath Government's deliberation at the very end of 1970 – which can be interpreted as a sort of 'reverse Solomonic sentence' – left the British civil aerospace sector with the worst of both worlds. In fact, not only did it deprive British industry, through the lack of support for the BAC Three-Eleven, of continuity in the independent development of large civil aircraft, but it also saw Britain lose the last opportunity to rejoin the Airbus consortium as an equal share partner of France and Germany. As we shall see in the next chapter, when Britain eventually decided to rejoin the Airbus programme in the late 1970s, the Airbus Industrie founding partners (France and Germany) had already established a viable product in the marketplace with the A300B, and were launching the first derivative, the A310. Britain was therefore accommodated in the consortium with a 20 per cent minority stake, basically representing the workshare that HSA had privately negotiated in 1969 after the Labour Government's decision to withdraw.

Not surprisingly, the news of the cancellation of the BAC Three-Eleven delighted the French and German Governments and their aerospace industries, which were relieved to see the removal of a serious, and feared, competitor to the A300B Airbus. The Times newspaper of 3 December 1970 reported that French officials had expressed satisfaction with Britain's decision to drop support for the BAC Three-Eleven airbus. The French added that this decision would eliminate destructive competition within Europe.

The cancellation of the Three-Eleven set in train the progressive marginalisation of Weybridge and civil aircraft within BAC. The military aircraft business at Warton had been on the ascendancy within the company since it had secured the Jaguar and Panavia Tornado military aircraft programmes. The status of 'Cinderella' for civil aircraft carried through to the newly formed British Aerospace. At the time of the nationalisation of BAC and HSA and the formation of British Aerospace, the BAC board decided to focus on the highly profitable and risk-free military aircraft and guided weapons businesses. For equity's sake, therefore, HSA's management was given responsibility for the civil aircraft business. HSA unsurprisingly promoted the Airbus and HS.146 programmes at the expense of promising Weybridge programmes such as further developments of the BAC One-Eleven and the new BAC X-Eleven 150-seat twinjet, projects which we will review in the next chapter.

With the termination of the Concorde programme, BAe became more and more defence-focused, and defence as core strategic business was crystallised with the formation of BAE SYSTEMS in the late 1990s. Now civil aircraft within BAE SYSTEMS consists only of the 20 per cent minority stake in Airbus, which BAE has now decided to sell to EADS, and the rump of the regional aircraft business (now a service-only business). This is what happens when the national champion loses the leadership in a particular sector of the industry. Warton preserved the design leadership on the Tornado and this leadership was carried through to the Eurofighter Typhoon. For Weybridge, the loss of the Three-Eleven proved fatal and signalled the beginning of its steady decline into oblivion.

The first immediate effect of the BAC Three-Eleven cancellation was the announcement of 900 redundancies at the BAC Commercial Division sites in Weybridge and Hurn, including 600 engineering and design staff. Several senior design engineers were made redundant and the redundancies were described by BAC as a 'serious depletion' of the world's most experienced airliner design team outside the US. Of course, also affected by the decision were the several equipment manufacturers, such as Elliott Automation, Ferranti, Marconi, Plessey and Smiths Industries, which would have played a key role in the development of the cockpit systems, computers and displays, in addition to helping BAC in the high-added-value area of cockpit systems, flight controls and overall systems integration.

The demise of the Three-Eleven wide-body airliner signalled the end of independent development of large civil transports by BAC and indeed by Britain, and project leadership on large civil aircraft, ceded to France on the A300B, was never recovered, as we shall see in the next chapter. BAC had invested over £3 million of company money and thousands of man-hours in the project, only to see it cancelled at the last minute by the British Government.

Of course many astute industry observers at the time were fully aware of the disastrous implications of the Three-Eleven cancellation for the British aerospace industry, none more so than the key people closely involved with the project. Sir Anthony Milward of BEA, in an interview with *The Times*, described the

Government's decision not to proceed with the Three-Eleven as 'an absolute disaster'. He said, 'This means the virtual withdrawal of Britain from the civil aircraft industry. The only new aircraft being built now is the Concorde, and I do not think anybody can feel really happy about the future of that. This decision really is a disaster...' BAC's chairman, Sir George Edwards, pulled no punches either when he described the decision as 'a tragic and stupid decision which Britain will regret for many years to come...'[44] For his part, Sir Reginald Verdon-Smith of BAC described the Government decision on the Three-Eleven as 'the biggest setback since TSR2 was cancelled', and added that 'In due course people will see how big an opportunity has been lost to Britain'.

In its editorial covering the cancellation of the Three-Eleven, *Flight International* stated that, 'there is no point in pretending that [the cancellation] is not a tragedy. Britain has all the rare skills needed to win a share of the biggest aircraft business of all, the mass market for subsonic jet airliners, and she has opted out.' The magazine added that there was nothing new between Concorde and Trislander to supply to the mass airline market of the future except for the A300B, in which Britain played a junior role. Looking to the long-term future for the industry, *Flight* concluded:

> What of the long term? Britain now has no direct stake in the truly prodigious subsonic airliner market of the future. The £144 million needed for the Three-Eleven and its engine will seem in 20 years' time a puny sum compared with the billion-dollar bills for imported American airliners. And there is no guarantee that indirect sales will be retained. However good a job Hawker Siddeley and Rolls-Royce and their suppliers do, their long term futures in this market are now in the hands of countries which, while espousing collaboration, as all sensible people do, will always put their national interests first.[45]

The reactions to the Three-Eleven cancellation in the national press ranged from the fatalistic and defeatist stance of the *Financial Times* to the angry and frustrated reaction of the *Daily Express*. The *FT*, in its leader of 3 December 1970, commented:

> The Government's decision not to support the development of the BAC Three-Eleven is sad news for the aircraft industry but it has seemed inevitable for some time past. It is true that BEA was eager, on purely commercial grounds, to order the Three-Eleven. On the other hand, the prospect of obtaining orders from other major airlines was doubtful [not true (author's note)]... For the demise of the Three-Eleven has shown that the British aircraft industry can no longer expect to embark on major projects alone: its future lies in cooperation with major manufacturers, and particularly in Europe.[46]

The *Daily Express* instead argued:

> ...but satisfaction about [support for the Concorde] must not be allowed to mask the setback caused by the Government's decision to kill the BAC Three-Eleven airliner. This

is as heavy a blow to British aircraft development as Labour's destruction of the TSR 2. The scrapping of the Three-Eleven means a loss of foreign exchange (to buy aircraft), the loss of technical know-how and the loss of many, many jobs for British workers. The keeping of Concorde will only partially compensate for this.[47]

Potential Negative Outcomes for the British and European Aircraft Industries of a BAC Three-Eleven Launch

There is little doubt in our mind that, had it been launched into production, the BAC Three-Eleven would have been a substantial commercial success. This was amply proven by the market penetration of the Airbus A300B and its smaller sister A310, together with their rivals from Boeing (the 767 and 757). The Three-Eleven was the right size of aircraft and had the competitive operational economics for the market that evolved from the late 1970s onwards. We believe that the Three-Eleven would have, in all probability, considerably outstripped the BAC One-Eleven's success both in sales volume and value. It is also possible to specu-late that, had the Three-Eleven been launched, Boeing might not have entered the twin-engine wide-body market with the 767 or launched the 757. However, in order to offer a balanced assessment of the project's prospects it is our duty to highlight the potential negative effects that a Three-Eleven launch could have had in the market place and, by reflection, on the British aircraft industry. These potential outcomes are reviewed below:

Destructive competition with the Airbus A300B

The main issue would have been the competition in the market place between the two wide-body twinjet offerings from Europe, namely the Airbus A300B and the BAC Three-Eleven. This could have resulted in either one or both projects failing to sell in sufficient numbers to make the ventures profitable. In this context the salutary and sombre lessons of the DC-10/TriStar rivalry in the US spring to mind. In that case the parallel development of the Douglas DC-10 and Lockheed TriStar to cater for the same market resulted in near identical solutions (medium-range trijet wide-bodies) which ended up cannibalising each other's relatively small market and selling in insufficient numbers and at prices too low to allow recovery of the development costs. The final result was that, due to the massive losses incurred on those programmes, first Lockheed, and then, several years later, McDonnell Douglas, exited the commercial airliner market.

There is, in principle, a realistic possibility that the price competition between the A300B and the Three-Eleven could have resulted in a similar outcome for BAC and the fledgling Airbus consortium. If the Three-Eleven had indeed prevailed in the market place, it could have been at the price of BAC having to sell below 'full cost', thus resulting in the financial failure of the programme and possibly of the company itself. On the other hand, Airbus's failure to sell the A300B in sufficient numbers could have resulted in Europe exiting the airliner business for good, and today we would not have Airbus as the world's largest producer of civil airliners.

However, a strong counter-argument to this pessimistic scenario is the fact that the market segment that the BAC Three-Eleven and Airbus A300B were addressing was much wider and with much higher growth potential than that addressed by the Lockheed TriStar and Douglas DC-10. As events have subsequently demonstrated, over 2,800 Three-Eleven-class aircraft have been sold since the first flight of the Airbus A300B (this total includes the aggregate of Airbus A300, A310 and Boeing 757 and 767 sales), thus making an outcome of both the A300B and the Three-Eleven being commercial successes and making money much more likely. It is also possible, as we have commented earlier, that the presence of the Three-Eleven in the market place and its early success could have convinced Boeing not to launch the 767 wide-body twin or its 757 single-aisle brother. Finally we must not forget that BAC's break-even figure on the Three-Eleven was only 200 units, not an ambitious number of aircraft given the way in which the market eventually grew. Best of all for British industry, Airbus Industrie years later would have been forced to make substantial concessions to the British (including design and project leadership) in order to eliminate the BAC Three-Eleven and its derivatives from the market place and to gain British participation in its future programmes. Instead, it was an emasculated and demoralised industry, without a major programme of its own, that came to the negotiating table with the French and the Germans in the mid-1970s.

The bankruptcy of Rolls-Royce

As we know, the bankruptcy of engine-maker Rolls-Royce was only around the corner at the time of the Three-Eleven programme cancellation. Rolls-Royce's bankruptcy not only would have seriously threatened or delayed the continuous development of the RB211-61 engine earmarked for the Three-Eleven (if indeed that variant of the RB211 had received Government support), but would also have cast a shadow on the development of the Three-Eleven itself. In fact, in view of the substantial sums of Government money that were in the event required to salvage Rolls-Royce from bankruptcy, it is not a wild guess to suggest that the UK Government might have pulled the plug on Three-Eleven launch aid. Therefore the death of the programme could have come anyway, only slightly later in its life.

Of course, the late proposal by BAC to power the Three-Eleven initially with General Electric CF-6-50 engines might have saved the programme from Rolls-Royce's predicament and from the ripple effects of the latter's bankruptcy. However, even in the most benign of scenarios (i.e. assuming that the British Government would have continued to support the Three-Eleven steadfastly as a means of retaining Britain's civil aircraft expertise), we cannot deny that Rolls-Royce's collapse might have severely delayed the Three-Eleven programme, with the potential outcome that the aircraft would have come to market too late.

Cost overruns

At the time of the financing discussions with HM Government, BAC had under-taken to carry any Three-Eleven project cost overruns on its own account. In this regard, it is a known fact that aerospace programmes are, by their nature, subject to cost escalation, the magnitude of which varies from programme to programme (see Chapter 5). BAC argued at the time that it was confident about its Three-Eleven development cost estimates, having already produced a jet airliner of similar size and complexity (the Vickers VC-10). Indeed BAC's claims were supported by the RAE's own estimates of programme costs. This might well have been the case, with BAC effectively being in a position to develop the aircraft within its budgeted costs. However, experience from the Airbus A300B development shows that initial cost estimates were substantially exceeded when the final product reached the market, and that therefore HSA may possibly have been right when it questioned BAC's ability to develop its aircraft for a total of £150 million.

In this particular instance, one major mitigating factor in favour of the Three-Eleven costing estimates is that the Airbus A300B was a cooperative venture, and that Aérospatiale and Deutsche Airbus in particular had at the time very limited experience of production of large airliners compared with BAC. In other words, the Airbus A300B development costs included a sizeable amount of 'learning curve' costs for the French and German partners, a factor which would have affected BAC to a far lesser degree. It is also a known fact that cooperative ventures and joint-venture developments in aerospace cost between 30 and 40 per cent more than similar programmes under the control of one single company.

Notwithstanding the above points, we must recognise that BAC's balance sheet at the time was not the strongest for a project of the Three-Eleven's magnitude. In addition BAC's key assumption of producing £5 million per annum of internally generated cash flow to help finance Three-Eleven development could have proved over-optimistic,[48] thus potentially leading the company into the hands of the receiver, as eventually happened to Rolls-Royce. Of course this is just pure speculation, but we do dare to suggest that, without a serious commitment on behalf of the British Government to see the Three-Eleven to fruition (and the Government's prepared-ness to inject further cash into the programme in the event of BAC's inability to do so), the project might have brought BAC to its knees. It is a known fact, for example, that without the French and German Governments' willingness to act as 'lenders of last resort' the Airbus programme would not have seen the light of day. We doubt that the more utilitarian and cost-conscious British Government would have been driven by a similar zeal to sustain the UK's civil aerospace industry, or that it would have parted with taxpayers' money with the same visionary abandon of the French and the Germans (although it did so – *obtorto collo* – in the case of Concorde).

The 1973 Oil Shock

In 1973 the OPEC Cartel decided to increase the price of oil threefold, precipitating a major world recession in the industrialised world which lasted several years. The air transport sector in particular was severely affected, and orders for new airliners rapidly dried up. Only by the late 1970s did order intake show any signs of recovery.

The BAC Three-Eleven was expected to fly for the first time in late 1973, and to enter service in 1975. It would therefore have reached the market at the worst of times, with airlines cancelling or deferring orders. This begs the question: how would BAC and the British Government have reacted to a situation where the Three-Eleven's development costs were peaking (with flight-testing, certification and initial production) while at the same time there was little or no revenue from orders and deliveries?

Indeed the Airbus consortium was faced with this very situation in the early days of Airbus A300B production (from 1975 to mid-1977), days that Airbus folklore calls the 'marketing desert'. The situation got so serious that the German Government demanded the termination of the Airbus programme. It was only due to the strong lobbying of Airbus's French chief executive, supported by French Government pleas, that the German Government agreed, reluctantly, to continue A300B production at a reduced rate of one aircraft per month. In short, the 1973 Oil Shock almost killed off the Airbus A300B and, with it, the Airbus venture.

Would the British Government have taken a similar stance to that of the French if presented with the same predicament in relation to the BAC Three-Eleven? Again, this is pure speculation, but we believe it is possible that the British Government would have allowed the programme to fold. It was only the single-minded French determination to succeed that kept both the Concorde and the Airbus programmes alive when the going got tough. Based on the British Government's past record in the sector, it would hardly have come as a surprise if it had allowed Three-Eleven production to terminate in the face of a 'marketing desert'.

Conclusions

Without strong Government backing, any of the events outlined above could potentially have killed off the BAC Three-Eleven at a later date even if it had received the go-ahead from the Conservative Government in December 1970. It is reasonable to assume that the aircraft could have survived any of the events described earlier only by way of the British Government's steadfast commitment to supporting the project and possibly also BAC itself during potentially criti-cal times. As we shall see through several examples in the next chapter, France's Government-backed ambition to retain design leadership on major civil and military aircraft encouraged its industry to abandon Pan-European consortia and to 'go it alone' when this goal could not be achieved through cooperative ven-tures. Would the British Government have shown the same resolve in the case of the Three-Eleven and its successive developments? It is difficult for us to give a definitive answer to this question, as the Heath Government did, in the end, sup-port Rolls-Royce's RB211 engine and the Concorde to completion, although in the latter's case only because the French refused the UK's request to drop the programme. However, a third major project (in the shape of the Three-Eleven) might well have proved a burden too heavy for the UK Government to bear.

1   As we shall see in the next chapter, a refined version of the Three-Eleven wing formed the basis for the evolution of the wing of the Airbus A320 single aisle aircraft in the 1980s.

2   HMG Files, 1969 and 1970.

3   In those years Boeing was evaluating a series of twins and trijets under the '767' designation. However, due to the major crisis the company faced in 1970, the definitive 767 would not emerge until 1978.

4   This total is the aggregate of Airbus A300/A310 sales (852), Boeing 757 sales (1,050) and Boeing 767 sales (950).

5   *Flight International*, 20 February 1969.

6   BAC's 'launch aid' application letter to MinTech of 25 November 1969 showed that, in the period 1951–69, BAC had sold 241 turbine-powered aircraft in North America (Viscount, Vanguard and BAC 1-11), compared with twenty sales from Sud Aviation (Caravelle), twelve from Nord Aviation (N262), nine from HSA (HS.748 and Argosy) and four from Handley Page.

7   See Charles Gardner, *British Aircraft Corporation: A History*.

8   *Ibid.*, p.173.

9   The author got confirmation of the minister's views at the time through recent private correspondence with the Right Honourable Tony Benn MP.

10 As we have seen in Chapter 2, the Plowden Committee recommended that any major aircraft projects should be carried out as a joint venture with Europe and that the UK should not carry out any new major project alone.

11 The key points are taken from British Aircraft Corporation, "The case for the BAC 3-11', October 1970.

12 BAC pointed out that it had exported 248 turbine-powered airliners to North America in the period 1950–1970 and that this total compared with only forty-five airliners exported to North America by all other UK and European manufacturers combined.

13 St John Elstub, *Productivity of the National Aircraft Effort* (London, 1969).

14 *Flight International*, 26 September 1968.

15 *Flight International*, editorial, 'Ce n'est pas la co-opération', 22 July 1970; *Flight International*, editorial, 'Two buses', 12 November 1970.

16 *Aviation Week & Space Technology*, editorial by Robert Hotz, 14 September 1970.

17 Senior insiders to the BAC Three-Eleven discussions with BEA have informed the author that support for the Three-Eleven within the airline was not unanimous. Whereas senior management like Sir Anthony Milward was definitely behind the British programme, several BEA engineers preferred an American aircraft.

18 Sir George Edwards, 'Maurice Lubbock Memorial Lecture', reproduced in *Flight International*, 16 July 1970.

19 There is consistent evidence in HMG files that several senior civil servants at MinTech
   and the MoA strongly supported the BAC Three-Eleven. One such senior official wrote
   in October 1970 that to drop the Three-Eleven 'would mean sacrificing the best chance
   of sharing in one of the world's larger growth industries over the next 20 years'. Another
   official wrote that not going ahead with the Three-Eleven would effectively imply the
   demise of the Weybridge team and would present the French with the opportunity to
   dictate the terms for collaboration on the next project. Then, he went on to say: 'we can
   hardly expect our friends across the Channel and the Atlantic to reserve a comfortable slot
   for us, and airlines generally prefer to buy from a successful manufacturer rather than from
   a Phoenix.'

20 Reported in Keith Hayward, *Government and British Civil Aerospace*.

21 *Ibid.*, p.97.

22 See Tony Benn, *Office Without Power: Diaries 1968–1972*: 'Charles Smith [Minister of State at
   the Ministry of Technology] looked in this morning about the BAC 3-11 and the RB211; I
   told him the Election was to be on 18 June and we would have to defer all decisions until
   after the Election.'

23 The difference between the lower and higher potential share for HSA depended on
   whether other European countries such as Italy and Belgium would join the Airbus
   consortium as full partners, as they were being invited to do at the time.

24 Christopher Hamshaw Thomas letter, dated 30 October 1970.

25 Strong support for the Three-Eleven at the Ministry of Aviation continued under the new
   Conservative administration. A senior civil servant in a memo to the minister, dated
   19 November 1970, wrote: 'in future years £20 million per annum of HMG investment
   will appear a puny sum to have saved against the huge market opportunities open to
   Britain in civil aircraft and the preservation of the most experienced civil aircraft design
   and sales team outside the USA.'

26 *Flight International*, 26 November 1970.

27 *Flight International*, 29 October 1970; Economic Models Ltd, 'Report on economic
   benefits to the British economy of BAC 3-11, A.300B and Lockheed L.1011 alternatives
   (econometric model)', 19 October 1970.

28 For the purpose of the study, Economic Models assumed that the Airbus A300B was a
   'foreign' plane to which the UK contributed exports. The study assumed the UK content
   of the A300B (in terms of exports) to be 20 per cent. It is worth noting how remarkably
   accurate this study was. In fact, since rejoining Airbus Industrie the UK share of Airbus
   wide-body airframes and systems has been 20 per cent!

29 An ex-BAC senior executive who acted as liaison manager with Douglas Hague of
   Economic Models at the time when the study was carried out has informed the author
   that the report showed that the BAC 3-11 project would have benefited virtually every
   industry sector under the SIC classification, and would have positively affected revenue
   and employment of British businesses in over 400 constituencies (out of a total of 630
   Parliamentary seats).

30 HMG, Ministry of Aviation files, 17 February 1970.

31 HMG, Ministry of Aviation files, SEP Draft Paper, February 1970.

32 *Ibid.*, 20 February 1970.

33 *Ibid.*, 24 February 1970.

34 *Ibid.*, 17 March 1970.

35 HMG, Ministry of Aviation files, 20 July 1970.

36 It was estimated that the BAC Three-Eleven would generate £20 million of revenue per annum for the UK's equipment suppliers, 20 per cent their total annual revenues of £100 million. HMG, MoA files, 8 October 1970.

37 HMG Files, CP (70) 25.

38 HMG, CP (70) 112. The full text of Mr Corfield's memorandum is reproduced in Appendix II.

39 The only notable dissident voice among the broad consensus in favour of a BAC Three-Eleven choice at MinTech, Ministry of Aviation, and Board of Trade was that of Chief Scientific Adviser Sir Solly Zuckerman.

40 HMG, Ministry of Aviation files, 6 March 1970.

41 Notes from conversation over dinner between Lord Delacourt-Smith, the Secretary of the Ministry of Aviation, and Lord Weinstock. HMG, MoA files, 5 February 1970.

42 The full text of Mr Corfield's statement is set out in Appendix I.

43 Mr Benn tabled a question to the Minister of Aviation asking him to disclose the economic calculations which formed the basis of the Government's decision to reject the BAC Three-Eleven. Mr Corfield replied privately to Mr Benn detailing the information on a 'commercial – in confidence' basis. From the minister's reply we can glean a better understanding of the reasons behind the decision. HMG files reveal that the following reasons were central to Government thinking:

> whatever [the MoA's] calculations may have been, the Cabinet rejected the project because it did not believe them… after all the decision on the BAC 3-11 was taken on different grounds – the size of the public investment required in relation to other calls on public funds… The BAC 3-11 would have earned a great amount of foreign exchange but at the cost of tying up a lot of scarce national resources and the risk of an unacceptable loss on the Government's investment… it is asking too much to expect projects of this size to be carried out by a small country alone… The BAC 3-11 was a promising proposal and under other circumstances – if large sums were not already committed to Concorde and if it had not been necessary to put more money into the RB.211-22 – the government might well have decided to support the BAC 3-11.

44 Charles Gardner, *British Aircraft Corporation: A History*.

45 *Flight International*, 10 December 1970.

46 *Financial Times* leader, 'Working with Europe', 3 December 1970.

47 *Daily Express* leader, 'Now – No further retreat!', 3 December 1970.

48 Countering this pessimistic assumption is the fact that BAC at that stage could rely on the strong cash flow expected from the Tornado and Jaguar programmes reaching full production, as well as the strong cash flow from the Saudi Al Jamamah support contract.

4

Civil Aircraft Developments in Europe since 1970

Introduction

The cancellation of the BAC Three-Eleven left a major hole in BAC's commercial aircraft division as far as new projects were concerned. The division was left with only two ongoing civil aircraft programmes: the BAC One-Eleven short-haul jet, whose annual sales were already down to a trickle by the early 1970s, and the joint development and production (with Aérospatiale of France) of the Concorde supersonic transport. In 1970 the latter boasted a relatively healthy provisional order book of some seventy-four options, but these soon evaporated in the aftermath of the 1973 Oil Shock. Total Concorde output was eventually limited to just twenty units (including two prototypes and two pre-production aircraft).

Hawker Siddeley, on the other hand, still had the HS.121 Trident in production, although this aircraft too was entering the twilight years of its life. Major orders from the People's Republic of China for thirty-three Trident 2Es and two 3Bs in 1972 and 1973, however, ensured that this British trijet continued in low volume production until 1978. HSA was also producing the HS.748 twin turboprop airliner, which successfully remained in production throughout the 1970s and 1980s with a grand total of 382 built. Last but not least, HSA was a major subcontractor on the A300B Airbus, designing the entire wing and producing the aircraft's wing boxes, a package equivalent to an 18 per cent share of the programme's development and manufacture.

France's Aérospatiale was without doubt the best placed of the European civil aircraft companies in terms of future prospects. In fact, in addition to co-developing the Concorde with BAC, Aérospatiale had won project leadership on the A300B Airbus wide-body twinjet. As we shall see, this was to place the French company at the very heart of European civil aircraft development, and to transform Aérospatiale's Toulouse base into Europe's main aerospace centre. However, France's other gamble in the civil arena, Dassault's Mercure twinjet 150-seat airliner, was to prove a total commercial failure, with only twelve aircraft produced between 1971 and 1975. Despite an abortive attempt in the mid-1970s to launch an 180-seat larger derivative of the Mercure (called the Mercure 200) with McDonnell Douglas and Aérospatiale, Dassault eventually exited the commercial airliner market for good and concentrated on business jets and military fighter aircraft.

Following the demise of the BAC Three-Eleven in December 1970, it became clear that any future airliner project would need to be squarely based on pan-European cooperation. The sheer cost of launching a new airliner meant that Britain, France, or any other European nation, could no longer afford a 'go it alone' approach. The only exception to this iron rule was the smaller, 70–100 seat regional jet segment of the market, where the HS.146 (later the BAe 146/Avro RJ) and the Fokker F.100/F.70 were launched as national programmes, albeit with international risk-sharing.

In the remainder of this chapter we shall analyse the key developments in European civil aerospace from the termination of the Three-Eleven project in December 1970 to the present day. These developments include the following:

The formation of the short-lived Europlane consortium by BAC, MBB, Saab, and CASA.

BAC's abortive attempts at developing larger and more advanced versions of the BAC One-Eleven twinjet.

The launch, suspension, and re-launch of Hawker Siddeley's HS.146 regional jet airliner.

The formation of the 'Group of Six' aircraft study group (later the Group of Seven), comprising Europe's leading civil aircraft developers, to evaluate the market for, and the development of, a twinjet 150-seater aircraft. The Group of Seven eventually metamorphosed into the JET study group.

Britain's decision to rejoin the Airbus consortium in 1978 as a full partner and the emergence of Airbus as Europe's only large civil aircraft producer.

Airbus's success in expanding from a single product consortium to being the supplier of an entire range of large civil aircraft, and its rise to the status of world's largest manufacturer of airliners.

Our review of the last thirty-five years of European civil aerospace will show how Britain failed to recover its leading position in Europe in the commercial aircraft sector (which it had held from the end of the Second World War up to the mid-1970s) and how France consolidated its leadership in the Airbus consortium by making it the focus of European civil aerospace. Britain did, however, retain leadership in civil aero-engine development and production through Rolls-Royce and its RB211 large turbofan family, and secured an important, if relatively junior, role in Airbus as the consortium's wing designer and manufacturer.

Notwithstanding these successes, however, it was in the wake of its exit from Airbus in 1969 and the subsequent cancellation of the Three-Eleven in 1970 that Britain missed the opportunity of playing the leading role in the consolidated European civil aerospace landscape, and was never again able to challenge France's position as large civil airliner design leader. In fact, France retained, project after project, the high-value-added roles of general aircraft definition, cockpit design, systems integration, final assembly, flight test and type certification for all Airbus aircraft. As anyone familiar with aircraft programmes will tell you, wing design and manufacture – important as they are – do not provide overall control of aircraft design and configuration.

Some readers may regard it as a moot point to suggest that the launch of the BAC Three-Eleven and its derivatives would have enabled Britain to preserve its position of European leader in large civil aircraft. Whatever the different opinions might be on the specifics, this author believes that the Three-Eleven's success in the marketplace may well have swung the pendulum towards the UK becoming the centre of European civil aircraft development and production instead of France, thus enabling the country to retain its hard-earned position in the sector. At the very least, the fact that the country would have been manufacturing a family of mainline civil aircraft at the time of its Airbus re-entry negotiations in 1978 would have resulted in the UK capturing a much larger share of the Airbus programmes (including systems integration, final assembly and flight testing) than the one it was otherwise able to negotiate from a position of weakness.

This chapter will also analyse the very different approach (compared to Britain) that France took when evaluating whether or not to participate in pan-European aerospace consortia. With examples taken from military aircraft as well as the civil aircraft segment, we shall show that France never agreed to cooperative ventures unless its industry was given project leadership. By following this highly self-interested but consistent policy, that country's aerospace industry was able not only to reach the same size as the UK industry, but also to challenge (and indeed overtake) the latter's position as the West's No.2 aerospace power.

The chapter closes with an estimate, in terms of revenues foregone, of the opportunity cost to Britain of having forfeited independent development of large mainline transport aircraft and of having a share of the Airbus joint venture which is roughly half that of France and Germany.

Europlane[1]

Now bereft of the Three-Eleven, BAC did not stand idle. After sounding out the other European aerospace companies with a view to joint development of future civil projects, in April 1972 BAC announced the incorporation at Weybridge of Europlane Ltd, a European airliner consortium tasked with studying new developments for the 1980s. Initially comprising BAC, Germany's MBB and Sweden's Saab (with equal shares of 33.33 per cent each), the consortium expanded to include Spain's CASA, and its shares were reapportioned equally among the four participants (25 per cent each). Based at Weybridge, Europlane had BAC's Alan Greenwood as chief executive and MBB's Heribert Flossdorf as technical director. Mr Flossdorf eventually was to play a key role in Airbus.

The initial studies concentrated on developments of BAC's own QTOL (Quiet Take Off and Landing) projects that had been on the drawing board for some time. Four aircraft categories were investigated, with capacities for 70, 80, 115 and 180 passengers. After further research, the partners decided to address the Boeing 737, HS Trident, DC-9, and BAC 1-11 replacement market. The project that was selected was a twin-aisle 180–200 seat aircraft, and details of this aircraft were unveiled at the 1973 Paris Air Show. The projected aircraft's basic parameters consisted of a double lobe fuselage with a diameter of 15ft 9in (4.8m), with twin-aisle seven-abreast seating (consisting of a two-three-two arrangement) for 191 passengers at 34in pitch, or a maximum of 219 seats. Powered by either two Rolls-Royce RB211 or GE CF-6-50 engines, Europlane had a range of 1,500–2,300 miles, with a take-off field length of 5,900ft (1,800m). The aircraft was designed from the outset to minimise noise footprint, being at least 10EPNdb quieter than the FAR Part 36 requirements. The engine choice would have enabled the aircraft to grow in size to 260–270 seats, or to have an increased range for the datum passenger load, by 1984.

BAC expected that full go-ahead would be given by mid-1974, with service entry slotted for 1979. Total launch costs were estimated at £180–200 million, and BAC envisaged break-even sales of some 350 units. Unit price was set at £5.3 million.

Europlane's basic configuration and general lines bore a striking resemblance to the BAC Three-Eleven, only slightly smaller in size, the main difference (apart from size) being the positioning of the rear engines. These were raised up from the fuselage on pylons in a V-shape, shielding forward noise by using the wing, the fuselage to mask downward directed noise and reducing rearward arc noise by acoustic treatment and full-length cowls. The arrangement also allowed for the addition of fuselage plugs without upsetting the position of the engines relative to the wings. The latter benefited from the advanced aerodynamics research that had gone into the stillborn Three-Eleven.

Table 4.1 Europlane key data

Overall length	48m
Fuselage length	42.5m
Wing span	38m
Wing area	192m²
Maximum take-off weight	110,000kg
Maximum payload	21,000kg
Take-off run (800km range)	1,200m
Take-off run (3,700km range)	1,700m
Passenger capacity	
Standard	191 at 34in pitch
High density	219
Stretched versions	260–270
Powerplants	2 x RR RB211 or GE CF-6 high bypass turbo-fans of 40,000lb (18,200kg) each

(Source: *Flight International*, 16 August 1972)

In many respects Europlane was a return to the original BAC Two-Eleven project of 1967, although it benefited from several more years of technological development and from a 'wide-body' fuselage. If launched, it would have competed with the subsequent Boeing offerings – the 757 and, in its stretched version, the 767. Europlane would have also been a competitor to Airbus's A310, the shortened version of the A300B launched in 1978. There is little doubt that, with BAC's pedigree in civil aircraft production, combined with the technical and financial muscle of MBB, Saab and CASA, Europlane would have been a fine aircraft, and would have achieved significant commercial success. As it happened, two factors contributed to Europlane's demise – the 1973 Oil Crisis and the subsequent worldwide economic recession (which hit the air transport industry particularly hard), and MBB's position as a key partner in the Airbus Industrie consortium. The latter situation meant not only that MBB was deeply committed financially to the A300B, but also that it found itself in a conflict of interest position when it came to launching the A300's smaller derivative, the A310. Europlane and A310 would have been direct competitors in the same way that the Three-Eleven would have provided direct competition to the A300B. In the end, the commitment of MBB and the German Government to their alliance with the French and to Airbus Industrie as the permanent European civil aerospace vehicle, won the day. It must also be said in all fairness that, at the time at least, Airbus had an aircraft about to enter airline service in the shape of the A300B, whereas the BAC-led Europlane consortium only had a paper aircraft.

By September 1973 the Europlane partners put the project in abeyance for a possible review in six months' time. This effectively put an end to the programme.

BAC One-Eleven Proposed Developments

While the Two-Eleven, Three-Eleven and Europlane sagas were winding their course, BAC studied a number of advanced, higher-capacity variants of its base-line short-haul twinjet BAC One-Eleven. The appearance in the marketplace of the Boeing 737 and the continuous development of the original Douglas DC-9 into higher-capacity versions were the spur for the BAC studies. Alas, for a variety of reasons, the principal of which was the bankruptcy of Rolls-Royce in 1971, none of these proposed developments ever saw the light of day. This sadly led to the One-Eleven being marginalised in the market place, to the point that the short/medium-haul twinjet market became a two-horse race between the Boeing 737 and the McDonnell Douglas DC-9/MD-80 series. Only the appearance of the Airbus A320 in the late 1980s allowed Europe (and indirectly Britain) to recover the lost ground. Again an excellent opportunity for Britain to capital-ise on the One-Eleven's early successes was missed.

The first proposed development of the One-Eleven emerged in 1967 and was dubbed the Series 600 (incidentally the first One-Eleven stretch, the '500', first flew in 1967). The One-Eleven 600 would have been some 3.6 metres longer than the series 500, increasing passenger capacity by about ten to 130 seats in high-density layout. Wingspan was also increased by 3m, and the powerplant was to be the 'aft-fan' Rolls-Royce Spey with a bypass ratio of 4:1 and thrust of 17,350lb (7,900kg).

The One-Eleven Series 700 was proposed in 1974. This again was a stretched, more advanced development of the Series 500. Fuselage length was to be increased by 12ft (3.65m), allowing maximum seating capacity to increase from 119 to 134 in a 'wide-body look' cabin. Power was to be provided by two new higher-bypass-ratio Rolls-Royce Spey 67C turbofans, each rated at 16,900lb (7,700kg). The Series 700's maximum range would have been 2,300 miles and the aircraft would have had 6 per cent better specific fuel consumption in the cruise than the Series 500. Maximum take-off weight was estimated at 117,000lb (53,200kg).

The Series 700 proposal was followed in 1975 by the larger Series 800 vari-ant. The Series 800 fuselage was some 32ft 6in (9.75m) longer than the Series 500, allowing capacity to be increased to 144–161 passengers. Power was to be provided by two new GE/SNECMA CFM-56 turbofans of 22,000lb (10,000kg) thrust each. Wingspan was also increased by 10ft (3.04m) over that of the Series 500. The maximum take-off weight was increased to 137,000lb (62,200kg) and maximum range to 2,400 miles. The BAC One-Eleven Series 800 was put for-ward by BAC as one of the proposals to be studied by the so-called 'Group of Seven' team (see relevant paragraph further on).

HS.146 and BAe 146

HSA was keen to retain a complete civil aircraft development capability to complement its Airbus work and to provide a successor to the Trident on the Hatfield production line. After several studies of feeder-liner jets dating back to the early 1960s, Hawker Siddeley settled on a high-wing, four-engine regional jet design powered by American Avco Lycoming ALF-502 turbofans. Dubbed the HS.146 (the 146th design from de Havilland at Hatfield), the project's definition phase was started in 1971. By August 1973 Hawker Siddeley and the British Government had agreed on a launch aid package for the aircraft whereby the Government would undertake the financing of 50 per cent of the project's non-recurring costs, with HSA covering the balance and undertaking to carry any cost overruns. The HS.146 emerged as a short take-off and landing (STOL), very quiet, regional jet, to be developed in two versions, an eighty-seater and a 100-seater. First flight was scheduled for 1975 and entry into service for 1977.

At the time the German-Dutch company VFW-Fokker protested and filed complaints in Brussels against the British Government's backing of the HS.146, which it saw as a direct competitor to its own Fokker F.28 and VFW.614 regional jetliners. VFW-Fokker argued that no EEC member state should launch a 'go it alone' aircraft when there were already similar European products in the market, and that in any case such aircraft project should be carried out on a European joint venture basis. However, the British Government and Hawker Siddeley stuck to their guns, countering that there was enough room in the market for a new aircraft, and that – save for larger and more complex projects like Concorde and Airbus – European cooperation was not necessarily the most efficient way to develop a civil aircraft.

Little more than a year after agreeing the launch aid package with the Government, in the autumn of 1974 HSA decided to terminate the HS.146 project unilaterally, on the grounds that the severe recession in the airline industry in the wake of the 1973 Oil Crisis had made the project no longer economically viable. However, after much lobbying by the trade unions and at the behest of the Minister of Technology, Tony Benn, it was decided that low-key design and development of the HS.146 would continue with Government backing, with a view to the project being reassessed at a later date by a new nationalised aircraft corporation. At this stage the Labour Party had returned to power and had pledged to nationalise the aircraft and guided weapon interests of BAC and Hawker Siddeley.

Eventually, in the summer of 1978 the newly formed British Aerospace decided to re-launch the HS.146 as the BAe 146 and obtained Government approval to do so in July 1978. The first BAe 146 was rolled out in May 1981 and first flew on 3 September 1981. It was the first new British jet airliner to fly in over eighteen years (the last having been the BAC One-Eleven in 1963).

Developed in three variants with different fuselage lengths (the 'roo' with capacity for 74–93 passengers, the '200' with 85–112 passenger capacity and the '300' able to carry between 100 and 128 passengers), the BAe 146 at first struggled in the marketplace, but then established itself and achieved good market penetration, especially after the early problems with its Lycoming ALF-502 engines were fixed and the new improved Avro RJ Series was introduced in 1993. However, the BAe 146 never made any money for British Aerospace and actually very nearly managed to bring down the whole group in 1992. This was the result of a commercial policy in the early days of the programme of leasing the aircraft to small, financially unstable regional airlines, whilst BAe retained the recourse obligation. The result was a £1.2 billion write-off of leasing obligations in BAe's balance sheet, and the company's near-collapse.

In the end total BAe 146/Avro RJ production reached 394, of which 390 were delivered to over sixty operators worldwide. The aircraft operated with the regional subsidiaries of major carriers such as United Airlines, Northwest, Air China, Air France, Alitalia, KLM, Lufthansa, Qantas, Swiss Airlines and Sabena, and was Britain's most numerically successful jetliner ever, and the country's second most successful airliner after the Vickers Viscount.

Unfortunately, in the wake of 11 September 2001, BAE SYSTEMS decided to terminate the development of the third generation of the BAe 146, the Avro RJX. This spelt the end of airliner production in the UK, symbolically not the proudest of moments for the country that had introduced turbine-powered airliners (both turboprop and jet) to the world.

The Group of Seven and JET[2]

In September 1974, at the Farnborough Air Show, the major European civil aircraft manufacturers announced the formation of the Group of Six (BAC, HSA, Aérospatiale, MBB, Fokker-VFW and Dornier) to study the market and the specifications for a 130–150-seat twinjet airliner that would compete in the marketplace with the Boeing 737 and Douglas DC-9 derivatives, as well as replace the various Boeing 727s, Caravelles, HS Tridents and BAC One-Elevens. In March 1975 Dassault-Breguet joined the team and the group was re-christened the 'Group of Seven'. Both derivative and new designs were proposed, based on the work that had been carried out by the individual manufacturers.

Amongst the new designs being evaluated were: Aérospatiale's AS.200 twinjet; several concepts studied by BAC at Weybridge in the mid-1970s under a UK Government-sponsored research programme; a number of single-aisle projects in the 150–190 seat bracket put forward by CAST (Civil Aircraft Study Team), a consortium formed by Hawker Siddeley, VFW-Fokker and Dornier with design offices at Hatfield and Bremen.

The general configurations of the Aérospatiale AS.200 and of the most conventional among the BAC Weybridge and CAST concepts were very similar, with two 10-ton engines mounted on pylons under the wing – in essence, a single-aisle equivalent of the Airbus A300B.

The derivative designs comprised four separate entries: BAC's One-Eleven Series 800 (described earlier), the Hawker Siddeley Trident 4 and Trident 5, and the Dassault Mercure 200. The Trident 4 was a three-engined stretch of the Trident 3, seating 180 passengers and powered by more powerful Rolls-Royce Spey engines, whereas the Trident 5 was a twin-engined 150-seat Trident development powered by two 10-ton engines and with a redesigned wing of 23° sweep as opposed to the original 35° sweep wing of the Trident. The Mercure 200 was instead a stretched, re-engined version of the original Mercure with capacity increased to 180 passengers and with greater range (the short range of the original aircraft was the main reason for its abysmal market performance).

In the end the Group of Seven decided to concentrate their studies on a derivative design, and the Mercure 200 was chosen as the preferred baseline design, leading BAC and HSA to drop their respective derivative proposals. Dassault therefore became project leader within the Group of Seven. At the time the specialist press reported that both BAC and HSA did not object to the Mercure 200 being the basis for the new pan-European 150-seater and that they accepted in principle French design leadership on the two new European civil subsonic jetliners (the A300-B10 and the Mercure 200).[3] The British groups' statements clearly seem to suggest that Britain's main civil players were by then demoralised and crestfallen. Aware of their Government's lukewarm attitude to launching new civil aircraft, they were prepared to play second fiddle to France as a means of getting at least some share of the action. On technical grounds the British teams, and HSA in particular, recognised the Mercure 200's superior six-abreast cabin cross-section (wider than either the Trident's or the One-Eleven's cabins) and general arrangement.

However, the Group of Seven eventually dispersed to be replaced by a new consortium called JET (for Joint European Transport). The Mercure 200 never saw the light of day, despite French attempts to keep it alive by forming a joint venture with McDonnell Douglas of the US and with other European companies. The plan was that Dassault would be the design leader with a 5 per cent stake in a joint venture, with Aérospatiale taking a 40 per cent stake with responsibility for final assembly and flight test, and McDonnell Douglas taking a 15 per cent share. The remaining 40 per cent industrial share would be available to other interested European parties. However, this French-led plan came to nothing and, as a consequence, Dassault exited the civil aircraft business for good.

The JET consortium which inherited the work done by the Group of Seven was established in June 1977 by the then Airbus partners Aérospatiale, MBB and VFW-Fokker, together with the newly formed British Aerospace, which had resulted from the combination and nationalisation in April 1977 of BAC, Hawker Siddeley Aviation, Hawker Siddeley Dynamics and Scottish Aviation. British Aerospace was invited to join by reason of the important role that HSA played in the A300B programme and because BAC itself had substantial expertise in civil aircraft design. The Joint Engineering Team of JET was based at BAC's Weybridge facility and was headed by HSA's Derek Brown.

In addition to studying all-new designs (of which more further on) the JET consortium seriously evaluated a new proposal from BAC, the derivative BAC X-Eleven. First proposed in the summer of 1976, the X-Eleven was again a further development of the One-Eleven Series 800, but this time the aircraft was given a wider six-abreast cabin of 143in (3.63m) in width. The X-Eleven would have shared about 40 per cent of its components with the One-Eleven, including the nose and rear fuselage sections, together with scaled-up wings, fin and tail-plane. Three versions of the X-Eleven were planned, the Series 100 with capacity for 130 passengers, the Series 200 (baseline aircraft) with 144 passenger capacity and the Series 300 for 156 passengers.

Table 4.2 BAC X-Eleven data (baseline aircraft)

Overall length	132ft 2in (40.30m)
Wing span	106ft 2in (32.36m)
Overall height	28ft 6in (8.69m)
Maximum take off weight	140,000lb (63,520kg)
Maximum range	2,300 miles (4,270km)
Powerplant	2 x CFM-56 turbofans of 22,000lb (10,000kg) thrust each
Powerplant –alternative	2 x P&W JT10D turbofans of 22,000lb (10,000kg) thrust each

Source: Richard Anthony Payne, 'Paper Planes' (*Air Pictorial*, November 1998)

BAC was predicting a break-even figure for the X-Eleven of 400 units, based on a go-ahead in the second half of 1977. British Airways, Lufthansa, Bavaria, American Airlines and South African Airways expressed considerable interest in the X-Eleven proposal, and BAC put the project forward to the HSA board for consideration in early 1977 in advance of the nationalisation of the two companies. HSA expressed doubts about the X-Eleven's attractiveness, preferring the Mercure 200 or any similar project, such as the Aérospatiale AS.200. Despite strong market interest in the BAC X-Eleven, which would have provided the aircraft with a sound launch base of prestigious customers, the JET partners, other than BAC, were not at all keen on a derivative aircraft.

Having discarded the X-Eleven, the multinational engineering team at Weybridge concentrated on an all-new design that drew strong inspiration from 'proof of concept' work done by BAC at Weybridge in the early 1970s and from the Aérospatiale AS.200 proposal.

Apart from the X-Eleven proposal, BAC Weybridge had studied all-new 150-seat designs in the early 1970s. These concepts had their origin in the joint company/Government-funded R/STOL (Reduced/Short Take Off and Landing) aircraft studies which started in the UK in 1972 and continued with the CTOL (Conventional Take Off and Landing) contract well into 1976.[4] For the overall design studies sequential numbers were given to each configuration, and the under-wing-mounted, twin CFM-56-engined aircraft was known as 'Aircraft 36' and was developed to a fairly detailed level. The final iteration of Aircraft 36 resulted in a twin-engined airliner with 145 seats at 34in pitch and a 23° swept wing. Aircraft 36 shows a remarkable configuration similarity to the definitive Airbus A320, the main difference being in fuselage cross-section, with Aircraft 36 having a double-bubble shape capable of taking full LD3 containers, while the A320 has a more nearly circular fuselage which gives a higher standard of passenger accommodation with the ability to accept cut-down LD3 containers below the cabin floor.

Using the Aérospatiale AS.200 and BAC's Aircraft 36 as blueprints, the JET team at Weybridge eventually designed two versions of a twin-engined transport with underwing-mounted CFM-56s: the JET 1 (150 seats – baseline aircraft) and JET 2 (180 seats).

Given France and Germany's commitment to Airbus Industrie as the permanent vehicle for European civil aircraft development, it was felt that the only route by which the JET aircraft could proceed was to sell the concept to Airbus, so the JET team arranged to present the proposals to them. Initially Airbus saw the aircraft as narrow-bodied and this did not fit their marketing image. The JET team eventually came up with the idea of single-aisle (SA) and twin-aisle (TA) aircraft, to distinguish between the JET project (SA) and the traditional Airbus wide-bodies A300 and A310 and their developments (TA). This nomenclature was accepted by Airbus at the presentation of the JET aircraft. The JET designs became SA1 and SA2, and the larger Airbus projects became TA9 (A330) and TA11 (A340).

A single-aisle engineering team was set up in the old airport terminal buildings at Toulouse, which over time became integrated with the main Airbus project office. Before proceeding too far with the SA projects, a limited marketing exercise was carried out in the USA and this, in addition to a meeting between Roger Beteille of Airbus, André Bord of Aérospatiale, and Roger Back of BAC (now BAe), led to an agreement to proceed with an aircraft midway between the SA1 and SA2, called internally the SA150. The original fuselage cross-section of the JET designs was modified to accommodate a cut-down LD3 container (20in off the top of a standard container) and an increase of 1in in each seat width and the aisle width. The latest BAe-designed wing iteration of the BAC Aircraft 36 with increased rear spar depth was also incorporated and the aircraft was eventually launched as the Airbus A320 (see further on for a full description of this aircraft).

With the shelving of the X-Eleven and the transfer of the JET project from its Weybridge base to Airbus in Toulouse, BAC/British Aerospace effectively ceded project leadership to Aérospatiale and to France on the European 'single-aisle' 150-seater, and accepted a subordinate role in the development of large civil aircraft. Thus the reversal of roles in civil aircraft between Europe's two leading aerospace industries, begun when the British Government decided not to support the BAC Three-Eleven, was confirmed once and for all with Britain's agreement to back France's project leadership on Europe's next mainline civil aircraft. In addition France retained leadership of the Airbus family of wide-bodies that were spawned from the original Airbus A300B.[5]

Ironically, it was during this very period of the early 1970s that Government ministers in charge of aerospace and aerospace industry leaders alike, woke up to the fact that Britain was losing the plot in the commercial airliner segment. In fact Michael Heseltine, Conservative Minister for Aerospace and Shipping, was to make the following comments at the *Financial Times* Aerospace Conference which preceded the 1973 Paris Air Show: 'It is unfortunately the case that the UK [aero-space] industry, one of the two major industries in Europe, is in the unenviable position of having no significant subsonic [civil aircraft] project. This is obviously bad for the UK, but is equally disturbing from the European point of view. It is not a situation which we can continue to accept.'[6] It was a bit rich and highly ironic that such a statement, albeit true, should come from the Aerospace Minister of the very same Government that, in December 1970, had refused launch aid for the BAC Three-Eleven airliner, thus precipitating the predicament that Mr Heseltine was referring to. But it is a known fact that British Governments and their min-isters come to power with an ingrained antipathy, or at best indifference, towards the aerospace sector, only to understand the high-tech content, excitement, and important contribution of this industry to the nation's economy when they have been in office for a long time, and are about to be voted out of office by the British electorate. Unfortunately for the British aircraft industry, Governments and ministers who had just started their terms in office were responsible for most of the deleterious decisions that caused the cancellation of major programmes.

Following Mr Heseltine's comments, a month or so later Mr Sisson, president of the SBAC, referred to the 'Tail-end Charlie' role played by UK aerospace in all the European Joint Venture programmes:[7]

> ...in musical terms, as I am sure the Prime Minister [Ted Heath] will clearly under-stand,[8] there is a frustration in always playing the second violin... And so the time has come when the British aerospace industry must take the lead, because to become an emasculated appendage of the French aerospace industry does not feature in our forward planning...

Unfortunately, the realisation, on the part of the country's decision-makers, that Britain had given away more than it had received in the European aerospace joint-ventures in which it participated, came too late to change the new status quo, at least as far as civil aerospace was concerned. The horse had already bolted, and trying to close that particular stable door was ineffectual. Through the establishment of Airbus Industrie with the Germans in 1970, France had wrested leadership of commercial aircraft development from Britain. Through its A300B wide-body twinjet airliner, Airbus Industrie had the most modern and competitive European subsonic jet transport in production and was beginning to gain market share from the Americans. Apart from HSA's participation in Airbus as supplier of the A300B's wings, Britain had no new large airliner in production, only paper proposals relating to developments of its long-standing One-Eleven and Trident jetliners. It came as no surprise, therefore, that France asserted herself when it came to the next major European project and that Airbus Industrie was the chosen vehicle to develop and produce the new 150-seater European twinjet airliner.

To the dejected and emasculated newly formed British Aerospace, the only future alternatives for its commercial aircraft business were either to rejoin Airbus Industrie as a full partner or to find some sort of partnership agreement with the American giants Boeing or McDonnell Douglas. We now turn our attention to these fundamental choices.

Britain Rejoins Airbus Industrie

The most pressing decisions for the nationalised corporation British Aerospace were in connection with its commercial aircraft business. The military side of the business was quite healthy: the Panavia Tornado multi-role aircraft was in full production, the Sepecat Jaguar ground attack and close support fighter was rolling off the assembly lines in quantity for the British, French and overseas air forces, and the Harrier/AV-8B and Hawk military aircraft also boasted healthy order books. The same was true for the combined guided weapons divisions of BAe, and to a lesser degree for its satellite and communications business. In addition BAe had a lucrative military support contract with Saudi Arabia.

The company's civil aircraft business was in a far less happy state. Production of the Concorde supersonic airliner would terminate with the delivery of the sixteenth production example in early 1979, after an agreement had been reached with France in 1974 not to proceed beyond sixteen production aircraft (divided equally between Aérospatiale at Toulouse and BAe/BAC at Filton, Bristol). The BAC One-Eleven twinjet airliner was nearing the end of its life, with little prospect of further major orders: indeed, only about twenty-five new One-Elevens (including the Romanian-assembled Rombac aircraft) were produced after the incorporation of British Aerospace. The same situation applied to the HS Trident trijet: the last order from China was taken in 1973, and by 1977 Hawker Siddeley had stopped direct marketing of the aircraft. Trident production would end in July 1978. The only bright spots within civil aircraft were the HS.748 twin-turboprop, which continued to sell steadily albeit in small numbers, and the HS.125 business jet, which still boasted a healthy order backlog.

As the management of the former BAC elected to concentrate on the profitable military aircraft and guided weapons businesses, it was decided to give overall responsibility for the civil aircraft side of the business to the ex-HSA management. Therefore the new BAe Board's decisions in terms of future civil projects came down in favour of launching the HS.146 regional jet as a 'go it alone' venture and of coming to some joint partnership agreement with either Airbus Industrie or the Americans as far as larger aircraft (upwards of 100 seats) were concerned. The BAe Board recognised that to launch a Three-Eleven or Airbus A300B Class large airliner would be far too expensive and risky to contemplate alone.

As early as 1976 (one year before the formation of British Aerospace) there had been informal meetings between Lord Beswick, BAe chairman designate, and General Jacques Mitterand, Aérospatiale's top man, to explore the shape of BAe's relationship with Airbus going forward. Talks ranged from the idea that BAe would continue as a privileged subcontractor on the wings to the possibility of rejoining AI as a full partner. Any firm decision, however, had to be postponed until the formation of the corporation.

The discussions and negotiations that eventually brought the civil airframe business of BAe back into the Airbus fold as a full partner were long, drawn out, difficult and politically sensitive, and were to take over one year to complete. The political sensitivity of the choice meant that Britain's then Prime Minister, Labour's James Callaghan, was directly involved in the discussions. For the purpose of this chapter we shall not rehearse in detail the dilemmas faced by British industry and HMG in choosing between a transatlantic alliance (notably with Boeing of the US) and Europe (represented by Airbus and its backers France and Germany).[9]

Simply put, British Aerospace had two realistic alternative choices at its disposal in terms of partnership on large civil aircraft. The first option was for BAe to formally rejoin the Airbus Industrie consortium as a full partner. BAe's Hawker Siddeley division was then designing and manufacturing the A300B's wings as a major subcontractor. The second option was for BAe to join Boeing in the development of the latter's 757 twinjet (a single-aisle replacement for the Boeing 727) which was to be powered by two high-bypass turbofans. A third, but much more nebulous, option was for BAe, McDonnell Douglas and Airbus to collaborate on a totally new mid-range mid-capacity twin. This third option, favoured in many respects by Prime Minister Callaghan, never really looked realistic.

The Airbus camp had the full political backing of the President of France, Giscard d'Estaing, and of the German Chancellor, Helmut Schmidt, as well as the support of the British Foreign Office and of the British ambassador in Paris, Sir Nicholas Henderson.

The Boeing proposal, on the other hand, was cleverly crafted: not only was British Airways, the UK's flag carrier, keen to order the Boeing 757 aircraft (with its twin-engined 180–220 seat capacity the 757 was in the same class as the still-born BAC Two-Eleven), but also the initial version of the aircraft (for BA and Eastern Airlines) was to be powered by Rolls-Royce's new RB211-535 turbofan, an advanced, reduced-thrust version of the original RB211. In addition Boeing was offering BAe the contract to design and manufacture the 757's wings, in this instance acknowledging Hawker Siddeley's advanced wing expertise as demonstrated in its work for the A300B. Therefore, from the start Boeing had the backing of two of Britain's premier civil aviation corporations (BA and Rolls-Royce), as well as the support of many Government departments, senior ministers and civil servants, especially in the Treasury. Many senior officials thought that the Boeing proposal had a far better chance of market success than any partnership with Airbus. They also believed that a transatlantic partnership with Boeing had the additional advantage of helping BAe achieve greater manufacturing efficiency and cost-effectiveness. Indeed, BAe's productivity at the time was not as good as Boeing's.

The British Aerospace Board was far less enthusiastic about the 757 and more suspicious of Boeing's intentions, feeling (correctly as it emerged later) that Boeing saw British industry merely as a subcontractor.[10] Boeing improved its offer to BAe on the 757 by suggesting that the British corporation would get further work on the empennage of the aircraft and some final assembly work, but at no stage was it prepared to form a partnership or joint-venture company with BAe to develop the 757. Indeed, Boeing's proposals left the British with no say in the marketing, systems integration and flight-testing functions. Moreover the Boeing fixed-price contract proposal on the 757 wings left little or no scope for cost inflation, thus subjecting BAe to the risk of losing money on the deal. As one senior BAe executive said at the time: 'They [Boeing] expect us to do all the clever bits on the aircraft and take all the risks, whilst they keep control of all the value-added processes.' In addition, Boeing was not in a position to guarantee any further collaboration beyond the 757. BAe soon came to the conclusion that a full partnership with Airbus Industrie offered a more secure future, a more senior role in the development of the aircraft and the preservation of the company's civil aircraft expertise.

After a meeting with Boeing's senior management in the US, James Callaghan himself developed an antipathy to what he perceived to be Boeing's condescension towards the British. He was reported as saying that, during his meeting with Tex Boullion and T. Wilson of Boeing, he felt as though he was 'talked down to' and that the Boeing chiefs treated the British delegation as 'representatives of an underdeveloped country'. Regardless of Callaghan's sensitivities in connection with Boeing's blunt style in the discussions, it was evident that Boeing saw BAe as a mere subcontractor, no more. As Matthew Lynn acutely points out in his book: 'Despite the best efforts of a powerful lobby within the [UK] commercial and political establishment, the British were not quite far enough along the curve of decline to accept serfdom as the best they could shoot for.'[11]

During his sojourn in the US, Callaghan also met with Eastern Airlines' chairman Frank Borman. Borman was happy to tell Callaghan that the Airbus A300Bs in his fleet were turning out to be very reliable and economical. This news was a pleasant surprise for Callaghan, and as a consequence he and the Cabinet warmed towards BAe rejoining Airbus Industrie, as the corporation's Board itself wished.

However, the Airbus partners (the French in particular) set down some conditions for Britain to rejoin the consortium, the principal of which were that the British Government should pay an entry fee of £200 million as a contribution towards A300B sunk development costs, and that British Airways should order a sizeable number of A300Bs or the new A310s to underpin Britain's commitment to the European aircraft. Of the various conditions, that of the 'forced' British Airways order was totally unacceptable to the British Government, which made it clear to the French that a UK Government could not overrule the independence of the corporation's Board in terms of commercial policy decisions. This the *dirigiste* French Government could not understand, as in France all of the state's corporations pull in unison in the same direction, for the greater benefit of the country: it was a given, therefore, that Air France would order the Airbus products.

All this haggling, intrigue and international horse-trading came to a head in the summer of 1978, when in July 1978 the French and the Germans decided to launch the derivative Airbus A310 'with or without the involvement of the UK'. At the same time the British Government approved British Airways' purchase of nineteen Boeing 757s powered by Rolls-Royce RB211-535s. Eastern Airlines' order for an additional twenty-one RR-powered 757s effectively launched the Boeing programme. In the same announcement by Trade and Industry Minister Eric Varley, the British Government authorised British Aerospace to complete negotiations for joining Airbus Industrie as a full partner.

The approval of the British Airways order for Boeing 757s incensed the French. Apart from the fact that the 757 was regarded as a direct competitor to Airbus's new A310, the French resented the fact that *Perfide Albion* wanted to have its cake and eat it by reaching a compromise that would indeed please all of the UK's big three aviation companies (BA, BAe and RR) but would also fatally weaken Europe's attempts through Airbus to build a durable competitor to the USA's stranglehold in civil aerospace. France, from President Giscard d'Estaing down, dug their heels in and issued an ultimatum: either there was a British Airways order for the Airbus or there was no deal for BAe.

Two concomitant events were to solve this impasse between Britain and France. The first was Airbus's failure to find a credible alternative source of wings for the new A310: despite the attempts to develop a German-French wing at Bremen, the best expertise in Europe as far as wing design was concerned still lay in Britain. Secondly, Sir Freddie Laker, chairman of British independent carrier Laker Airways, decided to order ten Airbus A300B4s to operate on a number of new medium-haul routes. In the end, Laker's order turned out to be providential, enabling the French to 'save face' by portraying the Laker deal as a British airline order, while allowing BA to stick to its choice of Boeing 757s. The British Government did also soothe French feelings by issuing a statement that BA may order A300Bs or A310s in the future if such aircraft were required in its fleet expansion plans. In fact, no A300s or A310s ever saw service with BA.

Tellingly, Sir Freddie Laker himself did not take too kindly to having to order Airbus A300Bs. In a press statement, Laker said: 'It's a terrible indictment that I'm having to buy a new aircraft built abroad which could have easily been supplied instead by British industry.' This statement was clearly a veiled reference to the stillborn BAC Three-Eleven project, the all-British alternative to the A300B that Laker, together with BEA, had supported to the hilt, only to see it killed by the British Government's refusal to support it financially. However, Mr Laker should have pointed out that the A300B was *at least partly* built in Britain (wings and fuel systems).

The Laker deal finally paved the way for British Aerospace to rejoin Airbus Industrie as a full partner. BAe was given a 20 per cent share in the consortium (thus reducing Aérospatiale's and Deutsche Airbus's holdings to 37.9 per cent each, while CASA's shareholding remained fixed at 4.2 per cent) and full Board representation. The qualified majority for Board decisions was raised from 75 to 80 per cent, in order to protect Airbus's two smaller shareholders, BAe and CASA, against collusion of the two main shareholders Aérospatiale and Deutsche Airbus. The British Government also agreed to contribute £50 million towards Airbus's marketing and launch costs, a compromise between the £200 million requested by the French and the £25 million initially offered by Britain. With effect from 1 January 1979, BAe became a full partner of Airbus Industrie.

The 1978 Airbus agreement concluded the long drawn-out saga of Britain's place in large civil aircraft manufacture. A long period of uncertainty for the UK civil airframe industry had started in 1969, when Britain withdrew from the original Airbus accord, and continued with the cancellation of the BAC Three-Eleven in December 1970. These two highly damaging decisions left a void that was only partially filled in 1978.

The 20 per cent share agreed in 1978 was about half the 37.5 per cent stake that Britain (via HSA) originally had in the consortium. It equated to slightly more than the manufacturing share that Hawker Siddeley had been able to negotiate as a private subcontractor in July 1969 and basically corresponded to the man-hours involved in the design and manufacture of the wing box (excluding the secondary structure and the moving surfaces such as flaps and slats). In the end the much-reduced share of the Airbus programmes that was given to Britain reflected the cost of the missed opportunities which had resulted from first withdrawing from Airbus in 1969 and then refusing to support the BAC Three-Eleven at the end of 1970. By 1978 the French and German-backed Airbus consortium had a fully operational large jetliner in service (the A300B) and were developing its advanced derivative, the A310. Why should these two countries, which had incurred massive start-up and development costs with the A300B, give away an equal share of the project to Britain, which had basically 'piggy-backed' for ten years by staying outside the consortium and by getting 60 per cent of its reduced share funded by Germany?

We also need to bear in mind two other important factors in relation to the smaller share accorded to Britain in Airbus. The first was the diminished status, and much weaker political leverage, of BAC Weybridge within the corporation. As we saw in the previous chapter, the loss of the BAC Three-Eleven in 1970 started a process of marginalisation of Weybridge and civil aircraft within BAC/BAe at a time when military aircraft at Warton were emerging as the rising star, with key programmes such as the Tornado, Jaguar, and the Saudi support contract. Therefore, by 1978 the former BAC management saw military aircraft and systems as its core business, as this activity, unlike civil aircraft, guaranteed almost 'risk-free' profits to BAe (this was before the days of 'smart procurement' policies, now commonplace in the MoD). At this point in time, Weybridge's voice was too marginal, both within the corporation and in Government circles, to support a BAe civil aircraft claim to a dominant role within Airbus. Therefore, as we highlighted earlier, the chickens hatched with the 1970 cancellation of the Three-Eleven had by 1978 come home to roost!

The second important factor related to with risk-taking and investment allocation assessment by senior people both within the newly formed British Aerospace Corporation and in the British Government (particularly in the Treasury). Civil aircraft development and manufacture, unlike military procurement, was perceived to be a high-risk business: any dominant share of the Airbus project for the UK would have implied the allocation of substantial funds by the corporation and by the British Government to projects whose future market prospects were still uncertain (by 1978 the A300B's sales were in the region of only 150 units and the days when Airbus would emerge as a serious competitor to Boeing were still far off).

In the end the British civil aerospace industry paid the ultimate price for short-term, risk-averse, myopic decisions by its leaders and political muddling by Government in civil aerospace policy. The price was the loss of large airliner design leadership to France and a junior position within Airbus.

On completion of the negotiations concerning the BA order for Rolls-Royce-powered Boeing 757s and BAe's re-entry into Airbus Industrie, British Prime Minister James Callaghan expressed great satisfaction as to the outcome achieved by the government. In fairness to the British government, it did achieve the goal of meeting the wishes of all three major corporations concerned and of exposing the British aerospace industry to both the US and European industries and markets. Tellingly, however, Callaghan made it quite clear as to whose company's future the Government had given its best energies: 'Rolls-Royce was the national asset we had to preserve, which meant that establishing it in the US market was the central consideration.' Unlike Rolls-Royce, the emasculated and demoralised British civil airframe industry was bereft of a major autonomous civil airliner programme or of a major share in the increasingly successful Airbus project, and found itself in a much weaker bargaining position. The British dislike for high-risk, long-term investment propositions, both at industry and at Government level, also played a key part in the scaling down of British ambitions in civil aircraft production. The industry was therefore left to agree a deal with the French and Germans that just about saved its collective face and honour.[12]

The Rise of Airbus

Following the substantial Eastern Airlines order for Airbus A300B4s in the spring of 1978, Airbus Industrie started an ascendancy in the world of civil aircraft manufacture that was to see it overtake Boeing of the US as the world's largest airliner manufacturer twenty-five years later.[13] The year 1978 also proved to be significant in two other respects:

The launch of the shorter fuselage derivative of the A300B, the A310; and Britain's decision to rejoin the consortium as a full partner.

The latter development meant that Europe's top three aerospace industries (France, Britain and Germany) were now firmly behind Airbus. Europe's fourth largest industry – that of Italy – continued instead to work as a subcontractor and risk-sharing partner with the US industry.

The original Airbus A300B was further developed with the introduction of the 600 and 600R Series, which benefited from improvements introduced with the A310. As a consequence, the A300's sales eventually overtook those of the BAC One-Eleven, the Sud Aviation Caravelle, and the Vickers Viscount, to become Europe's most successful airliner before the appearance of the Airbus A320 (total sales to date of all A300 models are 592)[14] and the first Airbus model is still in production in its freighter guise.

  The Airbus A310 derivative introduced an all-glass, two-crew cockpit, fly-by-wire for the secondary controls and a totally new highly efficient supercritical wing.[15]

After the British re-entry into Airbus Industrie, overall responsibility for wing development was given to BAe. However, despite the fact that the wings of the A300B and A310 were different, BAe's responsibility was limited to manufacturing the wing box, with the moving surfaces and secondary structure remaining the responsibility of Deutsche Airbus at Bremen. Completion of the wings was also left to the Germans at Bremen, despite the fact that manufacturing efficiency would have demanded that wing equipping be done where the wing is manufactured, an observation made by a number of BAe key executives.[16] Unfortunately the smaller share given to BAe on rejoining Airbus, and France's and Germany's entrenched positions as dominant shareholders at the time, limited the scope of Britain's claims.

The Airbus A310 achieved a moderate level of success competing against the Boeing 767 and 757 in the 220–280-seater category, with a total of 260 ordered as at 30 June 2005. Volume production of the A310 effectively ended in 2002 and the aircraft is only available on a 'to order' basis. However, this aircraft played an important role as a technological stepping-stone, introducing many features of the subsequent fly-by-wire Airbus aircraft. It also broadened significantly the A300B's customer base, gaining many customers in the former USSR and Communist Bloc countries (including Aeroflot, CSA, Interflug, Uzbekistan Airways and Tarom), Europe (Swissair and KLM), Asia (Singapore Airlines), Africa (Kenya Airways, Air Algerie) and the USA (Pan Am, Delta Airlines).

The single-aisle Airbus A320, launched in March 1984, represented a technological trailblazer for Airbus and catapulted the European manufacturer into the big league of airliner producers. As we commented earlier on, the A320's origins lie in the Weybridge-based JET studies, which addressed the 150-seat market, in those days dominated by the Boeing 727, Boeing 737 and McDonnell Douglas MD-80 Series.

When it first flew in February 1987, the Airbus A320 was the world's first digital fly-by-wire airliner. Its futuristic cockpit featured side-stick controllers (as in fighter aircraft) in place of the conventional control columns. More importantly the fully computerised fly-by-wire systems commanded all of the aircraft's primary flight controls (such as ailerons, rudder and elevators) and ensured full flight-envelope protection, lower aircraft empty weight and better fuel economy in the different flight regimes.[17] At first received with mixed sentiments by the worldwide pilot community by reason of its complex highly computerised flight deck environment,[18] the A320 and its derivatives went on to establish themselves as the benchmark aircraft in the 150–180 seat category. By 30 June 2005 the Airbus A320 family[19] had recorded over 3,600 firm orders, and close to 2,500 of the type were in operation worldwide. These numbers represent not only an unprecedented market success for a European design, but also make the A320 family the world's second most successful airliner programme of all time behind the Boeing 737 (whose sales total is over 6,400 units).

As a point of interest, it was with the Airbus A320 project that BAe tried, unsuccessfully, to reinstate its claim to project leadership on a major airliner programme. In summary, when the time came for internal project launch in 1981, BAe argued that it was against the partners' interest to specialise in only one area of the aircraft, and that the tasks should be rotated among the main partners. BAe therefore suggested that on the A320 it should undertake development of the front fuselage and cockpit, as well as carrying out final assembly and flight-testing at Filton, Bristol. This proposal had the backing of the company's then chief executive, Sir Raymond Lygo,[20] and a number of BAe senior people, but came up against the stiff and indignant opposition of the French.

Airbus's then chief executive Roger Beteille (one of the fathers of the Airbus project) was reported as saying: 'we are totally against people saying "we have made a wing, now we want to make cockpits and fuselages", this idea goes against the efficiency of the entire operation.' In another interview Beteille expressed opposition to 'those partners keen to play "musical sub-assemblies"'. In reality this tussle had less to do with issues of efficiency than with the desire to retain project leadership: it would have been anathema for the French to cede design leadership to the British after having achieved it originally on the Airbus A300B. In the end the French played a smart card: if the British wanted leadership they would need to almost double their financial contribution to the Airbus programme (i.e. increase their commitment from 20 per cent to about 36 per cent). This the BAe management felt they could not do, although in his memoirs Sir Raymond Lygo argues that the BAe Board should have insisted on trying to achieve their goals and let the British Government decide if it wished to back this up with the necessary cash.[21]

Again, as commented earlier on the Airbus share allocated to the UK when it rejoined the consortium in 1978, senior people both within BAe and the British Government/Treasury were opposed to the idea of heavy investment in a high-risk, very long-term activity like civil aircraft. They therefore elected to limit their exposure to a minority position and to responsibility for wing development and manufacture, where BAe had already gone down the 'learning curve' and had the production capacity in place. Undertaking development of the cockpit/front fuselage of the A320 together with final assembly and flight-testing would have implied a considerable investment in plant and equipment, with the associated higher risk of potential losses.

In order to at least partially meet BAe's aspirations, it was decided that wing equipping and finishing for the A320 family would be carried out at Filton, Bristol (the wing equipping was eventually moved to Chester when BAe rationalised its commercial aircraft sites). However, the Germans still retained design and production of the flaps. The work on some other wing components such as the spoilers and flap track fairings were also transferred to BAe. In addition, the British group was given responsibility for the aircraft's landing gear and related systems. In total, the British share of the A320 programme grew to approximately 26 per cent (as opposed to 20 per cent on the A300B and A310), with France still in the position of project leader with 36 per cent, Germany with 32 per cent and Spain with 6 per cent.

Germany in turn protested at French domination of all the Airbus programmes. In this instance the Germans had a stronger claim than the British, as from the Airbus programme's very beginnings the German Government had not only matched the French share of the financing, but also contributed significantly more through its subsidy to Hawker Siddeley on wing development. In the end the Germans achieved a partial victory when it was decided that the A321 and all other derivatives of the A320 would be assembled and flown from Hamburg. Up to then all final assembly work had been carried out at Toulouse. It was also agreed that Hamburg would become in future the Airbus 'centre of excellence' for single-aisle programmes.

BAe's valiant but futile attempt[22] to gain design leadership on the A320 family was the British industry's very last throw in the negotiations game aimed at achieving project leadership on large airliners.[23] The doctrine of site specialisation and of 'centres of excellence' (so reminiscent of Adam Smith's principles on the division of labour) eventually confirmed and cemented the status quo first set out at the time of the original Airbus A300 discussions in 1967, which established Toulouse and France as the centre of Airbus development.

In the end, by following through with the A300 and by getting full support from Germany, the French Government and aerospace industry established a pattern that Britain could do very little to change, bar launching an indigenous competitor or significantly increasing its financial contribution to the Airbus venture. Both of these strategies were unfeasible given Britain's unwillingness to commit financial resources on the scale required, leaving aside the fact that the launch of a competitor to the Airbus range was precluded to Britain by the Airbus Industrie partnership agreement.

It must also be noted that, apart from egotistical strategic considerations on the part of France, that country had another good reason in refusing Britain a larger role in the Airbus venture, and that reason rests in Britain's uneven record in supporting a long-term strategy of building an aerospace capability comparable to that of the USA. Britain's enthusiastic but somewhat doomed attempts to compete with the US on all fronts of the commercial aerospace market in the 1950s and early 1960s gave way to the defeatist attitude of the 1960s and 1970s (embodied by the Plowden Committee Report and a string of major programme cancellations). This attitude was compounded by the British desire to buy American aircraft off-the-shelf, only partly counterbalanced by the meagre consolation of achieving some subcontracting work for its aerospace industry. Therefore, in the French elite's mind, the risk must have loomed large that an Airbus programme driven by Britain would have been held hostage to the dithering, insecurities and changing priorities of different Governments in office, not to mention the all too recurrent policy of the British establishment to bow to US strategic and political priorities, often at the expense of its own industrial base.

Table 4.3 Airbus engineering centres of excellence and related tasks

Centre of excellence	Tasks
Toulouse (France)	Overall aircraft design, nose (including cockpit), centre fuselage, cockpit systems, avionics, fly-by-wire systems, centre wing box, engine pylons, final assembly (A300, A310, A320, A330/A340, A380), flight-testing, aircraft certification
Hamburg (Germany)	Fuselage, pressurisation systems, cabin interiors and systems, air conditioning systems, APU and systems, fin and rudder, final assembly (A318, A319, A321)
Filton (UK)	Wings, fuel systems, landing gear
Bremen (Germany)	Flaps and slat systems, cargo holds and cargo handling systems
Getafe – Madrid (Spain)	Horizontal tail planes and related systems

Source: Airbus SAS website, 2005

Before we close on the remarkably successful A320 family, it is worth noting that the aircraft's wing started life as an extrapolation of the wing of the subject of this book, the BAC Three-Eleven.[24] Starting with the Three-Eleven wing in 1970, in the mid-1970s BAC Weybridge, with the support of the RAE, developed a series of theoretical wings, codenamed W1, W2, and W3, which studied the effects of a kink in the platform and changes in root thickness. Subsequently, Weybridge developed the W4, W5, and W6 wing designs which used progressively higher Reynolds number design techniques. W5, the original wing used in the JET studies (BAC Aircraft 36), had a 23° swept outer wing. There were four versions of the W6 wing during the development of the A320 which had 25° of sweep and increased depth at the rear spar, giving the associated structural benefits: the fourth extrapolation of W6, W6-4, became the definitive A320 wing. This exceptionally efficient wing has been a major contributor to the good A320 performance economics that underpin its market success. It is therefore consoling to know that, despite the tragic demise of the Three-Eleven project, an important part of that aircraft contributed in its extrapolated form to making the Airbus A320 Europe's most successful airliner ever. One can only wonder as to the potential success of the Three-Eleven itself in the marketplace, had the programme seen the light of day.

Following up on the A320's success, in 1987 Airbus launched its first long-haul jet family, the twin A330/A340 programme. Based on stretched versions of the A300 fuselage (thus retaining the same twin-aisle cross-section as the original Airbus), the new jets have fully computerised cockpits, fly-by-wire controls and a completely new wing, whose aerodynamics are based on those of the A310. Cockpit and systems commonality with the A320 family enable crew cross-qualification on all Airbus fly-by-wire types via relatively short conversion courses, thus substantially reducing crew training costs for the airlines. The ultra-efficient wing of the A330/A340 allows the aircraft to achieve very attractive economics on the long-haul and very-long-haul routes. As a result the A330/A340 family was able to eclipse its competitor, the McDonnell Douglas MD-11 tri-jet, and also forced Boeing to launch the all-new 777.

The only difference between the A330 and A340 is that the former is powered by two engines whereas the latter is a four-engined jet optimised for the longer/thinner routes that do not require Boeing 747 capacity. The A330 and A340 share the same cockpits, fuselages, wings and systems.

In 1997 Airbus launched two higher-capacity, longer-ranged variants of the Airbus A340, this time powered by four Rolls-Royce Trent 500 high-bypass turbofans, as opposed to the smaller-thrust CFM International CMF-56s of the original versions. First flown in 2001 and 2002, the Airbus A340/500 Series is currently the world's longest-range aircraft, with ranges in excess of 15,000km,[25] and the A340/600 is the world's longest aircraft, boasting an overall length of over 75m and three-class passenger capacity of 380, making this version close to the Boeing 747 in terms of capacity for a given range.

Ironically, with the Rolls-Royce Trent-powered A330s and A340/500s and 600s (for these two A340 variants, Rolls is the exclusive engine supplier), Airbus goes back full circle to the original A300 programme of 1967, with British-designed wings and Rolls-Royce powerplant. It is some consolation, as many in the British aerospace industry like to point out, to know that Rolls-Royce-powered Airbus wide-bodies are close to 45 per cent British by value.

Despite having overall design authority on the A330/A340 wings, BAe's responsibility is again limited to the manufacture of the wing box. Flaps, spoilers, airbrakes and final wing equipping remain the responsibility of EADS Airbus Deutschland at Bremen. Overall, BAe's share of the A330/A340 programme lies between those of the A300/A310 and the A320 family, or approximately 22 per cent of the programme. BAe retains responsibility for landing gear development and relevant supplier selection. This underlines the fact, if indeed there is any need to, that the British never recovered the Airbus project responsibilities that originally belonged to Hawker Siddeley, namely the entire wing including all moving surfaces (flaps, slats, spoilers, ailerons), the engine pylons and the engine nacelles, as well as a share of the cockpit systems.

The A330/A340 family has achieved considerable market success, further consolidating Airbus's place in the large airliner market. By 30 June 2005, total sales for the A330/A340 were 908.

Finally, after years of studies into a replacement for the Boeing 747 Jumbo (including joint studies with Boeing in the early 1990s), in December 2000 the Airbus Board authorised the launch of the Airbus A380 double-deck, twin-aisle 'Super-Jumbo'. With standard three-class capacity of 555 passengers, a wingspan of over 79m, take-off weight of over 560 tonnes and range exceeding 13,000km, the Airbus A380 is now the world's largest airliner. It performed its maiden flight on 27 April 2005 from Toulouse's Blagnac airport. With over 150 orders to date from fifteen operators, the Airbus A380 looks set to achieve commercial success. The first flight of the A380 is without doubt the crowning achievement for the European company, which has gone, in the space of thirty-five years, from a non-existent presence in the jetliner market to overtaking the world's largest manufacturer, Boeing, first in order intake and then in total deliveries. In 2003, for the first time in history, Airbus was crowned as the world's largest civil aircraft manufacturer in terms of deliveries. In 2004 and 2005 Airbus confirmed its position as the world's premier aircraft manufacturer measured by aircraft deliveries. It is indeed an amazing achievement for the European industry, well beyond the wildest dreams of Airbus's founding fathers.

It is a source of some pride for the British aerospace industry that, on its first flight, the Airbus A380 was carried aloft by British-designed and manufactured wings and by Rolls-Royce Trent engines. Still, one cannot deny the fact that it was from Toulouse in France that the new leviathan of the skies took to the air, and not from the formerly glorious Filton (Bristol), Weybridge or Hatfield in England. In addition both flight test pilots were French, and two other Frenchmen acted as flight engineers on this maiden flight, together with a Spaniard and a German. Alas, not even a shadow of an Englishman on board!

Table 4.4 Airbus aircraft orders and deliveries[26]

	A300/A310	A320 family	A330/A340	A380	Total
Orders	852	3,611	908	149	5,520
Deliveries	798	2,483	660		3,941
Customers	87	157	77	15	239

Source: Airbus website, 30 June 2005

The French Strategic Approach to International Aerospace Cooperation

It is now the time to reflect on the very different French attitude to international aerospace cooperation, compared to that of Britain. After the Second World War, France's Gaullist Government set out a clear strategy aimed at rebuilding its shattered aerospace capability, as this industry was perceived to be essential to the country's aspirations as a world power. After a small number of successful national projects such as the Dassault Mirage fighter family and the Sud Aviation Caravelle passenger transport, in the early 1960s France's planners decided to adopt international cooperation with the objectives of tackling the issue of rising development costs of aerospace programmes, widening the market for the industry's products, and gaining access to the more advanced expertise and technology of other nations, principally Britain. Fully aware of the strategic importance of the industry, the ultimate French aim was to create a European aerospace capability large enough to counteract US dominance in the sector, with France at its centre.[27] Other goals were to enable the French aircraft industry to reach the size of that of the UK and eventually overtake it (which in due course they did) and to encourage specialisation within Europe, based on a sharing of tasks between the Continent's two major aerospace industries (the UK and France). In the early 1960s the French therefore put forward a proposal to their British counterparts that France would lead and specialise in airframes and related systems, whereas Britain would specialise in aero-engines and systems. The British did not go along with this strategy at first, but a review of the European industry forty years later cannot but reveal that the French strategy has indeed materialised.

Therefore it was not surprising that, when the two countries agreed to co-develop the Concorde supersonic transport in November 1962, France obtained leadership on the airframe and systems (including avionics and flight controls) and Britain was given lead on the engines and related systems. The same happened in the second major civil transport programme agreement, the one concerning the Airbus wide-body in 1967. Again France was given project leadership on the airframe, and Britain was to lead on the engines. France successfully negotiated for project leadership in spite of the fact that Britain's industry was more technically advanced at the time and had more experience in civil aircraft than France. However, from the viewpoint of Britain's negotiators, the trade-off was acceptable because of the country's wider political goals concerning France and Europe, namely Britain's eagerness to apply for Common Market membership.

France's strategy of leading on the airframe work was also followed in the military aircraft segment. In 1965 it agreed to a complex Franco-British military package that included the Jaguar air attack interceptor, the Anglo-French Variable Geometry (AFVG) fighter and three helicopters (the Sud Aviation Gazelle and Puma and the Westland Lynx) for the two countries' Armed Forces.

In the Jaguar project, again France led on the airframe (the basic design being the Breguet Br.121), with Rolls-Royce leading Turbomeca on the Adour engine. The AFVG was expected to be led by Britain's BAC with support from Dassault, while the engine development was to be led by SNECMA with support from Bristol-Siddeley. However, only a few months into the project France withdrew unilaterally from the AFVG, citing rising costs and shortage of funds. France's real motive emerged not long after when Dassault flew France's indigenous variable geometry fighter, the Mirage G-IV. The AFVG debacle left a very sour taste in British mouths, and fatally wounded any further cooperation in military aircraft between the two countries. In the end the truth was that Dassault and France had no intention of playing 'second fiddle' to Britain's industry and the AFVG was only a temporary counterbalance to getting Britain to agree to the Jaguar and helicopter packages.

Britain eventually recovered from the failure of the AFVG by launching the Panavia MRCA (Multi-Role Combat Aircraft, later called the Tornado) with Germany and Italy. However, in this latter venture Britain again had no clear leadership, and had to share the main role with a reinvigorated and assertive German industry.

The helicopter package did not work out in Britain's favour either. France was able to sell two of its helicopters (the Puma and the Gazelle) in quantity to the British forces, whereas France bought only a fraction of the Westland Lynx helicopters it had originally committed to purchase. To add insult to injury, Aérospatiale independently developed a new, much improved, helicopter which made the Gazelle technically obsolescent. In addition, at the engineering and project management levels, Westland managers were left with the feeling that they were playing 'second fiddle' to Sud Aviation (later Aérospatiale) and that they did not get a fair share of the action. A senior manager who worked for Westland in the early 1980s confided to the author that the company was under the French thumb and that the business was 'bound hand and foot' to Aérospatiale by the 1967 Tripartite Agreement.

History repeated itself more recently, in connection with the launch of the Future European Fighter Aircraft (FEFA). Initial discussions between the potential partners – British Aerospace, Dassault, Deutsche Aerospace and Alenia – about cooperation broke down when Dassault insisted on project leadership; this time BAe did not yield on the issue and the result was that four European nations (Germany, Italy, Spain and the UK) went on to develop the Eurofighter Typhoon, whereas France went solo with the development and production of the Dassault Rafale. Dassault did offer the Rafale to the other European participants, but their role would have been that of subcontractors, a role that they could not accept. In the end, France reverted to type by engaging in European cooperation only when its industry was given the task of project leader. The country was more than happy to 'go it alone' when this target could not be achieved. Any true supporter of the British aerospace industry wishes that the UK had done the same in the many instances (like in the BAC Two-Eleven and, more importantly, the BAC Three-Eleven decisions) when it found itself in a position to do so. Unfortunately, the British attitude to aerospace was very different from that of the French, its main drivers being risk aversion, short-term financial returns and wider political goals, such as the country's integration into Europe.

If one takes a snapshot of the two industries today, he or she cannot fail to notice that the French industry offers a complete gamut of civil and military aircraft either independently developed or led by France (Airbus airliners, ATR regional aircraft, Dassault Falcon business jet family, Dassault Mirage 2000 and Rafale fighters, Eurocopter helicopters) whereas the British industry is, with a few exceptions (Eurofighter Typhoon, BAe Hawk) a supplier of components and subassemblies to international programmes driven and led by other countries (Airbus, Joint Strike Fighter).

An industry observer may well argue that Britain has retained European leadership and control of large civil aero-engines and military engines through Rolls-Royce, now the world's second largest supplier of large civil engines. This is of course true, but one cannot overlook the fact that France too did not disregard its own aero-engine industry in its drive to lead on the airframe and systems in joint international projects. The French Government did encourage its national champion SNECMA to strengthen its civil aero-engine capabilities (SNECMA has always had a respectable share of the military market), even if this strategy demanded jumping into bed with the 'loathed' Americans. Through its joint venture with General Electric, CFM International, SNECMA developed the world's most commercially successful civil aero-engine family, the CFM-56. This has allowed the French company to occupy the respectable position of world's fourth largest aero-engine manufacturer, after GE, Rolls-Royce and Pratt & Whitney.

Any aviation historian looking at the standing of the British and French industries at the beginning of the 1960s and at their respective standings now, cannot but give full marks to the French for their unflinching ability to 'turn the tables' on their old rival, and to achieve leadership in Europe. To the people who remark that UK aerospace is still the world's second largest by turnover (even if this differential with France is only of the order of less than 10 per cent) one can point out that British industry is almost wholly dependent on programmes managed and led by overseas countries (including the no small part played by French-led Airbus) and does not lay claim to leadership on any significant aerospace programme.

Opportunity Cost to the UK Industry of the 1970 'Airbus' Decisions

We shall close this chapter by providing a rough estimate of the cost to the UK (in terms of revenues foregone) of first exiting Airbus when Britain was co-leader with France and then deciding not to back the wholly national BAC Three-Eleven wide-body airliner.

As we have seen earlier on, France secured leadership on the A300B and every single Airbus project that followed it. This leadership has translated into key responsibilities for high-value-added cockpit design, systems design and overall integration, final assembly and flight-testing. Moreover, due to the fact that almost all of Airbus's final assembly takes place in Toulouse, this major aerospace techno-pole has attracted a myriad of component suppliers to the area from all over the world, ranging from giants such as General Electric, Goodrich and Honeywell to small aerospace engineering and IT consultancies. This has created a substantial 'multiplier effect' for the local and national economy in both revenue and employment terms.

Also, Toulouse and France are in charge of Airbus pilot training, a highly lucrative business, and of maintenance engineers' training and formation. Several higher education institutions linked to the aerospace industry have also flourished in the Toulouse area. In addition, by being the aircraft integrator, France has won the lion's share of the major maintenance and modification contracts (with Germany in a strong position too). Heavy maintenance represents the cash flow over the life of the asset (the aircraft) and can easily match the original value of the aircraft over its useful life. French companies such as EADS's Sogerma and Air France Industries have benefited copiously from Airbus aftermarket activity over the years.

It is difficult to estimate, without carrying out a comprehensive economic study, the total benefit to France, vis-à-vis the UK, of having leadership in the Airbus business. However, with a view to giving just the order of magnitude, a conservative estimate can be derived by calculating the difference between EADS France's Airbus-related annual sales revenue (roughly US$8.5 billion) and the equivalent for BAE SYSTEMS (US$4 billion). The annual difference of some US$4.5 billion can be taken as a reasonable estimate, in today's money, of the last ten years of Airbus operations (1994–2003) and of the next thirty years (2004–33). Assuming that the difference in the first twenty years of Airbus (1974–93) was on average US$2 billion, again in current money's worth, to reflect the company's lower market share and smaller product line, the total estimated revenue foregone by the UK aerospace industry is a staggering US$220 billion.[28] Of course, we need to deduct from this sum the additional 'non-recurring costs' investment that the UK economy saved by playing a reduced role compared to France and Germany. A reasonable estimate of this would be US$5 billion for all the Airbus programmes to date. Deducting this from the foregone revenues stream still leaves an enormous 'loss' to UK aerospace of US$215 billion over a sixty-year span. It must be emphasised that these calculations are indeed a rough estimate, but still conservative as they do not take into account the Airbus aftermarket revenues accruing mostly to France and Germany. The aftermarket revenues foregone by Britain can easily add another US$200 billion to the total over the time horizon under consideration, giving a grand total of over US$400 billion.

There are three fundamental problems with the above estimates:

1) A proper cost-benefit analysis would consider not gross figures like revenues, but the net, i.e. the profits/cash flows accruing to the industry. In fact, Airbus was loss-making for the first twenty years of its existence, and achieved its first operating profit only in 1990.

2) The estimates do not reflect the potential revenues generated by the monies saved being employed in alternative investment opportunities (the so-called 'opportunity cost'). Indeed these alternative investment revenues could well exceed the amounts quoted earlier. While this is true, we can still assert that those alternative GDP benefits did not accrue to the British aerospace industry nor, we would venture to suggest, to UK manufacturing in general.

3) A stickler for a scientifically thorough cost-benefit analysis would also argue that future cash flows should be discounted to their Net Present Value (NPV) by reference to an appropriate 'cost of capital' discount rate to reflect investment and business risk.

However, the points made above do not invalidate the 'rough' scale of the loss to the UK aerospace industry that we have estimated.

Last but not least, as we mentioned in the book's introduction, account must be taken of the intangible benefits that accrue to a country that is identified with a high technology industry such as civil aircraft manufacture: these include international prestige, political leverage, broader international trade opportunities, etc. Although very difficult to quantify, these intangibles play an important role in the decision-making process of political elites the world over. It is therefore no surprise that all major industrialised countries (amongst them the USA, Britain, France, Germany, Canada, Italy and Japan) have aimed to play a major role in the aerospace industry, and that aerospace capabilities are a prized goal of several ambitious developing economies (China, Brazil, Korea and Malaysia, to name but a few).

1 For this paragraph the author is indebted to Richard Anthony Payne's excellent review of the UK's cancelled civil programmes, which appeared in three consecutive issues of *Air Pictorial* (September 1998–November 1998) under the title 'Paper Planes', and to the same author's recent book, *Stuck on the Drawing Board: Unbuilt British Commercial Aircraft Since 1945*.

2 The factual information for this paragraph is drawn from a number of sources, including Richard Anthony Payne, 'Paper Planes', *Air Pictorial*, November 1998; Bill Gunston, *Airbus: The European Triumph*; *Flight International*, various issues; R.F. Back and J.R. Wedderspoon, 'The A320 Wing – Designing for Commercial Success (*Aerospace*, January 1986).

3 Reported in *Flight International*, 8 May 1976.

4 For the background to the BAC studies at Weybridge the author has relied on a joint lecture on the A320 given at the Royal Aeronautical Society in March 1985 by BAe's Roger Back and Jack Wedderspoon and published in *Aerospace* in January 1986. See R.F. Back and J.R. Wedderspoon, 'The A320 Wing – Designing for Commercial Success' (*Aerospace*, January 1986) and on Roger Back's personal recollections of the Airbus A320 project.

5 Several senior BAC/BAe engineers who were deeply involved in the JET and A320 projects have pointed out to the author that these aircraft benefited from considerable design and engineering input from the British team at Weybridge, and that it is incorrect to portray the A320 as a 'French-led' project. While the author fully acknowledges this fact, the fact remains that the French at Toulouse were able to retain project leadership on the Airbus single-aisle family, with responsibility for overall project coordination, cockpit systems and systems integration, final assembly and flight-testing. Indeed the design authority on the A320 family rests with Airbus in Toulouse. Alas, as with the HSA 'hidden leadership' on the Airbus A300, the JET/A320 story is again a case of the British giving away their know-how and intellectual property to the other Europeans for little or no economic and technological benefit. To paraphrase Sir George Edwards, the BAC Weybridge team and Britain at large got no medals for providing the major A320 input 'behind the scenes': the core benefits accrued to France and, to a lesser degree, to Germany.

6 *Flight International*, 24 May 1973.

7 *Flight International*, 5 July 1973.

8 Conservative Prime Minister Ted Heath was an accomplished classical music conductor and pianist, as well as an experienced and enthusiastic yachtsman.

9 Britain's decision to rejoin the European consortium and the political intricacies thereof are dealt with at length in several books that cover the birth and rise of Airbus Industrie. For further reading we suggest: Ian McIntyre, *Dogfight: The Transatlantic Battle over Airbus*; Matthew Lynn, *Birds of Prey: Boeing vs Airbus – A Battle for the Skies*; Stephen Aris, *Close to the Sun: How Airbus Challenged America's Domination of the Skies*.

10 Former BAC/BAe Chief Engineer Mike Salisbury has confirmed to the author that the American 'Big Three' did not take BAC/BAe seriously as a competitor/senior partner. When confronted with the statement that BAC had considerable expertise in civil aircraft design, Boeing's answer was: 'we'll buy your men then, we don't need to collaborate with you as [an equal] partner.'

11 See Matthew Lynn, *Birds of Prey: Boeing vs Airbus – A Battle for the Skies*, p.156.

12 A very apt Italian expression for this state of affairs is '*Fare buon viso a cattivo gioco*', which loosely translates as 'To put on a brave face at a poor hand (of cards)'!

13 It is not the author's intention to provide here an exhaustive history of Airbus Industrie, but rather to briefly review the recent evolution of Airbus and especially the role played by British industry in it since rejoining the consortium in 1979. The emergence of Airbus Industrie as a powerful force has been covered extensively in numerous books, several of which are listed in the Bibliography at the end of this book.

14 Source: Airbus website, 30 June 2005.

15 Glass-cockpit means that the traditional analogue instruments are replaced by digital, computerised information, presented in flat-screen LCDs (Liquid Crystal Displays).

16 See Bob McKinlay's comments, as reported in Arthur Reed, *Airbus: Europe's High Flyer*. Also, Sir Raymond Lygo, former BAe CEO, in his autobiography, *Collision Course*.

17 The latter goal was achieved through Full Authority Digital Engine Controls (FADEC) for the engines.

18 Three notorious accidents in the aircraft's early career brought the A320's cockpit philosophy under intense scrutiny, but the subsequent accident investigations completely exonerated the aircraft's systems.

19 The family comprises the baseline 150-seat A320, the shorter fuselage A319 (125–150 passengers) and A318 (110 seats) and the stretched A321 (180–220 seats).

20 See Sir Raymond Lygo's autobiography, *Collision Course*, pp.456–457.

21 Sir Raymond Lygo, *Collision Course*, p.457.

22 As commented above, there was no consensus within BAe, especially at senior level, that the leading role on the Airbus A320 was a desirable outcome.

23 Large airliners are defined as transports carrying in excess of 100 passengers in a two-class, standard layout.

24 See R.F. Back and J.R. Wedderspoon, *The A320 Wing – Designing for Commercial Success* (*Aerospace*, January 1986). The author has also relied on Roger Back's own recollection of the genesis of the A320 project and of its wing.

25 This record is about to be broken by the introduction of Boeing's new 777-200ELR.

26 As at 30 June 2005.

27 History records that in 1965 General de Gaulle stood at the site of today's Rond Point Maurice Bellonte in Toulouse (where Airbus have got their HQ) and said: 'this is where the European aerospace industry will be based.'

28 Calculated as follows: US$4.5 billion @ 40 (years) = US$180 billion, plus US$2 billion @ 20 (years) = US$40 billion.

The Principal Factors Behind the UK Government's 'Airbus' Decisions in 1969 and 1970

Introduction

We have seen in the previous chapters how the April 1969 decision by the British Government to withdraw from the Airbus consortium and the subsequent December 1970 decision not to support the BAC Three-Eleven and not to accept an invitation to rejoin the Airbus consortium on favourable terms fatally undermined British industry's capabilities in civil aircraft manufacture. The December 1970 decision in particular put an end to Britain's ability to independently develop large mainline transport aircraft.

This last chapter analyses the several reasons why two successive British Governments, in the space of little more than one year, took decisions that proved so highly damaging to the future status of the country's civil aerospace industry. In fact, as any historian would point out, momentous changes for an industry, country or indeed an individual are seldom the result of one single factor. In the rest of this chapter we shall review the following factors which, in our opinion, played a fundamental part in the Government's 'double whammy' decisions not to back the BAC Three-Eleven and to withdraw from the Airbus partnership:

Poor commercial performance of previous British airliner programmes.

The aspirations to EEC membership of the post-war British Governments.

British Governments' modus operandi.

Concorde development costs.

The Rolls-Royce crisis.

BAC and HSA competing for the same Government backing with two distinct 'airbus' projects.

We shall deal individually with each factor below, before drawing our final conclusions.

Poor Commercial Performance of Previous British Airliner Programmes

A key factor that weighed heavily in the UK Government's assessment of the BAC Three-Eleven and A300B European Airbus projects was the poor performance, in terms of commercial success and market penetration, of the great majority of British-designed airliners produced from the end of the Second World War up to the mid-1960s. Failure in the marketplace was particularly true of the larger designs. The Bristol Britannia, Vickers Vanguard, Vickers VC-10 and Hawker Siddeley Trident all failed to achieve a significant share of the markets for which they were conceived. Of course there were a number of reasons as to why they failed, and these have been analysed at length in Chapter 1. But the fact remains that none of the above designs were commercially successful. And this fact is not limited to the aircraft mentioned above. Other major projects, like the Bristol Brabazon and Vickers V-1000/VC-7, in which substantial amounts of Government money were invested, did not even see commercial service.

Notable exceptions to this picture of repeated commercial failure were the Vickers Viscount turboprop and the BAC One-Eleven twinjet (incidentally both Weybridge designs), which achieved reasonable production runs and, more importantly, managed to gain a significant share of the North American market, the world's most important and most demanding aviation market, against strong local competition. Other notable British successes were achieved in the 'feederliner' segment, with the de Havilland Dove and Hawker Siddeley (Avro) HS.748 selling in their hundreds.

Continental Europe (in the shape of France) did not fare any better, with only the Sud Aviation Caravelle twinjet achieving a reasonable, but by no means impressive, production run. In summary, for Europe as a whole, only the Vickers Viscount, Sud Aviation Caravelle and BAC One-Eleven scored a moderate degree of commercial success. It should be noted, however, that two out of three of these European successes stemmed from the Weybridge design and marketing team, the same stable from which the BAC Three-Eleven came.

The British aircraft industry must take a fair share of the blame for the repeated commercial failure of the majority of its designs. Too many airliners were launched into production without first assessing if there was a sufficiently large market for them. Some projects reached the market too late to make a significant impact (Bristol Britannia, Vickers Vanguard) whilst others were ill-conceived in terms of general specification or size (Bristol Brabazon, Vickers VC-10 and the resizing of the HS Trident). In fairness to the industry, many projects were Government sponsored, and the necessity to satisfy the limited specifications of the nationalised airlines did hinder the scope of what the manufacturers could do. However, it was still the responsibility of the industry, not the Government, to come up with projects that had the broadest possible market appeal. The aircraft manufacturers should have refused to bid for specifications that conflicted with their better judgment, even if that meant going against the often-flawed requirements of the nationalised airlines. This last point is particularly true of the narrow requirements of BOAC and BEA that led to the launch of the Vickers VC-10 and the Hawker Siddeley Trident in its revised lower-capacity version.

Why did industry make the wrong choices in terms of aircraft specifications? Several senior people who worked in the industry in the 1950s and 1960s have explained to the author that engineers in senior management positions dominated the British aircraft companies' decision-making process. These engineers gave scant consideration to the views of the marketing people, the only ones who were actually aware of what the customers really wanted. So it came to pass that engineers decided on aircraft layout and technical solutions without first considering if those solutions satisfied the broadest customer base. As one Airbus old hand later said, 'the European engineers used to design airliners just to please themselves.' The British industry's attitude to the design of new airliner projects was in stark contrast to the approach of their American competitors. The latter designed an aircraft around specifications that reflected the best compromise of the requirements of the broadest possible customer base. In Europe, prior to Airbus, only BAC at Weybridge had learned the lessons of its past mistakes (Vanguard and VC-10) and went on to design successful airliners like the Viscount and BAC One-Eleven. The BAC Three-Eleven was the result of the most thorough and detailed study of world airline requirements ever undertaken in Europe and was entirely market-driven in its specifications. The author has no doubt that, had it been allowed to go ahead, the Three-Eleven would have achieved substantial market penetration and a worldwide success well in excess of both the One-Eleven and the Viscount.

Table 5.1 overleaf shows HMG's launch aid contributions and receipts for civil aircraft and engines for the period from the end of the Second World War up to early 1974. We can see from the table that only the Viscount and its Rolls-Royce Dart engine managed to repay in full the British Government's launch aid and to provide a profit to HMG. On the airframe side, of a total of £340 million invested by the British Government in civil aircraft, only £21 million was recovered. On the engine side only £41 million was recovered out of a total £407 million invested. Of course the Concorde and its engine exaggerate the loss to HMG. Without Concorde the total loss would amount to only £88 million on the airframe side and £194 million on the engine side. Notwithstanding this latter point, the civil aircraft sector must indeed have appeared to the Treasury to be a huge drain on the nation's resources.

Table 5.1 UK Government Launch Aid for Commercial Airliners and their Engines

Aircraft type	Year	Contributions to 31/3/74 (£ m)	Contributions to 31/3/74 (£ m)	Receipts to 31/3/74 (£m)	Receipts to 31/3/74 (£ m)
		Current prices	1974 input prices	Current prices	1974 input prices
Shetland	1945	See below	See below	See below	See below
Sandringham	1945	See below	See below	See below	See below
Solent	1945	See below	See below	See below	See below
Tudor	1945	See below	See below	See below	See below
Air Horse	1945	See below	See below	See below	See below
Total for 1945		2.25	11.7	N/A	N/A
Apollo	1948	1.25	6.5	Nil	Nil
Brabazon	1948	6.45	32.8	Nil	Nil
Hermes	1949	1.3	6.4	N/A	N/A
Comet 1 – 4	1956	10.25	38.0	4.1	12.2
Ambassador	1951	1.85	7.6	0.15	0.4
Princess	1951	9.1	47.1	Nil	Nil
Viscount	1951	1.8	8.4	3.0	9.8
V.1000	1955	2.35	7.8	Nil	Nil
Twin Pioneer	1955	0.05	0.1	0.05	0.1
Britannia	1955	6.4	24.8	5.1	16.0
Rotodyne	1956	3.05	7.8	Nil	Nil
Argosy	1961	0.1	0.2	Nil	Nil
Herald	1962	0.1	3.0	0.05	1.1
VC10	1963	10.25	27.1	1.05	2.1
Trident	1965	26.1	53.5	0.75	1.6
One-Eleven	1965	19.05	45.3	3.3	6.1
Islander	1968	0.05	0.1	0.05	0.1
Jetstream	1968	1.2	2.4	0.1	0.2
A300	1968	1.15	2.2	Nil	Nil
Concorde	1968	233.8	406.8	3.15	5.8
HS.146	1972	1.25	1.6	Nil	Nil
Total aircraft		340.1	741.2	20.9	54.5
Engines					
Dart	1949	5.3	21.7	8.45	20.8
Proteus	1950	19.45	72.2	3.5	9.2
Eland	1952	10.9	34.8	0.05	0.1
Tyne	1958	4.0	12.6	2.1	4.0

Orion	1959	4.75	14.9	Nil	Nil
Avon	1958	8.5	26.7	6.95	17.1
Conway	1960	6.65	15.9	5.85	13.4
Spey	1965	9.9	23.7	6.6	11.2
RB.178	1967	1.3	2.8	0.1	0.1
Trent (RB203)	1968	2.5	5.1	0.6	1.0
RB.207	1968	2.0	3.8	0.05	0.1
M45H	1973	6.6	8.6	Nil	Nil
RB.211	1971	146.7	224.4	6.25	10.4
Olympus 593	1968	178.1	297.0	Nil	Nil
Total engines		406.7	746.2	40.5	87.4
Grand total		746.8	1,505.4	61.4	141.9

Source: N.K. Gardner, 'The Economics of Launching Aid', reproduced in *Flight International*, 28 February 1976

It is hardly surprising, therefore, that in an era when 'value for money' concepts in relation to public expenditure were rapidly gaining ground, the UK Government carefully assessed the market potential of any major project for which a substantial demand on taxpayers' money was expected. It is a fact of life that past performance is a key parameter and evaluation tool in the assessment of any investment opportunity. As a consequence the commercial failure of past commercial transports would have weighed heavily in estimating the future viability of new civil aircraft. In the case of the BAC Three-Eleven, as we have seen in Chapter 3, very conservative production volumes (in terms of potential units sold) were used in the Government's economic assessment models.

Table 5.2 Cost Escalation on Civil Projects

Project	Initial estimate (£ million)	Actual or latest estimate (£ million)	% increase
VC-10/Super VC-10	36.2	39.5	9
BAC 1-11	26.5	33	28
Trident 1	23.3	23.2	Nil
Concorde airframe	100	480	380
BAC 3-11	140	N/A	N/A
Spey (civil variants)	32.2	33.9	5
Olympus for Concorde	50	320	540
RB211-22	65.5	137.5	110
RB211-61	50+	N/A	N/A

Source: HMG, Ministry of Aviation Supply files, 26 October 1970

Possibly the most deleterious consequence of the lack of commercial success of the majority of British airliner programmes launched in the 1950s and 1960s was that it did not allow the commercial aircraft divisions of BAC and HSA to generate the necessary cash flow and retained equity required to launch new generation designs without substantial Government backing. Unlike the situation in the US, production runs of British airliners were, in the majority of cases, insufficient to guarantee a recovery of the non-recurring costs. In other words, the revenues generated by these aircraft programmes did not yield sufficient cash flow to allow a substantial build-up of retained equity capital. As a result of this, the share of the companies' equity capital available to back the launch of a new airliner was relatively small, while the cost of raising funds in the open market was prohibitive due to the high-risk profile of the required investment. Thus, towards the end of the 1960s, the British Government was being asked to underwrite the lion's share of the financing of the non-recurring costs, a proposition which was becoming less and less palatable to the Treasury as launching costs increased with each new generation of aircraft.

But what about the French and German decision to back the A300B European Airbus despite the fact that at that point in time the aircraft did not have a single order to its name? Their decision can be explained by the fact that, in this instance, the French and Germans had a totally different mindset from that of the British. The French saw the Airbus, as they had seen the Caravelle and the Concorde before it, as a means to strengthen the technological base and capabilities of their aerospace industry, with the aim of reaching parity with, and eventually overtaking, the British industry. The Germans, in a similar fashion, saw the Airbus project as a tool to recover their strength in aerospace, which had been artificially stunted by the post-Second World War moratorium on aircraft development, which was lifted only in 1955. Unlike the British, value for money was a secondary consideration in the minds of both the French and Germans when assessing the merits of the project.

Does this suggest that the Germans and French took a longer-term view than the British as far as major aerospace projects are concerned? The simplistic answer, and probably the truthful answer, is yes. However, we must not forget that other factors were also at play. For one, Britain had inherited a large, over-manned and substantially intact aircraft industry from the Second World War, with several design centres and production facilities scattered all over the country. France and Germany, on the other hand, had to rebuild their industries almost from scratch, following the destruction or impairment of most of their production facilities during the war years. As one acute observer has pointed out, it is easier to plan investment and modernisation starting from a small base than it is when trying to rationalise a much larger capacity.[1] Another point to bear in mind is that Britain had launched into production a relatively high number of civil aircraft since the end of the war compared to France (whose turbine-powered aircraft experience was limited to the Caravelle and to the then 'in development' Anglo-French Concorde SST) and Germany (who had no experience to speak of at that stage). Most of the British designs had turned out to be commercial failures. It is hardly surprising, then, that by 1970 the British decision-makers were suffering from civil aircraft 'fatigue' compared with the more enthusiastic and eager French and Germans. This in turn led the British Government 'mandarins' to take a much less sentimental and more 'hard-nosed' or cynical view of civil aerospace than their French and German counterparts. It is, after all, a peculiar characteristic of human nature that when one plays a game several times, and loses most of the time, eventually his interest in the game fades: the opposite is true of the neophyte.

The Aspirations to EEC Membership of the Post-war British Governments

After the end of the Second World War the British elite slowly came to the realisation that the halcyon days of the British Empire and of the country's 'Splendid Isolation' were over. Granted, Winston Churchill was there among the 'Big Three' at Yalta's conference, together with US President F.D. Roosevelt and USSR leader Josef Stalin. However, the war effort had cost Britain dearly, not only in lives, but also in the form of a massive foreign debt to the US for the latter's support during the war. The US-conceived Marshall Plan was eventually put in place with the aim of helping Europe (Britain included) out the economic mire of the post-war years. At the same time the plan achieved the political goal of Western Europe's allegiance to the US.

British politicians in the post-war years started charting a new course for Britain's future, in the full knowledge that the end of the war had left only two effective superpowers, the USA and the USSR. This course eventually matured under Harold Macmillan's Conservative Government in the early 1960s with the decision to apply for membership of the recently formed European Economic Community (EEC). It is at this point in time that Britain's aircraft industry became a bargaining pawn in a larger political game. General de Gaulle's France was at the heart of the EEC and was very much the initiator as well as the political heavyweight of the new Community at a time when Germany and Italy were still trying to recover from the defeat in the war and from the aftermath of their undemocratic regimes in the war years. The French, therefore, saw themselves as the catalyst of a new powerful Europe, which would act as counter-weight to the USA and USSR. The French identified the aerospace industry early on as an essential element of their strategy of world leadership within the framework of a united Europe, and set about rebuilding the industry's technical and industrial capabilities.

It came as no surprise then, that Britain – with Europe's most powerful and technically advanced aerospace capabilities, and France – with its ambitions in the sector – found common ground for discussion on aerospace cooperation. The Concorde agreement of 1962 was the first of such joint venture projects, which the Macmillan Government hoped would convince France of Britain's good faith towards Europe. In the end de Gaulle rejected Britain's application to join the EEC in 1963, citing the fact that the British were too much aligned with the US to make them trustworthy partners. This did not deter Britain's political elite from again using aerospace as a bargaining tool with the French.

The Labour Government under Harold Wilson signed up to a comprehensive package of joint venture projects with the French in 1965–67, covering military aircraft (Sepecat Jaguar, AFVG), civil aircraft (Airbus, this time including the Germans) and helicopters (Gazelle, Lynx and Puma). With a couple of notable exceptions, in all these aerospace joint ventures the French demanded and obtained design leadership. This happened despite the fact that the French at that time had less experience in aerospace than the British. The two exceptions were the BAC/Dassault AFVG variable geometry fighter and the Westland Lynx helicopter. Predictably, the French pulled out of the AFVG only a few months later and went on to develop a wholly national alternative, the Dassault Mirage GIV. Understandably, the British Government and the industry were very angry and upset at this French *volte face*. In the end, despite these Government-inspired major concessions on the part of British industry, the country did not gain EEC membership, de Gaulle rejecting the British application for the second time in 1967. It was only in 1973, several years after de Gaulle's death, that Britain eventually joined the EEC.

Most industry commentators, when reviewing the British Government's policy decisions with regard to international cooperation in aerospace in the 1960s, agree that the UK industry's interests were sacrificed in the pursuit of membership of the EEC. It was entirely acceptable to successive British Governments for the country's aerospace industry to play a junior role in French-led joint venture projects. In fact, the industry was encouraged to transfer its hard-earned know-how and expertise to the French (and the Germans) for virtually no consideration. The British Governments of the time saw this as a small price to pay in order to achieve a place in Europe. We must not forget, however, that international cooperation was also meant to achieve another important goal for the British Government, namely the reduction in the substantial risk and cost of major projects, with a consequent reduction in taxpayers' money invested in aerospace. In this respect the Government took the Plowden Report's recommendations to heart. In the end international cooperation as devised by Government pleased the Foreign Office and the Treasury, but left the industry in a much weaker position in relation to France and Germany.

In the June 1970 election the surprise defeat of Labour saw a new Conservative administration taking office. It was Edward Heath's stated intention to finally get

Britain into the EEC. Therefore, when it came to evaluating the Three-Eleven
project, overriding considerations of European politics must have coloured
Government thinking. These translated into the view that launching a competitor to the European Airbus would greatly upset the French and the Germans,
the EEC's main partners. Although Government papers reveal that the Foreign
Office advised that a Three-Eleven launch could be made palatable to the French
and Germans with a carefully and sensitively planned PR exercise, there is no
point denying that Heath's Government regarded the aircraft's launch to be a
poor move for a country wishing to join the EEC. In the end, the major financial
crisis of Rolls-Royce helped the Conservative Government extricate itself from
this political dilemma. Although the reasons given for the decision not to back
the Three-Eleven were the necessity to fund Rolls-Royce and Concorde, it is fair
to suggest that broader political goals connected with Europe played an important part in its demise.

British Governments' Modus Operandi

This explanatory factor refers to the planning horizon of British Governments
and to the modus operandi of their civil servants in the Treasury and other minis-
tries when it comes to the appraisal of long-term investment opportunities. First,
the Parliamentary timescale of five years tends to be skewed against long-term
projects. In practice, Government spending plans tend to be set against the life of
one Parliament. This, however, explains only in part the refusal to back projects
like the Airbus A300B and the BAC Three-Eleven, as British Governments have
financed long-term military procurement programmes such as the Panavia
Tornado and Sepecat Jaguar which cover several Parliaments.

   More relevant to our Three-Eleven story is the introduction of Discounted
Cash Flow (DCF) project evaluation techniques in the Treasury in the late 1960s
and the conservative attitude of most civil servants in relation to projected market
volumes and values. In fact, on the first point we must remember that, in those
days, the Treasury's DCF models were based on relatively short-term horizons of
five or ten years maximum. As we know, the value of a civil aircraft programme,
including spares and support, spans anything between thirty and fifty years. It
logically follows then that an evaluation by the British Treasury of a programme
like the Three-Eleven based on, say, a ten-year investment horizon would have
resulted in a substantial underestimate of the value of the programme to HMG.
The second point relates to the 'timid' or conservative mindset of most civil servants working for the Treasury, MinTech or the MoA when it came to estimating
the market share or potential of a particular project. As we know from Chapter 3,
very conservative sales numbers were assumed for the BAC Three-Eleven project,

although in all fairness BAC itself underestimated the aircraft's market potential. It is clear, therefore, that the combination of low sales volumes assumed in the evaluation models and a short DCF horizon yielded negative cash flow results for HMG, and helped make the case for rejection of the project. However, to be fair to the British Government, the sales track record of most British mainline transports that had gone before (with the exception of the BAC Viscount and BAC One-Eleven) was so poor as to make conservative sales assumptions for the Three-Eleven wholly understandable.

Concorde Development Costs

Concorde holds a very special place in the hearts and minds of the British people. The great majority of the British public saluted Concorde's withdrawal from commercial service at the end of 2003 with a mix of pride, sadness and nostalgia. The Anglo-French Supersonic Transport (SST) holds an almost iconic value in Britain's collective psyche and is a source of great pride for many. However, it is in the light of Concorde's effect on the future of the British civil aircraft industry that we wish to assess its legacy.

When we view Concorde's contribution under the light of its effect on other civil aircraft programmes, only one conclusion is valid: the programme was disastrous, as it absorbed almost all the available Government funds that could have gone to finance more commercially viable civil transports, such as the BAC Three-Eleven.[2] By the time the Three-Eleven decision was taken at the end of 1970, the total estimated cost of the Concorde airframe alone to the UK Exchequer (and by implication to the British taxpayer) was a staggering £480 million, a 380 per cent increase on the original estimate. The development cost of the Olympus engine added another £320 million, representing a 540 per cent increase on original estimates.[3] The aggregate amount of £800 million for estimated completion of the Concorde airframe and engine development represented about ten times what BAC was expecting the Government to contribute to the Three-Eleven project (i.e. £84 million). It is no wonder then that projects like the Three-Eleven found themselves struggling for Government funds when the Concorde had such a gargantuan and voracious appetite for taxpayers' money.

To be fair to the British Governments of the day, they did try to extricate themselves from the Concorde commitment on several occasions, only to find that they were locked in by a clause in the original 1962 agreement that forbade unilateral withdrawal. The November 1962 agreement had the legal force of an international treaty (ironically, the clause forbidding unilateral withdrawal from the project was included in the treaty at the express request of the British Government!). It is also fair to point out that, at the time of the Three-Eleven decision, Concorde's manufacturers, BAC and Aérospatiale, still held seventy-four options for the aircraft from some of the world's largest airlines such as Pan Am, TWA, Lufthansa and Japan Airlines. BAC and the Government at the time would have therefore regarded the SST's commercial prospects to be reasonable. With the Concorde's future assured, the necessity for another major aircraft programme such as the Three-Eleven would have appeared to be less urgent. Alas, the seventy-four provisional options for Concorde were to evaporate completely by the time the great Oil Shock hit the Western World in 1973.

Ironically, it was France that reaped the greatest rewards from the Concorde programme. A sizeable amount of British technological know-how and expertise was transferred to the French during the Concorde project. In addition French partner Aérospatiale, by virtue of being allocated the responsibility for the Concorde's avionic systems and flying controls, i.e. the 'brains' of the airplane, built up substantial expertise in systems integration. This expertise, gained in the main with the Brits as willing 'givers', allowed Aérospatiale to demand leadership of the European Airbus and to establish Toulouse as the centre for European large airliner development and production. What is instead the Concorde's legacy for the UK aircraft industry and for the British taxpayer? Ten splendid but now useless aircraft scattered in various museums across the country, as well as in the US and in Barbados…

The Rolls-Royce Crisis

When the Minister of Aviation, Frederick Corfield, announced in Parliament that the BAC Three-Eleven would not get Government financial backing, he referred to the need for continued funding of Rolls-Royce and its RB211 engine as a key reason behind the decision. The necessity to fund Rolls-Royce also prevented the Government from accepting the invitation to re-enter the Airbus consortium as a full partner, and from backing the launch of the RB211-61 engine to power the proposed A300B7 version, on which Hawker Siddeley would have had design leadership.

There is little doubt that the Rolls-Royce financial crisis, which came to a head during 1970 and which was triggered by the complexity and associated development cost overruns of the RB211-22 high bypass turbofan for the Lockheed TriStar, played a major part in the demise of the BAC Three-Eleven programme.

On 11 November 1970, only three weeks before the Three-Eleven announcement, Mr Corfield made a statement[4] to Parliament to the effect that the Government was providing a further £42 million towards the RB211-22 engine development costs. This sum was in addition to the £47 million that the previous Government had provided to Rolls-Royce in 1968. The development costs of this engine were originally estimated at £65 million but by the end of 1970 the revised estimate for its development costs had more than doubled to £135 million. With the additional financing, total Government contribution to the engine now amounted to £89 million, on top of which Rolls-Royce had obtained an £18 million loan from a consortium of banks and £10 million from the Industrial Reorganisation Corporation, the latter sum in effect another Government loan. On the same day as Mr Corfield made his announcement to Parliament, Rolls-Royce released a financial statement showing prospective losses of £48 million. Interestingly, *The Times* newspaper of 3 December 1970, reporting on the cancellation of the BAC Three-Eleven, had written: 'Weeks ago, before the announcement of the bridging loan by the Government to Rolls-Royce, it seemed likely that the Government would inject funds into the British airframe industry to support the BAC 3-11 airbus.'[5] Whether this statement was based on private soundings of Government ministers, or was the newspaper's own speculation, we do not know.

All this propping up of Rolls-Royce was to no avail, however, as just a few weeks after the 2 December 1970 'airbus' announcement Rolls-Royce went bankrupt and had to call in the receivers. The date was 4 February 1971. The collapse of Rolls-Royce sent shockwaves through British industry and was a major embarrassment for the British Establishment. It also proved to be an embarrassment and a major headache for Edward Heath's Conservative Government, who had won the June 1970 election backing a non-interventionist policy in industry ('no more lame ducks' cried the party's manifesto). It was therefore ironic to see the Conservatives forced to nationalise the aero-engine assets of Rolls-Royce under the umbrella of a new state-owned company called Rolls-Royce (1971) Ltd. The nationalisation of Rolls was indeed a forced choice for the Government, as it turned out to be the only viable option to protect the strategically important military engine interests of the company and to safeguard against the heavy penalties demanded by Lockheed Corporation in connection with the RB211 engine.

The considerable delays on the RB211 and the collapse of Rolls-Royce almost brought Lockheed Corporation down with them: only a US Government bail-out scheme which was approved by the American Senate with a majority of a mere one vote saved the day for the prestigious US aerospace and defence contractor. A painful and tortuous renegotiation of the RB211 contract followed, with the UK Government, Rolls and Lockheed as key participants. Discussions among the three parties lasted for the best part of 1971 and pitted the British Government against the charismatic chairman of Lockheed, Dan Haughton. Eventually, Lockheed relented a little, and allowed a new agreement to be struck which saved both the Lockheed TriStar and its RB211 engine.

The reasons for the Rolls-Royce debacle have been analysed at length in other books[6] and in several newspaper and specialist press articles. Suffice to say that three factors played a major part in the company's undoing:

A gross underestimate of the complexity and associated development costs of the new RB211 three-shaft high bypass turbofan.

A poorly negotiated contract with Lockheed, which did not allow for cost escalation. This latter situation arose by reason of Rolls' relatively weak bargaining power vis-à-vis Lockheed, with the British company very eager to get onboard a major US wide-body airframe.

Rolls-Royce's takeover of British rival Bristol Siddeley in October 1966 at a cost of £67.5 million. The takeover of Bristol Siddeley was driven, inter alia, by Rolls' desire to thwart a potential deal between Bristol Siddeley, SNECMA of France and Pratt & Whitney to produce the JT-9D high bypass engine under licence in Europe for the A300 European Airbus. In any case, Rolls-Royce would sorely regret this major cash outlay only a few years later when its own RB211 programme ran into problems.

In the end, it was the arrogance and self-belief of the then Rolls-Royce management that brought the company to its knees. Believing that they were almost invincible, Rolls-Royce's management took on more than they could chew, with two complex programmes at the boundaries of the then existing knowledge (RB207 and RB211) running in parallel. The company's collapse in 1971 forced the proud Rolls-Royce to 'eat humble pie'.

It is a known fact within UK aerospace circles that Rolls-Royce has always been regarded as the 'golden boy' of the industry by successive British Governments, and that its interests have always taken precedence over those of the airframe manufacturers. Even the infamous Plowden Report of 1965 made an exception for Rolls-Royce when it described the small scale of the UK aircraft industry players, emphasising by contrast the aero-engine maker's global presence. It was the Government's insistence that Rolls-Royce should provide the engine for the European Airbus (the ill-fated RB207) that allowed France and Sud Aviation to demand design leadership on the A300 airframe, despite the fact that the latter's basic design was a Hawker Siddeley-led project (the HBN.100), and the fact that HSA was the more experienced of the two constructors as far as jet-powered subsonic civil aircraft were concerned.

It was the Airbus consortium's decision in late 1968 to open up the engine competition for the scaled down A300B[7] to General Electric and Pratt & Whitney, thus reneging on Rolls-Royce's exclusivity, that triggered the UK Government's decision to withdraw from the three-nation partnership.

Finally, the financial woes of Rolls-Royce in 1970 were a contributing factor in leading the newly elected Conservative Government to refuse launch aid for the BAC Three-Eleven or for HSA's proposal to rejoin the Airbus partnership on an equal footing with France and Germany.

Rolls-Royce's commercial interests again took precedence over those of British Aerospace when the UK was considering its civil aircraft options in 1978. At the time, Prime Minister James Callaghan made it clear that: 'Rolls-Royce was the national asset we had to preserve, which meant that establishing it in the US market was the central consideration.' By then, however, Britain's civil airframe industry was a shadow of its former self, emasculated and demoralised following the BAC Three-Eleven cancellation and the withdrawal from Airbus. In the end the airframe side of the industry, in the new guise of British Aerospace, could only negotiate for a supporting role either with Boeing or with French-led Airbus Industrie. Wisely, as it turned out, BAe opted for Airbus.

All things considered, was it worth it for Britain to sacrifice its civil airframe industry on the altar of Rolls-Royce's interests? As most people know, the great Derby-based company bounced back from the mire. The RB211 was successfully developed for the Lockheed TriStar, and increased thrust versions found application on the Boeing 747 Jumbo and Boeing 767, while a redesigned lower thrust model (the '535') became the leading engine on the successful Boeing 757 airliner.

The RB211 eventually provided the platform for the development of the highly successful Rolls-Royce Trent family of large fan engines. All the major wide-bodies now in production have RR Trent engines either as an option (Airbus A330, Boeing 777, Boeing 747-400) or as exclusive powerplant (Airbus A340-500 and A340-600). The success of the Trent family of engines has propelled the British company to No.2 amongst the world's Top Three aero-engine makers (after General Electric of the US). In 2004 Rolls actually achieved the No.1 slot in terms of commercial engines orders, with a 40 per cent share. The cherry on the cake came recently when the Rolls-Royce Trent 900 engine, as the lead engine, powered the first flight of the world's largest airliner, the Airbus A380 'Super-jumbo'. Rolls-Royce has a share of about half the total A380s ordered to date. In addition, it has already established a strong position on the new Boeing 787 Dreamliner with its Trent 1000 turbofan. In summary, Rolls-Royce has recaptured its mantle of UK's best-known and admired engineering company.

Concluding the review of the Rolls-Royce crisis of the early 1970s, one cannot overlook the possibility that a similar success in the marketplace could have greeted BAC and its Three-Eleven project, had the Government shown the foresight to back it. Like the RB211 that was earmarked to power it, the Three-Eleven would have, in all probability, achieved substantial market success, and this commercial success could have spawned a whole family of modern jetliners, possibly on a European joint-venture basis along the lines of what Airbus Industrie eventually achieved.

BAC and HSA Competing for the Same Government Backing with Two Distinct 'Airbus' Projects

At the time of the 'airbus' decisions, the British aerospace industry was blessed (or should we say cursed!) with two powerful aircraft groups, BAC and Hawker Siddeley Aviation (HSA), both of whom had world-class civil aircraft design and development facilities at Weybridge and Hatfield respectively. France, by contrast, had only one group with a similar level of civil aircraft expertise, Toulouse-based Sud Aviation (later Aérospatiale). Moreover, as befits two major centres of civil aircraft development, both BAC and HSA had their own ideas in terms of how to best address the 'airbus' market, the former promoting its Three-Eleven design, and the latter backing the cooperative European Airbus A300B, of which it had been a founding member.

The 'curse' for the British Governments of the day (Labour and later Conservative) was to decide who of the two British aviation powerhouses had the most economically promising proposal for the 'airbus' market. As it happened, both BAC and HSA had powerful arguments in favour of their own designs.

BAC Weybridge was undoubtedly the more experienced civil team, and the Ministry of Aviation and its advisers readily recognised this fact as we have seen in Chapter 3. In addition to having produced Europe's largest jetliner at the time (Vickers VC-10) and to being involved with Aérospatiale in the development of Concorde, BAC Weybridge had twice successfully penetrated the difficult North American market with two successive generations of short-haul airliners (Vickers Viscount and BAC One-Eleven). The team also had the largest customer base of any European civil aircraft manufacturer. BAC promoted these facts strongly on several occasions in its correspondence and in meetings with Government officials relating to BAC Three-Eleven launch aid. BAC also emphasised that the Three-Eleven was the result of the most extensive customer survey ever undertaken by a European manufacturer and that the project's specifications reflected substantial airline feedback. The company also pointed to the forty-three conditional orders from eight airlines already received for the Three-Eleven, versus nil orders for the Airbus A300B.

HSA, on the other hand, still believed in the commercial soundness of the Airbus A300B, despite having been demoted from senior partner on the project, on an equal footing with France's Aérospatiale, to subcontractor, as a result of the British Government's withdrawal. After all, the blueprint aircraft that formed the basis for the A300B was the Hatfield-designed HBN.100. HSA insisted that it was madness for Britain to back a 'stand alone' Airbus competitor, and that the future lay in European cooperation. HSA also argued that, in their view, BAC's estimates of Three-Eleven development costs were too optimistic and that the new aircraft would cost much more to develop than what BAC was predicting. The company made the point that to rejoin the Airbus consortium would be cheaper for the UK taxpayer than to support the BAC Three-Eleven. As a rebuttal to BAC's claims of greater civil transport expertise, HSA reminded the Government of its own track record of two generations of medium-haul jetliners (the world's first jetliner, the Comet, and the advanced second-generation Trident trijet) which, combined with Aérospatiale's own success with the Caravelle, gave the consortium sufficient credibility in the marketplace.

As one industry insider said at the time, the 'airbus' battle between BAC and HSA turned into a 'competition for the esteem of the British government'.

It is fair to suggest that, had Britain had only one major civil airframe group, as was the case with France, or had BAC and HSA collaborated on the same 'airbus' project, then it would have been much more difficult for the British Government not to provide support for the project, as a much larger constituency would have been affected by a negative decision. As it happened the Conservative Government in December 1970 acted as a 'reverse Solomon' and decided, in its wisdom, to back neither the all-British BAC Three-Eleven nor the re-entry of HSA in the European Airbus consortium.[8]

Conclusion: The Price of Lack of Vision

The BAC Three-Eleven represented Britain's last chance of remaining in the large mainline airliner market as an independent producer. Its demise at the end of 1970 signalled the end of Britain as a major civil aircraft producer for the world markets. The death of the Three-Eleven also marked the end of the road for BAC Weybridge, which was then Europe's most successful civil aircraft design team. This team had sold close to 800 turbine-powered airliners, 250 of which were exported to North America, the world's largest and most demanding aviation market. The several reasons why this course of events was allowed to materialise have been analysed earlier in this chapter. But the underlying cause for this major failure of British industrial policy was undoubtedly the lack of vision on the part of the British decision-makers from the early 1960s onwards. Whereas in the 1950s Britain had valiantly striven to build a world-class aircraft industry on the back of her leadership in turbine and jet-powered engines, by the early 1960s the country had lost the enthusiasm for things great and bold. It has been said elsewhere that an almost pathological defeatism gripped the British ruling classes in the 1960s and 1970s.[9]

This lack of self-belief was particularly evident in the choices that the British Governments of the time made for the aerospace industry. Unlike their French counterparts, the British – only at the political level, it must be emphasised – lacked inspiration, vision and aspirations for their *then* great industry. The British Government was apparently happy to play 'second fiddle' to the French in joint venture projects and, almost true to the classic Napoleonic stereotype of the 'shopkeeper', it became obsessed with 'value for money' and petty short-term savings for the Exchequer. The commercial failure of several post-war commercial transports, issues of European foreign policy, the problems at Rolls-Royce, and the cost overruns on Concorde no doubt all played their part in this change of mood. The end result of this lack of vision was, however, that the country missed the (air) bus at the very point when air travel was about to grow exponentially. By not entering the market for wide-body twinjets at the start, Britain lost out not only in terms of use of its undoubted technical expertise but also in terms of huge revenues foregone (exports and frustrated imports) as we have seen in Chapter 4. When the country rejoined the Airbus consortium on 1 January 1979, it was given a 20 per cent minority stake and a relatively junior role in the programmes. As Geoffrey Owen rightly points out in his book, the 1969 and 1970 Government 'airbus' decisions resulted in 'giving the airframe side of the industry the worst of both worlds – neither a position of leadership within Europe nor a close link with the US.'[10]

With the termination of the BAe 146/Avro RJ programme in November 2001 and the last delivery of an Avro RJ to Blue1 of Finland in 2003, Britain exited civil aircraft production altogether. This was indeed the end of an era: in fifty-three years of continuous manufacture Britain had produced over 930 jetliners of six different models.[11] This tally, however, compares unfavourably with France (over 3,100 deliveries – and counting – from Toulouse, of which over 2,800 Airbuses) and even Germany (over 1,000 Airbuses delivered to date from Hamburg).

The successor company to BAC and HSA, BAE SYSTEMS, is now basically a defence contractor with emphasis on military electronics equipment and subsystems integration, and a strong focus on the US Defence market. Its only significant exposure to civil aircraft is its 20 per cent stake in the Airbus SAS integrated company. As Airbus is now an 80 per cent subsidiary of the huge Franco-German-Spanish EADS group, British influence on the company is even weaker than it was at the time of the Airbus consortium. BAE SYSTEMS has already decided to sell its minority stake in Airbus to EADS, as it concentrates more and more on winning US Defence contracts. Therefore it is not an exaggeration to claim that Britain has not got an aircraft industry to speak of anymore, if by this we mean having leadership or control over major civil or military platforms: the country is now effectively a designer and supplier of subsystems and components for aircraft designed and manufactured elsewhere.

In the civil aircraft arena, the evolution of Britain's status in the last thirty years is, to use a property metaphor, tantamount to someone who used to live in a country mansion and now lives in a small one-bed town flat. Whereas since the early 1970s Toulouse has gone from strength to strength, Weybridge and Hatfield, once world-renowned civil aircraft design and manufacturing centres, are now simply suburban towns in the expensive London hinterland where property development and property sales are the major economic drivers. It was from Toulouse, France, that the world's largest ever airliner, the Airbus A380, made its first flight on 27 April 2005. Toulouse is the headquarters and the key centre of the world's largest airliner manufacturer.

Some people will argue that Airbus is a European joint venture, where Britain plays a significant role. While superficially this is true, the reality is that the French dominate the Airbus organisation at every level: the company's chief executive is French (and has always been so),[12] senior directors including the engineering director are French, the company's headquarters are in Toulouse, where aircraft final assembly, flight-testing and certification take place. Indeed the most important elements in the design of the Airbus range of aircraft (cockpit and avionics, fly-by-wire systems and systems integration) are a French responsibility. Many people and countries outside Europe identify Airbus as a French aircraft manufacturer. This state of affairs is reinforced by the fact that successive French Presidents and Prime Ministers have promoted Airbus while on foreign visits, and major Airbus contracts have been signed in the presence of French Presidents or Prime Ministers. The Airbus CEO and the company's senior officials always form part of French Government delegations on overseas visits. Leaving aside the prestige element, the choice of Toulouse as the Airbus base has triggered a prodigious growth in the number of subcontractors, systems developers, R&D centres and support services. These businesses have set up bases in the Toulouse hinterland, generating impressive 'multiplier-driven' economic and financial benefits for the French economy.

As far as Britain is concerned, while wing design and production is an important element of the overall project, this cannot hide the fact that Britain is very much a junior partner in the Airbus project.[13]

In summary, a good theatrical metaphor for Britain's current standing in Airbus is that of a supporting actor taking part in a play set in Toulouse, led by a French director and with French thespians in the leading roles.

When Noël Forgeard, CEO of Airbus, delivered the Lindbergh Lecture on the history and evolution of Airbus at the Royal Aeronautical Society in London on 4 March 2003, he said that both Britain and France had to forego their rightful ambitions in order to cooperate for the common good of the European commercial aircraft industry. This diplomatically worded comment for British audience consumption glossed over the fact that it was Britain, not France, that lost out the most in the unfolding of the Airbus story. In fact, while the latter country, through Airbus, achieved a European (and indeed world) pre-eminence that it could only have dreamed of in the late 1960s, Britain lost its leading role in Europe in civil aircraft forever, and is now reduced to a designer and manufacturer of subsystems for a family of aircraft that most people now identify with France. For this state of affairs the British have only got themselves to blame.

1 Geoffrey Owen, *From Empire to Europe – The Decline and Revival of British Industry since the Second World War*.

2 Geoffrey Owen, in his book *From Empire to Europe – The Decline and Revival of British Industry since the Second World War*, states in his coverage of the aerospace industry: 'The most expensive folly was the Concorde, a waste of national resources on a gigantic scale.' Brian Trubshaw, BAC test pilot, draws the reader's attention to the commercial viability of the BAC Three-Eleven in relation to Concorde in his book *Concorde – The Inside Story*.

3 HMG, Ministry of Aviation Supply files, 26 October 1970.

4 *Flight International*, 19 November 1970.

5 *The Times*, 'Aid for airbus and 3-11 refused', 3 December 1970.

6 See, for all, Keith Hayward, *Government and British Civil Aerospace*, and the same author's *The British Aircraft Industry*.

7 The scaling down of the Airbus A300 to the definitive A300B was inspired by the unveiling of the Three-Eleven in the summer of 1968.

8 The Italians have a proverb that goes like this '*Tra i due litiganti il terzo gode*', which loosely translates into 'between two quarrelling parties the third party runs away with the prize'. This was definitely the case with BAC and HSA, whose rivalry over the Airbus in the end benefited France's Aérospatiale, to the detriment of both British companies.

9 Matthew Lynn, in his book *Birds of Prey: Boeing vs Airbus – A Battle for the Skies*, says: 'Britain was gripped by an almost pathological defeatism in the 1970s, and nowhere more so than among its commercial and political elite. Pessimism was the ruling philosophy, and with good reason. A generation had come to power whose lives had coincided with the slide of the country from world's strongest military and industrial power to a nearly bankrupt bit player on the world stage. Defeat was what they knew best, and they believed it was unstoppable: "managed decline", to use a phrase popular at the time, was the best that could be hoped for…' (p.150).

10 Geoffrey Owen, *From Empire to Europe – The Decline and Revival of British Industry since the Second World War*, p.326.

11 These are the de Havilland Comet (114 produced); Hawker Siddeley Trident (117); Vickers VC-10 (54); BAC One-Eleven (244); BAC/Aerospatiale Concorde (10 British built); and BAE 146/Avro RJ (394).

12 From 1 July 2005 the new Airbus CEO is the German Gustav Humbert. However, the French still control Airbus affairs via the chairmanship of the Airbus board and the position of chief operating officer.

13 Britain at present has a 20 per cent share of European jet airliner production through its Airbus shareholding. This compares with a share of 60 per cent of European capacity (measured by order intake) in 1970 (see Appendix III).

Appendix I

Text of the statement made by the Minister of Aviation, Frederick Corfield, to the House of Commons on 2 December 1970 announcing the cancellation of the BAC Three-Eleven:

The House will be aware that the British Aircraft Corporation and Rolls-Royce have asked for launching aid for the BAC Three-Eleven and its RB211 engine at a cost to the Government estimated at some £144 million at present prices. We have also had an invitation from the French, Federal German and Netherlands Governments to rejoin the A300-B project. The initial cost to the Government would be some £30 million if we took a share in the airframe part of the A300-B project alone, or some £100 million if, in addition, the RB211-61 engine were also launched for this aircraft. This takes no account of further costs likely to be incurred during the production phase.

After very careful consideration, the Government have decided that they cannot support either of these proposals, in view of the size of the public investment required. We have to take into account the large sums of money already being devoted to the support of civil aircraft and engines, and to bear in mind other calls on public funds.

In the light of this BEA will have the opportunity to choose between two alternatives, the Lockheed L.1011 TriStar and the A300-B. Both include a large contribution by British Industry. The Lockheed L1011 has Rolls-Royce RB211-22 engines, for which Her Majesty's Government recently announced an increase in launching aid up to a limit of £89 million. As for the A300-B, Hawker Siddeley are designing and manufacturing the main part of the wing.

The decision in regard to the A300-B does not imply any weakening of our interest in joint projects such as the MRCA, Jaguar and of course Concorde, to each of which HMG is making very substantial contributions.

I have already discussed with my colleagues in the other Governments concerned proposals for a joint study of the possibilities of increased cooperation between European aero-engine industries, and they have recently proposed that we should meet. I welcome these proposals and hope that they can be extended in due course to the rest of the aircraft industry.

Appendix II

Memorandum presented to the Cabinet by the Minister of Aviation Supply, Frederick Corfield, on 26 November 1970:

At its meeting on 3 November 1970 the Cabinet decided to put certain questions to the French, German and Netherlands Governments to establish more clearly the basis on which the Rolls-Royce RB211-61 engine might be adopted for the A300B European Airbus. The answers have been fully discussed with officials of the other Governments. They give us no assurance either that the European national airlines would buy (or even be pressed by Governments to buy) the aircraft with RR engines or that other Governments would contribute to engine launching costs.

The way is now clear for consideration of the various options open to us. This paper summarises them briefly. The cost and out-turn for each are set out at Annex I; the figures are necessarily tentative, but I believe they are a sufficiently reliable guide for comparative judgment about the courses available.

RE-ENTRY INTO A300B WITH RB211-61 ENGINES

The RB211-61 would be too late for the present A300B1, and would therefore be launched in the stretched version of the aircraft, the A300B7. The engine launching cost to HMG is unlikely to be less than say £75 million when allowance is made for the fact that extra engine development would probably be required to match the needs of the A300B7. In the absence of a firm German undertaking to contribute, nothing has been assumed.

The engine would be in direct competition with the General Electric CF-6, which would already have been firmly established in the aircraft, and it would have no assured market. BEA would understandably be unwilling to use the A300B7 with Rolls-Royce engines unless some other major airlines use the same powerplant.

Neither Rolls-Royce nor we believe that, in these circumstances, the A300B represents an adequate launching base for the engine; there would be a serious risk of worsening Rolls-Royce's financial situation. Our view might change if Lockheed also placed an order, but this is most unlikely before the middle of 1971.

My conclusion is that we should not launch the engine for the A300B. I am satisfied that the other Governments would understand and accept our reasons.

RE-ENTRY INTO THE A300B (WITH GE ENGINES)

This means taking up the current proposal by the European Governments that we should re-enter as full partners, with an equal share of the rights and responsibilities. The launching cost of the A300B is given as £175 million at 1968 prices (on a fixed price contract with an escalation clause), plus the cost of launching the larger A300B7, whose launching cost has not yet been established, but is expected to be some £20 million. Our estimates of sales lie between 175 and 275 aircraft.

The UK share of this would be some 27 per cent or £52 million at 1968 prices, but the Germans and Hawker Siddeley are already bearing £30 million of this and will continue to do so. The remainder would fall as direct cost to HMG. With an allowance for contingencies, the amount is likely to be at least £30 million at current prices. On the basis proposed by the other Governments, HMG's recovery would be nil at 175 sales and £10 million at 275 sales. There would be no unilateral right of withdrawal.

There are certain conditions of re-entry which involve certain contingent liabilities beyond the £30 million and whose impact we cannot estimate in advance. Firstly we are asked to indemnify Hawker Siddeley against loss in respect of that part of the UK share which they are financing (about £13 million). A similar suggestion that we should indemnify the Germans should be negotiable. Secondly we should be expected to share responsibility for risks of loss if aircraft are unsold or have to be sold at subsidised price. While we should try to limit our liabilities in negotiation, the others would argue that we should share the liabilities as equal partners. Losses under these arrangements might wipe out or exceed our recoveries by an amount which is impossible to quantify at this stage, leaving us with a final cost in excess of our original £30 million contribution as the price of our ticket to entry in the project.

The UK share of the airframe production work, mainly at Hawker Siddeley but with a small proportion at equipment firms and subcontractors, would rise from the present 16 per cent to perhaps 27 per cent, representing extra work to the value of some £250,000 per aircraft. There would not be a proportionate increase in development work.

The A300B would rank third, after the BAC 3-11 and Lockheed L1011, in BEA's choice. BEA estimate that it would probably cost them more to run than the other two aircraft, and that there is danger of the aircraft being late and short on performance. My Department shares these views. We understand that BEA would accordingly seek formal indemnities from HMG if they are made to buy the A300B. The officials' discussion has, however, made it clear that, just as the other Governments feel unable to direct their airlines, they would not expect us to direct BEA, who could thus be left free to make a commercial choice if we so wished.

We could expect good political dividends from re-entry into the A300B. It would generate goodwill and lead to further proposals for cooperation. There are signs that the time is now ripe for a serious dialogue on the possibilities of cooperation in particular between Rolls-Royce and the Continental engine firms. Thus, it would be a step towards a European aircraft industry.

On the other hand there are significant risks that the project will fail to come up to expectations, and the effectiveness of French (SNIAS) management under competitive pressures is suspect, particularly as they will be heavily stretched on Concorde at the same time as the A300B. Re-entering at this stage we would exert little influence on design or project policy, and differences of opinion on production policies and underwriting could be continuing sources of friction. Governments are meeting by far the greater part of the costs and risks of the project. This may have been unavoidable but it is not a good precedent for the future, and it is more lax than our own policies for launching aid which, for example, has always stopped short of sharing production risks (except for Concorde).

Furthermore, the discussion between officials has established that, provided we do not launch the BAC 3-11, we could open negotiations for wider cooperation with Europe without formal re-entry into the A300B, though in this case, not unnaturally, the other side would be less enthusiastic and progress would be at best slower. Our case would rest not only on present collaborative projects but also on the fact that we should be bringing into the partnership far greater experience and resources than any other European country. The

French and Germans appreciate the critical value of Rolls Royce as a potential nucleus for a future European aero-engine industry which would be strong enough to withstand American penetration.

In summary, on our usual basis of economic appraisal the A300B project is too dear and risky to be attractive; bur re-entry carries with it potential advantages of a broader type which we may otherwise find it more difficult to achieve.

BAC 3-11 WITH RB211-61 ENGINES

The Cabinet has already looked at this proposal; the main figures are repeated at Annex I (they are presented on a slightly different basis to ensure comparability with the other options and assume 100 per cent Government funding of the RB211-61 engine, since Rolls-Royce are no longer able to contribute to the launching cost). It is unlikely that any additional funds will now be forthcoming from the private sector.

The cost to HMG would be £144 million spread as follows (£ million):

	1970–71	1971–72	1972–73	1973–74	1974–75	1975–76	Total
Airframe	4	13	16	20	20	11	84
Engine	-	9	18	18	7	8	60
Total	4	22	34	38	27	19	144

To these figures should be added an appropriate share of any national wage and material cost escalation.

At 240 sales, the Government's cash break-even point, the project would produce exports or import savings worth some £1,400 million in cash terms (the comparable discounted figures are a Government loss of £50 million and earnings of £550 million). This does not of course represent a net gain to the balance of payments since alternative use of the resources (e.g. in the engineering industry) will produce exports or save imports, but we are talking of the decade 1975–1985 and beyond and the alternative resources use and output so far ahead is quite impossible to forecast.

Full responsibility for the cost overruns on the airframe (apart from HMG's share of escalation) and for financing production would rest with the British Aircraft Corporation. With their additional £12 million of capital for which firm underwriting arrangements have been made, BAC should have sufficient resources for this task.

For Rolls-Royce the position is less clear pending completion of Sir Henry Benson's examination of the Company's finances. By the relevant period (1974 and later) they should, on the basis of their current forecasts, have returned to a position of profitability. But we cannot be certain of this. Nor can we be certain that that the launching cost can be contained within the estimate of £60 million. Following the experience which they have gained with the RB211-22 there seems no reason to doubt that Rolls-Royce have the technical and managerial ability to develop and manage the RB211-61 successfully.

Nevertheless the new Rolls-Royce Board have confirmed that they regard the RB211-61 engine in the BAC 3-11 (with possible later applications in the Lockheed aircraft) as the best course for them commercially, and as providing the best prospects for HMG's of recovery of its investments in the RB211 series of engines as a whole. They have expressed confidence in their estimate of £60 million.

The advantages of the BAC 3-11 in preserving BAC's successful civil aircraft team at Weybridge, and in providing employment in the aircraft equipment and other industries (including Shorts in Northern Ireland) have been dealt with in CP (70) 74, paragraphs 38–43. Collaborative arrangements with European countries were outlined in paragraph 49 of the same paper.

If we develop the RB211-61 for the BAC 3-11 the engines would be available to meet Lockheed's probable needs, for an additional installation cost estimated at £10 million. Sales of the RB211-61 in a stretched Lockheed aircraft should improve sales of the RB211-22 in the basic L1011.

At a later stage, BAC might wish to offer a slightly smaller version of the aircraft with the RB211-22 engine for American airlines who have already bought tri-jets. The airframe and engine costs of this version have not been assessed but would be unlikely to exceed a total of £30 million. It would not be embarked upon unless sufficient sales could be assumed and the manufacturers found a major part of the launching cost.

If it is felt that we should support the BAC 3-11 but could not commit ourselves fully to the RB211-61 until Rolls-Royce's financial position is clearer and more progress has been made on the RB211-22, it would be feasible for BAC to keep the option open for some four months to the end of March 1971. If, at the end of that period, it was decided not to proceed with the RB211-61, BAC could fall back on the GE engine without losing time (see paragraph 27 below). If we wished to adopt this course, however, we should have to give full authority for the BAC 3-11 straight away, and limited contract cover (within a maximum of, say, £2.5 million) for the RB211-61.

BAC 3-11 WITH GE ENGINES

The cost to HMG would be £84 million, plus a share of escalation, on the assumption, yet to be established, that GE would finance the costs of adapting their engine, which would be imported from America (Rolls-Royce believe that it would be commercially damaging for them to manufacture a rival engine). The aircraft would be acceptable to BEA and would be likely to command a slightly higher market share, particularly in the USA, than a Rolls-Royce-engined version.

Though this course is a fall back position if the RB211-61 is dropped, it would be regarded as strongly anti-European and would damage Rolls-Royce's reputation.

TAKE NO ACTION

BEA would be left free to decide between the L1011 and A300B. The total foreign exchange savings (as compared to buying a wholly foreign aircraft like the Douglas DC-10) would be about £120 million (if BEA buy the L1011) and about £24 million (if BEA buy the A300B).

If BEA (unexpectedly) decides to order the A300B, we should gain some political advantage, and more work for Hawker Siddeley.

If BEA ordered the L1011 we should gain the following advantages:

1. A boost for Lockheed and the L1011 and an increased return on our investment in the RB211-22.

2. Termination of our underwriting liability of up to £5 million on the Air Holdings arrangements.

The British work proportion of the L1011 over the life of the project is higher than that proposed in the A300B (without Rolls-Royce engines).

It still seems probable that Lockheed will pull through their present financial difficulties; the L1011 has just made a successful maiden flight and is due in service in a year's time.

CONCLUSIONS

RE-ENTRY INTO A300B

1. Launching the RB211-61 in this project is not justified by prospective sales.

2. The costs and uncertainties of re-entry into the airframe must be weighed against the gains of political goodwill in Europe, and of a better foundation for future European aircraft collaboration.

BEA need not be compelled to buy the aircraft against their will.

STAY OUT OF A300B, BUT DIRECT BEA TO BUY IT

This half-way course has nothing to commend it.

BAC 3-11

1. With RB211-61

Costs are high but are spread over a number of years.

Would bring considerable benefit to the airframe industry and Rolls-Royce (and hence to our large present investment in the RB211) and to the aircraft equipment industry.

2. With GE engine

Would be a blow to Rolls-Royce, and would substantially impede progress towards a European aero-engine industry built around Rolls-Royce, but shares the other advantages of the BAC 3-11 with Rolls-Royce engines.

Though success cannot be guaranteed and we must recognise that we should be jeopardising an early move towards a unified European aircraft industry, I believe that the balance of national advantage lies in supporting the BAC 3-11. This should preferably be with the RB211-61 engines, but the GE engine represents a useful fallback position if we wish to avoid a full commitment to the RB211-61 now (see paragraph 24 above).

DO NOTHING

We leave BEA free to buy L1011, with gains for Rolls-Royce and Lockheed, or the A300B, with gains for Hawker Siddeley.

 Need not close the door to discussions aimed at establishing closer permanent links with Europe, though progress would not be as rapid and our negotiating position would be weaker. FVC (Frederick Corfield)

Ministry of Aviation Supply SW1
26 November 1970

Annex I

	BAC 3-11 RB211-61	BAC 3-11 RB211-61	A300B GE CF-6	A300B GE CF-6
	150 sales	240 sales	175 sales	275 sales
Government spend	£ million	£ million	£ million	£ million
Airframe	84	84	30	30
Engine	60	60	–	–
Total	144	144	30	30
Government gain/loss	-49	7	-43	-30
Forex benefit	875	1420	70	100
Discounted to 1970 NPV				
National resource cost	460	600	59	72
Government loss	-68	-50	-29	-24
Forex benefit	390	555	30	45
Excess of resource cost over forex benefit (1)	18	8	85	60
Govt loss as % of forex benefit (2)	17	9	91	53

(1) Implied preference

(2) Implied subsidy

Appendix III

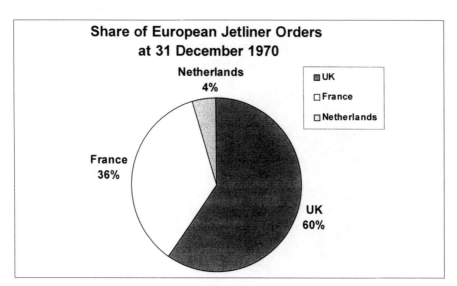

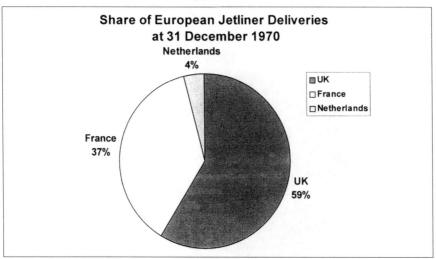

Source: *Flight International* magazine; manufacturers' data.

Appendix IV

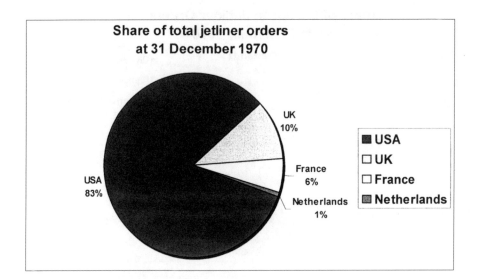

Share of total jetliner orders at 31 December 1970

UK 10%

France 6%

Netherlands 1%

USA 83%

- USA
- UK
- France
- Netherlands

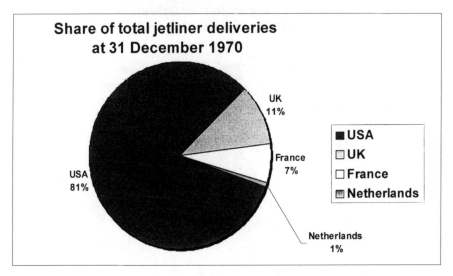

Share of total jetliner deliveries at 31 December 1970

UK 11%

France 7%

Netherlands 1%

USA 81%

- USA
- UK
- France
- Netherlands

Appendix V

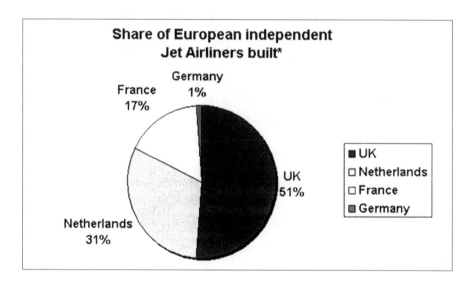

Above: Manufacturers' data.

Opposite: Manufacturers' data.

Appendix VI

Order status of Western turbine-powered airliners at 31 December 1970

Jets			Turboprops	
USA				
Boeing				
707	852			
727	869			
737	277			
747	198			
	2,196			
McDonnell Douglas				
DC-8	552			
DC-9	656			
DC-10	113			
	1,321			
Lockheed				
L1011 TriStar	150		L188 Electra	170
	150			170
Convair (General Dynamics)				
880	65			
990 Coronado	37			
	102			
Total USA	3,769			170
UK				

BAC				
Vickers VC-10	54		Vickers Viscount	444
BAC 1-11	204		Vickers Vanguard	44
	258		Bristol Britannia	85
				573
HSA				
de Havilland DH106 Comet	114	*	Hawker Siddeley HS.748	246
Hawker Siddeley HS121 Trident	82		Hawker Siddeley Argosy**	73
	196			319
Total UK	454			892
France				
Aerospatiale				
Sud Aviation SE-210 Caravelle	274		Nord N-262	92
Dassault				
Mercure	–			
Total France	274			92
Germany				
Vereingte Flugtechnische Werke				
VFW 614	26	***		
Total Germany	26	***		
Netherlands				
Fokker				
Fokker F-28 Fellowship	34		Fokker F-27 Friendship	552
Total Netherlands	34			552

   *   Including 2 Comet 4Cs converted into Nimrod prototypes

  **   Including 56 Argosy C1s for RAF Transport Command

***   Options. No firm orders

Source: Manufacturers; *Flight International*.

Appendix VII

European nationally developed turbine-powered commercial aircraft – production totals at 30 June 2005

First flight	United Kingdom Model	Jets	Turboprops	Total
1949	de Havilland DH106 Comet	114		114
1950	Vickers Viscount	-	444	444
1952	Bristol Britannia	-	85	85
1959	Vickers Vanguard	-	44	44
1959	Handley Page Herald	-	50	50
1960	Hawker Siddeley HS748	-	382	382
1962	Hawker Siddeley HS121 Trident	117	-	117
1962	Vickers VC-10	54	-	54
1963	BAC One-Eleven	244	-	244
1969	BAC/Aerospatiale Concorde	10	-	10
1974	Shorts SD-3-30	-	136	136
1981	BAe 146/Avro RJ	394	-	394
1981	Shorts 360		164	164
1991	BAe Jetstream 41	-	104	104
1986	BAe ATP	-	63	63
	UK total	933	1,472	2,405
	France			
1955	Sud Aviation SE210 Caravelle	282		282
1962	Nord Aviation N-262		111	111

1969	Aerospatiale/BAC Concorde	10		10
1971	Dassault Mercure	12		12
	France total	304	111	415
	France–Italy			
1984	ATR 42/ATR 72		739	739
				739
	Netherlands			
1955	Fokker F-27 Friendship		787	787
1967	Fokker F-28 Fellowship	243		243
1985	Fokker F-50		212	212
1986	Fokker F-100/F-70	327		327
	Netherlands total	570	999	1,569
	Germany			
1971	VFW 614	19		19
1991	Dornier 328		120	120
1998	Dornier 328JET	105		105
	Germany total	124	120	244
	Europe total			5,134

Source: Manufacturers; *Flight International.*

Appendix VIII

Manufacturers of jet airliners of more than seventy seats at 30 June 2005

Manufacturer	Country	Orders	Deliveries*	% orders	% deliveries
Boeing Excl. Boeing 717 (ex-MD95)	USA	12,917	11,570	51.6	53.5
Airbus	Pan-European	5,520	3,941	22.1	18.2
McDonnell Douglas Incl. Boeing 717 (ex-MD95)	USA	3,640	3,628	14.6	16.8
British Aerospace Incl. UK Concorde production (10 units)	UK	933	933	3.7	4.3
Fokker	Netherlands	570	570	2.3	2.6
Aérospatiale Incl. French Concorde production (10 units)	France	292	292	1.2	1.3
Lockheed	USA	250	250	1.0	1.2
Bombardier	Canada	364	269	1.5	1.2
Embraer	Brazil	412	66	1.6	0.3
General Dynamics	USA	102	102	0.4	0.5
Dassault	France	12	12	0.0	0.1
Total		25,012	21,633	100.0	100.0

*Includes prototypes and development aircraft

Source:

Manufacturers; *Flight International*; Roach/Eastwood *'Jet Airliner Production List – Volume 2'*

Glossary

APU	Auxiliary Power Unit (turbine)
BAC	British Aircraft Corporation
BAe	British Aerospace
BEA	British European Airways
BOAC	British Overseas Airways Corporation
CAST	Civil Aircraft Study Team
CP	Cabinet Paper
CTOL	Conventional Take-Off and Landing
EADS	European Aeronautics, Defence & Space Company
FCO	Foreign & Commonwealth Office
HMG	Her Majesty's Government
HP	High pressure (turbine)
HSA	Hawker Siddeley Aviation
IP	Intermediate pressure (turbine)
JET	Joint European Transport; Joint Engineering Team
MinTech	Ministry of Technology
MoA	Ministry of Aviation Supply
MoU	Memorandum of Understanding
MRO	Maintenance, repair & overhaul
Nm	Nautical miles
NPL	National Physical Laboratory – Teddington
RAE	Royal Aircraft Establishment – Farnborough
R/STOL	Reduced/Short Take-Off and Landing
RR	Rolls-Royce
SST	Supersonic Transport

Bibliography

Books

Aris, Stephen, *Close to the Sun. How Airbus challenged America's domination of the skies*, Aurum Press, London, 2002

Benn, Tony, *Office Without Power: Diaries 1968-1972*, Arrow Books, London, 1989

Gardner, Charles, *British Aircraft Corporation, A History*, B.T. Basford, London, 1981

Gold, Bonnie, *Politics, Markets, and Security. European Military and Civil Aircraft Collaboration 1954-1994*, University Press of America, 1995

Gunston, Bill, *Airbus, The European Triumph*, Osprey Publishing, London, 1988

Hayward, Keith, *Government and British Civil Aerospace (A case study in post-war technology policy)*, Manchester University Press, 1983

Hayward, Keith, *The British Aircraft Industry*, Manchester University Press, 1989

Hayward, Keith, *International Collaboration in Civil Aerospace*, Frances Pinter (Publishers), London, 1986

Henderson, Scott, *Silent Swift Superb: The Story of the Vickers VC-10*, Scoval Publishing Ltd, Newcastle-upon-Tyne, 1998

Heppenheimer, T.A., *Turbulent Skies: The History of Commercial Aviation*, John Wiley & Sons, Inc. New York 1995

Jarrett, Philip (Ed.), *Modern Air Transport: Worldwide Air Transport from 1945 to the Present*, Putnam, London, 2000

Kingsley-Jones, Max, *Classic Civil Aircraft: Hawker Siddeley Trident*, Ian Allan Publishing, 1993

Lygo, Sir Raymond, *Collision Course: Lygo Shoots Back*, The Book Guild, East Sussex, 2002

Lynn, Matthew, *Birds of Prey: Boeing Vs. Airbus, a battle for the skies*, Mandarin Paperbacks, London, 1996

McIntyre, Ian, *Dogfight. The Transatlantic Battle over Airbus*, Praeger Publishers, Westport, CT, 1992

Newhouse, John, *The Sporty Game: the high-risk competitive business of making and selling commercial airliners*, Alfred A. Knopf, New York, 1982

Owen, Geoffrey, *From Empire to Europe: The Decline and Revival of British Industry Since the Second World War*, HarperCollins, London, 1999

Painter, Martin, *The DH.106 Comet. An Illustrated History*, Air Britain (Historians) Ltd, Tunbridge Wells, 2002

Payne, Richard, *Stuck on the Drawing Board: Unbuilt British Commercial Aircraft since 1945*, Tempus Publishing Ltd, Stroud, Gloucestershire, 2004

Reed, Arthur, *British Aircraft Industry: What Went Right? What Went Wrong?*, J.M. Dent & Sons, London, 1973

Reed, Arthur, *Airbus: Europe's High Flyer*, Norden Publishing House, St Gallen, Switzerland, 1991

Simpson, Rod, *Airlife's Commercial Aircraft and Airliners. A Guide to Postwar Commercial Aircraft Manufacturers and their Aircraft*, Airlife Publishing, England, 1999

Skinner, Stephen, *BAC One-Eleven: the whole story*, Tempus Publishing Ltd, Stroud, Gloucestershire, 2002

Trubshaw, Brian. *Concorde: The Inside Story*. Sutton Publishing, Stroud, Gloucestershire, 2000

Weldon Thornton, David, *Airbus Industrie. The Politics of an International Industrial Collaboration*, St Martin's Press, New York, 1995

Wilson, Stuart, *Viscount, Comet & Concorde. The Story of Three Pioneer Airliners of the Postwar Era*, Aerospace Publications Pty, Australia, 1996

Wilson, Stuart, *Airliners of the World*, Aerospace Publications Pty, Australia, 1999

Wood, Derek, *Project Cancelled (British Aircraft that Never Flew)*, The Bobbs-Merrill Co., Inc. Indianapolis/ New York, 1975

Government Files

HMG, Cabinet/Ministry of Aviation Supply/Ministry of Technology/Treasury files as follows:

- AVIA, 63/142	- AVIA, 65/2221	- MoA, Supp 29/126
- AVIA, 65/2178	- CAB, 164/767	- MoA, Supp 29/127
- AVIA, 65/2179	- CAB, 164/768	- Treasury, T225/3746
- AVIA, 65/2180	- MoA, Supp 29/124	
- AVIA, 65/2220	- MoA, Supp 29/125	

Manufacturer's Literature

British Aircraft Corporation, *BAC Three-Eleven Tour: Interim Report*, November 1968

British Aircraft Corporation, *BAC Three-Eleven: World Market Study Tour. General Brief*, October/November 1968

British Aircraft Corporation, *BAC Three-Eleven: Specification for Sales Engineering Department Mock-up Demonstration Centre*, 24 November 1969

British Aircraft Corporation, *BAC Three-Eleven: Presentation to SABENA Belgian World Airlines* (5 documents), June 1970

British Aircraft Corporation, *The Market Assessment Programme and Results*, June 1970

British Aircraft Corporation, *BAC Three-Eleven: Technical Features*, Sales Engineering Department, Weybridge, August 1970

British Aircraft Corporation, *The case for the BAC Three-Eleven*, Press Release and Attachments, 23 October 1970

Periodicals, Newspapers, Papers and Correspondence

Aerospace, 'The A320 wing: designing for Commercial Success', Roger Back and Jack Wedderspoon, January 1986

Air Britain Digest, 'Lost Opportunity: the "British Airbus" which might have been', Richard Payne, autumn 2001

Air Pictorial, 'Paper Planes', Richard Payne, September, October and November 1998 issues

Aviation Week & Space Technology, 'The European Challenge', editorial by Robert Holtz, 7 September 1970

Aviation Week & Space Technology, editorial by Robert Holtz, 14 September 1970

Benn, Tony (Rt Hon. MP), Private correspondence with the Author, 2003

The Bournemouth Evening Echo, '£8 million Hurn hangar if 3-11 goes ahead', 10 November 1970

The Daily Express, 'Editorial: Now – No further retreat!' 3 December 1970

Economic Models Ltd, 'Report on the benefits to the British economy of BAC 3-11, A.300B and Lockheed L.1011 alternative programmes (econometric model)', 19 October 1970

The Financial Times, 'Leader: Working with Europe', 3 December 1970

Flight International, 'Several issues covering the years 1968-1976'

The Journal of the Long Range Planning Society, 'Product Forecasting: the BAC Three-Eleven Airliner', Christopher Hamshaw Thomas, June 1970

The Putnam Aeronautical Review, 'The Basic Strategy of Airbus', Roger Béteille, September 1990

The Putnam Aeronautical Review, 'Airbus: the Formative Years', Derek Brown, September 1990

The Putnam Aeronautical Review, 'Airbus: Expanding the Product Range', Derek Brown, September 1990

The Royal Aeronautical Society, 'Airbus – The First Thirty Years', lecture by Bob McKinlay, February 1999

The Royal Aeronautical Society, 'A Flight into the Future: the Airbus Way', Lindbergh Lecture by Airbus CEO Noël Forgeard, 4 March 2003

Surrey Advertiser, 'Redundancy fears over 3-11 airbus', 13 November 1970

The Times, Aid for airbus and 311 refused'; also, 'State funds refused for airbus projects: European talks on aero-engine cooperation', 3 December 1970

Index

If you are interested in purchasing other books published by Tempus, or in case you have difficulty finding any Tempus books in your local bookshop, you can also place orders directly through our website
www.tempus-publishing.com